Hotel Finance

ANAND IYENGAR

Institute of Hotel Management

Aurangabad

OXFORD

OXFORD

UNIVERSITY PRESS

YMCA Library Building, Jai Singh Road, New Delhi 110001

Oxford University Press is a department of the University of Oxford.
It furthers the University's objective of excellence in research, scholarship,
and education by publishing worldwide in

Oxford   New York
Auckland   Cape Town   Dar es Salaam   Hong Kong   Karachi
Kuala Lumpur   Madrid   Melbourne   Mexico City   Nairobi
New Delhi   Shanghai   Taipei   Toronto

With offices in
Argentina   Austria   Brazil   Chile   Czech Republic   France   Greece
Guatemala   Hungary   Italy   Japan   Poland   Portugal   Singapore
South Korea   Switzerland   Thailand   Turkey   Ukraine   Vietnam

Oxford is a registered trade mark of Oxford University Press
in the UK and in certain other countries.

Published in India
by Oxford University Press

ISBN-13: 978-0-19-569446-8
ISBN-10: 0-19-569446-5

Typeset in Baskerville
by Tej Composers, New Delhi
Printed in India by Radha Press, Delhi 110031
and published by Oxford University Press
YMCA Library Building, Jai Singh Road, New Delhi 110001

Dedicated to my mother
Smt. Padma Ramprasad Iyengar

Preface

Finance is an extremely interesting and dynamic discipline that deals with all aspects of a business. If you can understand finance, you will be able to understand the finer nuances of any business because the purpose of every business is essentially value addition and profit generation. Business success depends on the efficient management of finance, that is, the translation of business visions and dreams into monetary terms. Modern businesses do not require ordinary employees. They need managers who have an astute sense of business and are profit oriented and executives who can read the writing on the wall much ahead of anyone else. This is possible only if you have a good grasp of one subject—financial management.

ABOUT THE BOOK

Hotel Finance has been specially designed to meet the needs of undergraduate and postgraduate degree/diploma students of hotel management and hospitality courses. Aimed at providing a practical view of financial management in the hotel business environment, the book fills a void in Indian publishing that hitherto had no textbooks in the area of finance specific to the hospitality industry. Whereas most available books in financial management tend to delve into the generic, this book discusses the principles and practices of the discipline as applied in the context of hotel management, exploring all the relevant theoretical concepts and incorporating current industry practices.

Descriptive explanation is accompanied by numerical illustrations and solutions wherever necessary. The solved numerical examples and additional test questions will help students gain precise conceptual clarity. The case examples and references provide an opportunity to synthesize the classroom experience to the real-world situation. The case studies have also been drawn from the hospitality industry.

COVERAGE AND STRUCTURE

The book, divided into six parts, discusses the types of financial decisions confronted by hospitality managers, the relevant tools and techniques used to make appropriate decisions, and the financial environment of the hospitality industry in India.

The introductory aspects of finance are dealt with in Chapters 1–3. Chapter 1 details the objectives of financial management in the hospitality industry, the functions of finance, and the position of financial management on an organizational chart. Chapter 2 considers the hospitality business and its legal and other environment-related issues. Chapter 3 discusses the fundamental concepts in valuation.

Chapters 4, 5, and 6 help in understanding the toolkit available to assess the financial performance of hospitality organizations and in planning finance.

Chapters 7, 8, 9, and 10 deal with the importance of management of current assets and liabilities. Chapter 7 highlights the importance of working capital. Cash, receivables, and inventory management are the focal point of Chapters 8 and 9. Chapter 10 highlights the sources of short-term loans available to hospitality firms in India.

Chapters 11–14 deal with capital expenditure decisions. The implications of estimating cash flows are dealt with in Chapter 11. Chapter 12 clarifies the use of tools and techniques available to hospitality firms in deciding on the capital expenditure budget. Chapter 13 deals with the processes and approaches to hospitality firm valuation. Chapter 14 pertains to the risk and return characteristics in the hospitality business.

Chapter 15 expounds the financial system in India, and Chapter 16 looks at the sources of long-term finance.

Chapter 17 deals with franchising and management contracts, and Chapter 18 looks at the options of leasing in the hospitality business scenario.

ACKNOWLEDGMENTS

While there are many who are responsible for the completion of this work, I would like to thank the team at Oxford University Press, New Delhi, for the momentous support and extreme patience, devoid of which this book would not have been possible, much less successful. Acknowledgments are due to my colleagues at the Institute of Hotel Management, Aurangabad, for the kind support extended during the development of the manuscript.

Anand Iyengar

Contents

Financial Management in the Hospitality Industry

> *The significance of a man is not in what he attains but in what he longs to attain.*
>
> **Kahlil Gibran**

Learning Objectives

After studying this chapter, you will be able to

➢ Understand the meaning and importance of financial management in the context of hospitality operations

➢ Understand the goal of the firm and the constraints in relation to the goal

➢ Examine the position of financial management in the organization chart of a hospitality firm

➢ Explore the relationship between finance, micro/macro economics, and accounting

Success at Hilton Hotels Corporation

Hilton Hotels Corporation is a leading global hospitality company, with more than 2800 hotels and 4,90,000 hotel rooms in more than 80 countries across the globe. The company offers great choices to its customers, whether travelling for business or leisure. Hilton guests and customers can choose from four-star city centre hotels (more 1000-plus room hotels than any hotel, including the Waldorf=Astoria, the Palmer House, and the Hilton San Francisco); convention properties (more than any other company); mid-priced focused

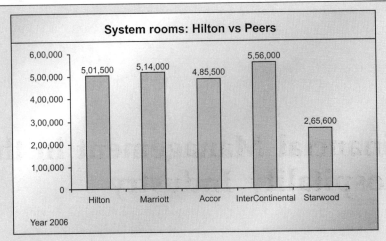

Source: www.hilton.com.

service hotels (the Hilton Garden Inn and the Hampton Inn); long-term extended stay hotels (the Homewood Suites by Hilton); destination resorts on the beach and/or golf course (including the famous Hilton Hawaiian Village and Pointe Hilton Resorts in Phoenix); luxury leisure resorts in the Waldorf=Astoria Collection (including The Grand Wailea, Arizona, Biltmore, and La Quinta Resort and Spa); airport hotels (nearly 40 in such cities as Chicago, Los Angeles, Atlanta, Miami, New York, and Dallas-Ft Worth); vacation ownership (in such locations as Orlando, Miami, and Las Vegas), or conference centres.

The Hilton Hotel Corporation example is that of resounding success of a large global hotel chain. The growth of its business can be attributed to the efficient allocation of resources available to the corporation. *Finance* is a term used to describe all the monetary resources available to an organization. The focus, however, is on the management aspect of finance. Therefore, financial management deals with the acquisition, management, and financing of resources for corporations by means of money, but with due regard for prices in external economic markets.

Effective management of finance is pivotal to the success of hotel companies, and with rapid globalization the role of finance managers is getting more complex. Modern finance managers are expected to play a more dynamic role than that of just raising funds and managing cash flows of the corporation. Managers at various levels of the organization have to be well versed with the subject matter of financial management. Finance is the common thread that runs through all the departments and units of an organization. Majority of managers appreciate financial expertise, and do not consider it as an impediment in their areas.

FINANCIAL MANAGEMENT IN HOSPITALITY INDUSTRY

Modern day hospitality managers face challenges from all quarters. There is rapid development in technological aspects of the hotel business, while increasing operating costs make it necessary to check costs at all levels to maximize profits. With increase in the competition, it is necessary that the hospitality managers focus on profitability and cash flows without triggering an adverse effect on guests or customers. It is imperative that all executives appraise the financial implications of their actions. It is also necessary that managers be aware of the correct techniques to forecast trends, and be able to identify and address potential problems through discussions with the concerned executives. Estimating revenues and profits accurately is essential for developing the financial side of the business. This calls for appropriate investment in people and infrastructure, and also ensuring adequacy in training and development of the employees and staff.

Financial management in the hospitality industry deals particularly with investment decisions (one of the most important functions of financial management), which begins with the determination of total assets required for operations. The management has to estimate and assess the financial implications of investment in a proposed project or asset. The other side of investment—disinvestment—also needs to be given due consideration. Assets that are not economically viable may be eliminated or discarded.

We are building a culture at IHG that's focused on producing strong returns for our owners while creating shared social benefits in the communities we are part of.

Andrew Cosslett, Chief Executive, Intercontinental Hotels Group

My personal commitment over the next few years will be on building sustainable value for our shareholders. I believe the key to long-term value building is growth: growth in investments, growth in earnings; and growth in the return on capital employed.

Capt. C.P. Krishnan Nair, Chairman, Hotel Leela Ventures Ltd

Source: Annual Report, 2005–2006.

Financing decision is the second major decision in the sequence. It is necessary for managers to determine the source of finance. An examination of the mix of financing across the hospitality industry gives a varied result. Some firms have a relatively high amount of debt, whereas others are absolutely debt free. Does a particular type of financing make a difference? Can a certain mix be thought of as the best? These are some questions pertaining to the financing decisions in the hospitality industry. Dividend policy must also be viewed as an integral part of the financial decisions. The dividend payout ratio would determine the amount of funds to be retained in the firm. Larger the dividend payout, lesser will be the amount of current earnings. A firm needs to balance the value of dividends paid and the amount of funds to be retained in the firm for further expansion.

The third important financial decision of the firm is the asset management decision. Asset management decisions call for responsible use of current and non-current assets. The managers must be concerned about employing current assets and non-current assets to provide optimum results.

INCREASING SHAREHOLDER VALUE

Throughout the book, we shall assume that the primary goal of any hotel organization is to maximize shareholder wealth. Shareholders too would invest in companies that show potential for growth. With spurt in the tourism sector, most of the investors look at hotels as a profitable investment avenue. Tourism statistics indicate a phenomenal growth in the industry. This would definitely increase earning opportunities in the hospitality sector. Therefore, the shareholders would definitely look forward to increasing their wealth by investing in the hotel companies. These companies can increase shareholder wealth by increasing profits. This can only be done by increasing revenue from the rooms, and food and beverage sales.

The service sector in India has been burgeoning over the past years. Sectors such as financial services, ITES (information technology-enabled services), and the like have shown a remarkable growth. The Incredible India campaign launched

---

Ten ways to increase shareholder wealth

- Do not manage earnings or provide earnings guidance.
- Make strategic decisions that maximize expected value, even at the expense of lowering short-term earnings.
- Make acquisitions that maximize expected value, even at the expense of lowering near-term earnings.
- Carry only those assets that maximize value.
- Return cash to shareholders when there are no credible value-creating opportunities to invest in the business.
- Reward CEOs and other senior executives for delivering superior long-term returns.
- Reward operating-unit executives for adding superior multi-year value.
- Reward middle managers and frontline employees for delivering superior performance on the key value drivers that they influence directly.
- Require senior executives to bear the risks of ownership just as shareholders do.
- Provide investors with value-relevant information.

Source: Rappaport A. (2006), 'Ten ways to create shareholder value', *Harvard Business Review*.

---

by the government of India has featured India on the world tourism map. The change in policy as regards to civil aviation has allowed the sector to grow. The receipts from tourism have shown an increase of 50 per cent in India. The number of private airlines has increased dramatically over the past five years. As a consequence, the demand for hotel rooms is constantly on the rise. Due to such favourable conditions, hotel companies have emerged as profitable investment alternatives. See Table 1.1 for earnings per share (EPS) of the top three Indian hotel companies.

Table 1.1 EPS of top three Indian hotel companies

	2005 (Rs)	2006 (Rs)
Indian Hotels Co. Ltd	20.06	31.47
Hotel Leela Ventures	6.59	9.69
East India Hotels Ltd	5.58	36.04

Average room rates in star hotels have shot up in the last couple of years (see Table 1.2).

Table 1.2 Rising room rates

	2001–02 (Rs)	02–03 (Rs)	03–04 (Rs)	04–05 (Rs)	05–06 (Rs)	12-month growth* (%)	Growth** (%)
Overall average	3467	3269	3569	4299	5318	23.7	5.8
Five-star deluxe	4668	4335	4686	5606	7099	26.6	5.9
Five-star	3277	3114	3372	3897	5019	28.8	7.2
Four-star	2368	2246	2580	3088	3799	23.0	10.4
Three-star	1696	1669	1670	1830	2044	11.7	5.4

*Growth in 2005–06 (in absolute terms) expressed as percentage of the figure for 2004–05. **Compounded.

Source: HVS International.

Earnings per share does not specify the duration of expected returns, risk involved in the project, and the effect of the dividend policy on the *market price of the shares*. Hence, maximizing shareholder value may not be the same as maximizing market price per share. Market price of a share is the judgment or perceptions of all the market participants as regards to the value of the firm. It considers all the factors that influence prices. The market price is a reflection of the business performance and an indicator of effective or ineffective management. This brings the management under continuous scrutiny. Unsatisfied shareholders have the option of moving to another company. If the number of unsatisfied shareholders is high, the market price per share will fall due to excessive selling. It is the responsibility of the management to create value for shareholders. Hotel companies will be able to increase shareholder value only by focussing on products, and market strategies such as building market share or increasing guest satisfaction, to increase shareholder value.

SHAREHOLDERS VERSUS MANAGEMENT

The basic premise is that the benefit of the shareholder is most important. The reason is very simple. Let us consider the example of a small restaurant or hotel business where the owner is also the manager of the firm. Here the owner has the primary goal of earning good income and increasing his own wealth. When the operations of a business are limited, the owner supplies all the resources and bears all the risks. Perhaps the owner may have borrowed money from a bank or elsewhere, but the ultimate rewards of good or bad performance, and the major risks, go to the owner alone.

The increase in the size of operations demand a larger quantum of resources, which may be beyond the reach of a single individual. Major corporations today invite the participation of the general public to raise capital. In return for the investment, the shareholders get residual (or last) claim on the firm's stream of cash flows. The shareholders benefit by way of cash dividends and/or increase in the market price of the share. But if the firm fails, they may even lose everything because they have a last claim on the assets.

One of the characteristic features of the modern corporation is that the ownership is distinct from the management. Managers are empowered by the owners (shareholders) to make decisions. This is also one of the reasons for conflicts between owners and managers regarding individual interests. In certain cases, there is very little or no control or influence of shareholders due to a large shareholder base, and the management has complete autonomy. Consequently, management may act in its own interests rather than the interests of the shareholders. Managers often work towards mere satisfaction of shareholder interests rather than maximizing them because they focus on ensuring their own security and advancement, rather than maximizing the value of the shareholders.

In this context, the management of the firm is addressed as the *agent* of the owners. Since the shareholders cannot manage the operations of the organization, they delegate the decision-making authority to the managers in a democratic manner. *Agency theory* states that the managers (agents) may have different interests or goals than the shareholders (principal). The shareholders exercise control by casting votes on issues raised in the AGM (annual general meeting) or at any other meeting that is convened by the organization. The agents would act in the best interests of the principal, provided there are adequate incentives, schemes, and monitoring mechanisms. Incentives such as performance bonus linked to the performance of the firm and perquisites (perks) like company cars are provided to the executives. Monitoring devices include external audit and other reporting mechanisms. The direct and indirect monitoring costs are called *agency costs*. While we do not know the implications of agency costs, they appear to hamper the objective of shareholder value maximization.

The acid test of the firm's performance is the judgment of the financial markets, reflected in the market price of the share. Firms with low share prices are acquired by larger corporations either by mergers or takeovers. The consequence of mergers and acquisitions is restructuring and retrenchment of the work force. In some cases, good managers are retained. The well-being of the managers and the shareholders depends on the success of the firm. Although, the interests of the managers and shareholders do not coincide at all times, there are common factors that ensure some amount of similarity of objectives.

As long as there is misalignment of shareholder and management interests, the objectives of the firm will never be achieved.

SHAREHOLDERS VERSUS CREDITORS

Shareholders are not the only suppliers of funds to the organization. There is another set of people who lend money to the organization on a short-term or long-term basis. They are called *creditors*. In certain cases, there may be a clash of interest between the shareholders and the creditors. Consider the example of long-term creditors who seek timely payment of interest and repayment of the principal amount. In such a case, the firm will have to balance between the interest and the dividend payout. This cost is borne by the equity shareholders by way of accepting lower cash dividends or a lower market price of the shares.

SHAREHOLDERS AND SOCIAL RESPONSIBILITY

A great deal has been said about the social responsibility of business in recent years. It is true that maximizing shareholder wealth does not mean that management should ignore social responsibilities like protecting consumer rights, ensuring fair payment of salaries to employees, maintaining fair business practices, and supporting other social causes like education, welfare, and the like.

In the context of hotel organizations, it is necessary to support the cause of environment by conserving and protecting it. The Orchid is a hotel that is committed to environmental excellence and follows a *mantra*: deluxe need not disturb, comfort need not compromise, and entertainment need not be insensitive. The hotel participates in environmental protection by involving the local community, educating the employees, ensuring solid-waste management, and conserving energy and water. Likewise, most hotels in India have a policy on the protection of environment. It has become necessary to balance social responsibility with business sense. The whole idea of social responsibility is complex. Most firms have resolved the issue by undertaking to maintain a desired level of commitment to society by sponsoring community projects and projects that are socially responsible. Let us consider two firms similar in all respects, the only difference between the two being that one is more socially responsible, supports social causes, and has lower revenues, whereas the other does not and has higher revenues.

Endangered species: Whose social responsibility?

Industrial fishing has wiped out almost 90 per cent of the large predatory fish. Most of the world's oceans are facing the problem of overfishing. Surprisingly, majority of the world's fishing fleet is found in Asian waters. Many restaurants, especially in some of the Asian countries like Indonesia, attract divers searching for lobsters, the last remaining valuable species. Biologists are concerned about popular increase in taste for the fancy, novel, coral reef fish in mainland China. Experts believe that in the wake of massive and hi-tech slaughtering the fish do not stand a chance of survival. This problem can be resolved to some extent by ensuring that countries limit export quotas, create protected areas and encourage consumers to select less endangered species. Legislations will certainly benefit the process of developing marine ecosystems but the fundamental reform that must precede is a change in people's mind. Only when fish are seen as creatures deserving protection that the depletion of the world's ocean will cease.

Source: National Geographic, April (2007), nationalgeographic.com.

The lower revenues of the former mean lower cash flows and possibly a lower market price of share. Can this situation continue? In an intensely competitive environment, this gross difference between the two firms may not be accepted by the shareholders. The socially responsible firm will have to change policies to correct disparities between revenues and market values to avoid a negative impact on its very existence. Is social responsibility at odds with the objective of shareholder wealth maximization? The answer is yes and no. But it places some restrictions on the freedom to make financial decisions based on the objective of shareholder wealth maximization.

The Practice

With such diverse interests, it is appropriate for the firm to consider the interests of *stakeholders* other than shareholders. These stakeholders include customers, creditors, suppliers, society, employees, and others. The ability to address issues of genuine concern to the stakeholders will ensure the ultimate goal of shareholder wealth maximization.

The objective of shareholder wealth maximization is theoretically correct and provides a proper basis for decision making. There are constraints but the objective provides a clear and precise framework to judge decisions. It provides a ground for comparison and allows one to determine the quality of managerial decisions.

HOW DO HOTEL COMPANIES ACHIEVE THE OBJECTIVE?

After considering the objective of the firm, it is imperative for us to understand how hotel companies endeavour to achieve the objective. Hotel companies have become a lucrative investment proposition in recent years due to the increasing demand for hotel rooms. However, the value to an investor is determined by (a) the quantum of future returns in terms of cash flows to be gained from the investment, (b) the timing of these cash flows, (c) risk involved in the investment, and (d) the market value, which is the fallout of cash flows, timing, and risk involved in the investment.

Cash flows refers to the actual cash to be received or paid. This is not to be equated with earnings or profits in the accounting terminology. Accountants would watch earnings, while managers would be concerned about cash flows. Earnings or profits depict the ability of the firm to earn profits, while cash flows focus on the firm's ability to maintain a healthy flow of cash.

The second fundamental concept relates to *timing the cash flows*. Timing is of paramount importance as far as cash flows are concerned. For instance, if you had to make a choice between Rs 1000 today and Rs 1000 after a year, you will choose Rs 1000 today. This will be an obvious decision if you are rational, even when you may not require the amount till the next year. By investing the money elsewhere, you will be able to achieve more than Rs 1000 in a years' time. Managers often hasten the collection process and try to delay the payments to a practical extent. Hotel companies do not battle the problem of collections as most of the transactions are purely based on cash and there is no problem of default from corporate debtors. Therefore, most hotel companies do not face a difficulty in maintaining healthy cash flows.

The third aspect relates to *risk*. The uncertainty of something happening or an event less than desirable is known as risk. Rational investors expect a higher return for assuming higher risks. The risk and return consideration is fundamental to the study of financial management.

Valuation is the fourth important financial concept. Valuation means the process of determining the worth of a company's assets, based on expected risk and return associated with the asset. The magnitude, timing, and risk associated with future cash flows, from the investor's point of view, influence the demand and supply for the shares and thereby determine the market price of the share. It is important to note that management actions that affect the magnitude or timing of, or reduce the risk associated with, the firm's future cash flows will increase the value of the firm.

ORGANIZATION OF FINANCE FUNCTION IN THE HOTEL INDUSTRY

You may become either a chef, a food and beverage manager, a front office manager, or an executive housekeeper, and so it is important to understand the role of financial management in the operation of hotels. Figure 1.1 provides a view of the finance function in a majority of hotel companies in India.

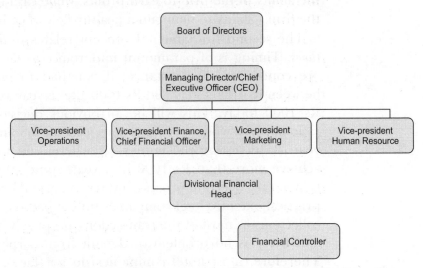

Fig. 1.1 Financial management in a hospitality organization chart

The head of one functional area of the firm, the vice-president of finance or the chief financial officer will report to the chief executive officer (CEO). The vice-president of finance is assisted by heads of finance for different divisions, who are in turn supported by financial controllers at the unit levels. The controller's responsibilities largely pertain to the accounting function that includes cost accounting, budgets and forecasts, and monitoring internal consumption finalization of the unit level financial statements.

The divisional finance head is the link between various functional units (hotel properties) and the chief financial officer (CFO). The divisional financial head is responsible for capital budgeting decisions, financial requirements of strategic business units, cash management, credit management, etc.

FINANCE: AN INTERDISCIPLINARY APPROACH

Financial management has a close association with economics and accounting. In effect, financial management is the application of microeconomics. Key macroeconomic indicators like growth rate of the economy, the domestic savings rate, developments in the tourism sector, tax environment, and the availability of funds to the hospitality industry define the framework for the firm to operate. Managers must be tuned into economic developments taking place in the country. Thorough knowledge of macroeconomic concepts will help managers to spot opportunities and threats existing in the environment, while a scrupulous understanding of microeconomic principles is a prerequisite for making effective decisions pertaining to financial aspects of hospitality operations.

Finance and accounting functions invariably fall into the same domain of knowledge and are therefore considered to be the same. But as students of finance, we need to distinguish between the nuances of both disciplines. Accounting is concerned with scorekeeping whereas finance is about value maximization. Accounting pertains to a routine system that reports the financial performance of the firm in the past whereas the principal objective of financial management is to maximize shareholder value by investing in profitable projects and ventures. This does not mean that finance and accounting are exclusive to each other. Financial decision making requires substantial accounting data and information.

The focus of accounting is earning, whereas cash flows are central to financial management. The accrual concept (a detailed discussion on the concepts of accounting is provided in Chapter 4) advocates that the earnings for a period must be recorded irrespective of receipt of cash and similarly expenses must be documented irrespective of payment of cash. Financial management on the other hand is associated with the magnitude, timing, and risk associated with the cash flows, as this serves as the basis for valuation.

Accounting is the systematic recording of financial transactions that have happened in the past. Therefore, it is static and certain. On the contrary, financial management is forward looking and futuristic, therefore dynamic and uncertain.

Need to Study Finance in a Hotel Management Programme

The knowledge of finance is essential to gear up, for the workplace of the future. One may be an excellent chef or a food and beverage service person, or even a housekeeping professional, but organizations would prefer employees who are multi-skilled and have cross-functional expertise, which has become the rule of our modern corporate work environment. Therefore, knowledge of basic financial management skills will be a key ingredient of success in the career of non-finance professionals.

SUMMARY

- Acquiring, financing, and managing assets with some overall goal is financial management.
- Financial management is largely associated with investment, financing, and asset management decisions.
- The goal of a firm is to maximize the wealth of current shareholders. Shareholder wealth is represented by the market price per share of the firm.
- The market price of a firm's share is the reflection of the perception of all the market participants as regards to the value of the firm.
- Agency theory states that managers (agents), particularly in large firms, may have different goals than the shareholders (principal). The shareholders ensure that the managers are working towards their (shareholder's) interest by providing incentives and monitoring the performance of the managers.
- The firm is obliged to act in a socially responsible manner. The objective of maximizing shareholder wealth does not absolve the firm of its responsibility towards the society in which it operates.
- Major aspects of the finance function at the helm of affairs are dealt with by the vice president finance, or the chief financial officer, who is usually supported by divisional heads and finance controllers at the business unit levels.
- Financial management has a close association with economics. It is vital for hospitality managers to know the concepts and principles of macro and microeconomics, to understand the hospitality business environment.
- Accounting is concerned with recording transactions of the past and is, therefore, static and objective. Financial management is forward looking, hence dynamic, and contains an element of subjectivity.

KEY TERMS

Accounting Accountancy (profession) or accounting (methodology) is the measurement, disclosure, or provision of assurance about financial information, primarily used by managers, investors, tax authorities, and other decision makers to make resource allocation decisions within companies, organizations, and public agencies.

Assets In business and accounting, an asset is any economic resource controlled by an entity as a result of *past* transactions or events, and from which future economic benefits may be obtained. Examples include cash, equipment, buildings, and land.

Chief executive officer A chief executive officer (CEO), or chief executive, is the highest-ranking corporate officer, administrator, corporate administrator, executive, or executive officer in charge of total management of a corporation, company, organization, or agency.

Corporate social responsibility (CSR) CSR is a concept that organizations have an obligation to consider the interests of customers employees, shareholders and communities and ecological considerations in all aspects of their operations.

Earnings per share (EPS) Earnings per share are the earnings returned on the initial investment amount.

Expense An expense is a general term for an outgoing payment made by a business or an individual.

Finance A term used to describe all the monetary resources available to any organization.

Financial controller The person responsible for the control of finance at unit level operations.

Income Income, generally defined, is the money that is received as a result of the normal business activities of an individual or a business.

Shareholders A shareholder is an individual or company that legally owns one or more shares of stock in a joint stock company. A company's shareholders collectively own that company.

Stakeholders A corporate stakeholder is a party who affects, or can be affected by, the company's actions. The stakeholder concept was developed and championed by R. Edward Freeman in the 1980s.

REVIEW QUESTIONS

1. Explain the following terms:

   (a) Financial management
   (b) Share capital
   (c) Cash flow
   (d) Valuation

2. What is the importance of financial management to hospitality organizations?

3. What are the broad areas of financial decision making in the hospitality industry?

4. Financial management is in many ways an integral part of the job of hospitality managers. Explain.

5. Why should managers not take actions that are unfair to the shareholders?

6. Explain the relationship between finance, economics, and accounting relationships.

CRITICAL THINKING QUESTIONS

1. Comment on the following statement made by the vice-president–operations of a large five-star hotel company. 'Sharma, I'm in a dilemma since I'm going to be judged by the shareholders on the basis of market price over which I've no control. In fact, I can't even control the sales or earnings that are the primary determinants of market price.'

2. Socially responsible firms will perform no worse in the market place than those that are less socially responsible. Comment.

3. Discuss the three broad areas of financial decision making.

4. Comment on the relevance of the maximization of shareholder wealth in the light of environmental and other regulations being imposed on hospitality business firms.

PROJECT WORK

1. Collect and discuss the mission and vision statement of two global hospitality companies.

2. Collect and analyze data of two Indian hospitality companies as to the sales turnover, earnings per share, and market value of the shares on the Bombay Stock Exchange.

CASE STUDY

GOLDIE'S PALACE

Goldie Singh is in the business of hotels since 1980. He opened a 50-room hotel property, Goldie's Palace, in Mumbai after graduating from a well-known hotel management school in India. The hotel is known for its excellent service, and the restaurant Café Gold is the talk of the town due to the food served. Though the restaurant serves a spread of multi-cuisine fare, it is renowned for the Indian regional variety on the card. The popular items were a result of Goldie's extensive research on Indian cuisine. The restaurant has been rated as *numero uno* by food critics and gourmets of Mumbai. Goldie's business has flourished in the recent years and he wants to benefit from the business opportunities. The hotel has forty-two employees, including Goldie and his daughter Lovely, to take care of the rooms and the food and beverage activities as well. The list of clientele is elaborate and draws from major cities and towns of India. Some of the guests have been staying with the hotel since its inception. Goldie's pleasant approach to his guests has played a vital role in the success of his business.

Lovely has recently graduated from an international hospitality school and her father has provided her with an option of working in his hotel. Goldie feels that she will be able to provide financial management expertise and international hospitality perspective to the business. Lovely is inclined towards the family business due to the challenges and opportunities involved. Goldie is conservative, while his daughter is aggressive and wants to achieve success at the earliest. Goldie had struggled very hard to establish a business whereas his daughter will inherit a successful business. He feels that his daughter should learn the nuances of managing the business with him before she is capable of managing things on her own. Lovely desires to expand the business and even wants to incorporate a company at a later stage. Though Goldie has complete confidence in his daughter's ability and is intrigued by her ideas, he is concerned about the changes in the operations after expansion. Goldie has been always committed to social and environmental cause. He introduced environment-friendly amenities in the rooms and abandoned Shark fin soup on the menu (after he read about numerous sharks being killed for fins) even though the revenue generated from the sales was substantial. The guests are also advised to conserve water and contribute towards a healthy environment. Goldie is apprehensive of the fact that incorporation would bring in outside shareholders, who may force him to compromise on the social, ethical, and environmental practices of the business.

Goldie and Lovely decide to discuss all the issues concerning their future course of action. Lovely is organized and has outlined a series of questions for them to address.

1. What are the important financial management decisions taken in the hospitality industry today?
2. What should be the primary goal of the firm?
3. What is the meaning of shareholder wealth maximization?
4. Will Goldie's commitment for social and environmental issues be an impeding factor for the growth of his business?

Factors Affecting the Hotel Industry

> *The truth is we are all caught in a great economic system which is heartless.*
>
> **Woodrow T. Wilson**

Learning Objectives

After studying this chapter, you will be able to

➢ Understand the effect of culture on the hotel business
➢ Examine the significance of tourism as a major influence on hotel business development
➢ Assess the importance of legislation in the hotel business environment
➢ Review different ownership structures and forms of business organization
➢ Understand the tax framework

INTRODUCTION

It is essential to understand the business environment in order to appreciate the role of managers in the hotel industry. Government regulations, tax laws, and the financial system that govern financial decisions influence hotel operations to a large extent. This chapter sets a broad framework for discussion on the nature of hotels while highlighting the international hospitality business environment. The term 'hotel' is derived from French, and means commercial hospitality organizations. Such establishments catered to the requirements of the affluent population in the mid-eighteenth century. The evolution of railways affected the quantity and quality of accommodation in conjunction to travel. Increasing urbanization in the nineteenth century propelled the practice to dine outside in Europe. This influenced changes in tastes and preferences of the guests. Towards the end of the nineteenth century, the ownership compositions of hotels underwent change. With increasing popularity of the company form of organization, the management of hotels passed on to companies. This also led to the formation of hotel chains with several establishments under the same management. Luxury hotels began to emerge on the scene, offering exquisite and comfortable services to the wealthy class. Development of a network of roads and rail routes also facilitated the growth of travel inns and transit hotels.

Jamshedji Nusserwanji Tata established the first luxury hotel in India—the Taj Mahal Palace. Soon many other hotel companies like the Oberoi group and Welcomgroup emerged and contributed to the total luxury and five-star rooms' inventory in India. The hotel industry in India has recorded phenomenal growth over the last twenty years. An open economic policy and subsequent efforts to liberalize have contributed to the development of the service sector in general and the hospitality industry in particular. With privatization in the airlines, the need for hotel rooms has increased exponentially. The tourism sector has also witnessed growth due to government policy and support. The following discussion highlights some of the important factors that impact hotel business environment.

CULTURE: AN INTEGRAL ASPECT OF THE HOTEL INDUSTRY

From an international perspective, it is necessary to see hotels as a phenomenon bound by cultural factors. Tourism and international business have facilitated the confluence of many cultures. Customs govern hospitality provisions and providers to a large extent; for instance, some of the hotel locations are specifically chosen to attract a particular set of people. In other instances, establishments have to refrain from using a particular kind of food in certain countries. McDonalds refrains from using beef-based or pork-based products in India. Restaurants in Israel modify their products during the seven days of Passover. There are many such variants in the global hotel industry environment. Failing to understand cultural factors can doom a hotel from expanding into the international arena. Hotels must decide the extent to which they will adapt their products and marketing programmes to meet unique guest requirements. It is interesting to note that there are various connotations for hotels based on the perceptions of various cultural groups. Commercial accommodation is referred to as inns, (youth) hostels, guesthouses, lodges, holiday camps, and the like.

One common method used worldwide to resolve the problem related to perceptions of various cultural groups is the star rating of hotels and restaurants. Higher stars indicate greater luxury in the products and services provided to the guests. Similarly, restaurants are awarded stars from one to five as per the guidelines introduced by the Michelin Red Guide. The Michelin system awards from upto one star, which denotes a very good restaurant in its category, to three stars, which denotes a restaurant with exceptional cuisine worth a special journey. Hotels are also awarded stars according to the luxury and the standard of services provided. For instance, Restaurant Gordon Ramsay, London, is a three-Michelin-star restaurant. In some countries, there is an official body for classifying hotels, but in many countries there are no provisions for classification. Though the five-star rating is generally accepted all over the world, there are some issues surrounding the acceptance of six-star and seven-star ratings. Huge differences in the quality of accommodation and food within one category of hotels in the same country pose serious problems to the efforts made to bring uniformity in the rating mechanism. Therefore, from a cultural perspective, it is rather difficult to find a ubiquitous definition and standards for conventional hotel products.

LEGISLATION

Hotels are subject to various legislations and regulations. There are variations across countries including the method of registration, licensing, classification, and grading of commercial establishments. Legislative provisions with respect to premises, food and beverage, personnel, and business govern hotels in India. Select legal provisions are discussed in this section.

The aim of hotel legislation is to facilitate operations of hotels and other tourist establishments. It is binding on the establishments to fulfil certain legal obligations. There is a statutory or legal commitment binding on the establishments to fulfil the requirements regarding the health and safety of people. The state of legislation is also an incentive for capital investments in hotels and restaurants. The laws that relate to hotels can be classified under two broad heads:

1. *Food laws* Laws that affect production and service of food
2. *Labour laws* Laws that affect people working in those establishments

It is necessary to note that the laws are amended from time to time, in accordance with the changing patterns and needs of society. The modern hotel industry comprises of units that provide all services such as accommodation and food and beverages to people travelling for pleasure and business. It is necessary for hotel managers to possess a basic understanding of the legal obligations that arise while conducting business.

For example, it is important to know the difference between a hotel, motel, or a boarding house. More often than not, courts do not differentiate between hotels and motels because they offer similar services. Boarding and rooming houses do not qualify as hotels because they do not cater to absolute public requirements. A boarding housekeeper is free to provide or refuse accommodation as per his will, and the terms of accepting guests (room rate, length of stay, and the like) may also vary, but a hotel cannot arbitrarily accept or reject guests.

Similarly, everyone using a hotel is not a guest. The law recognizes categories of guests as invitees and licensees. Registered guests and also customers and patrons visiting restaurants and bars are considered as invitees. A licensee is one who is not specifically welcomed or invited, but may be allowed an entry into the premises. This category would include various service providers, visitors at an exhibition or convention, or even a person wanting to use the washroom facility at the hotel.

The licensee cannot proceed beyond public areas and an attempt to do so would be called trespassing.

Provision and Refusal of Accommodation

A hotel is obliged to accommodate all travellers seeking accommodation under condition of availability of rooms. Accommodation can be legally refused on the following grounds:

1. There are no rooms available.
2. The hotel has a reason to believe that the prospective guest might create annoyance or disturbance to other guests due to his behaviour. If the guest is in an inebriated condition or is suffering from a contagious disease or there is any other reason that deems the guest unfit to be received, accommodation may be refused.
3. The guest is known to be a criminal or is in possession of illegal objects such as arms, narcotics, etc.
4. The guest does not agree to the terms of payments such as an advance, or demands a rate lower than the specified room rate at the time of negotiation.

Provision and Refusal of Food and Beverages

The food and beverage service provider can legally refuse to provide food and beverage service for the following reasons:

1. There is constraint of space and there is no available space.
2. The person is intoxicated or is under the influence of drugs.
3. The person is not attired according to the standards of the restaurant.
4. The person is known to be a troublemaker or is an associate of a troublemaker.
5. The guest is below the prescribed age limit for the use of services.

Other legal obligations with regard to food and beverage production are as follows:

1. The guests should be informed of the prices of *table d'hôte** menus.

---

* A French term used in restaurant business, meaning 'host's table'. It indicates a menu in which multi-course meals with limited choices are charged at a fixed price.

2. It is necessary that the order corresponds to the requirements of the guest. For example, if the guest orders grilled fish but is served with poached fish, she can refuse to pay.

3. The food items must be edible. It is a legal offence to understate or overstate the products. It is crucial to be careful when describing menu items to the guests.

Safety of Guests

Hotels are legally obliged to provide safety to guests. The liability for protecting guests encompasses the following:

1. The guest has to be safeguarded against danger arising from defective equipment or due to lack of maintenance of the building and premises.

2. The guest has to be protected against the carelessness of employees.

3. Hotels are responsible for the protection of guests against improper conduct or discourtesy of employees.

4. Hotels are also expected to be conscientious towards maintaining privacy and safety of the guests, and following good food hygiene practices, including protection against contaminated or poisonous food items.

Right to Lien

It must be noted that unlike in other businesses, hotels do not have the legal right to select customers and are obliged to receive all guests, which at times leads to the problem of unpaid bills. The law offers certain compensatory rights to the hotel to safeguard against non-paying guests. In the event of non-payment, a hotel can withhold the guest's property and this is called the right of lien. Lien means the right to retain property belonging to others, under certain circumstances, till the time a claim is settled. The hotel has a general lien on the goods of its guest and can retain them till the time the bill is paid. The hotel, however, cannot detain the guest or confiscate the clothes worn by him. Such an attempt would amount to an assault. Therefore, to avoid complications and the consequences arising out of non-payment of bills, most hotels insist on payment in advance.

International Hotel Regulations

Economies across the globe are experiencing transformation due to widespread growth in tourism, rapid globalization, and technological advancement. The hotel industry today cannot remain untouched by this development and is experiencing a sea change in the way it operates. The rules and regulations that govern this process are being reviewed and altered, as per requirements.

The International Hotel Regulations were published sixty years ago with the aim of coding the generally accepted international trade practices that govern the contract of hotel accommodation and define the contracting parties. The person staying in a hotel may not always be a contracting party because the contract of hotel accommodation may have been concluded on his behalf by a third party. Under these circumstances, the term 'customer' means an individual or a legal person responsible for the payment (refer to the discussion on companies in the next section). The term 'guest' refers to the individual intending to stay at the hotel.

International Hotel Regulations governs the relationship between the hotels and any customer or guest. The first part deals with the contractual relationship as mentioned above and is divided into eight articles dealing with the formation of the contract, the form of contract, duration of the contract, performance of contract, remedies available for non-performance of the contract, termination of contract, payment, and breach of contract.

The second part, consisting of six articles, deals with the obligations on the part of the both the contracting parties. Articles 1 to 6 encompass the liability of the hotelkeeper, the liability of the guest/customer, retention of the guest's property, guest behaviour, domestic animals, and occupation of rooms.

TOURISM SCENARIO

Tourism influences the hotel industry to a large extent. These factors are diverse and include economic, social, political, and technological parameters. The tourism sector in India has witnessed tremendous growth over the past decade. Tourism has shown an upward surge due to factors such as an increase in personal disposable income. India and China, two densely populated countries, have a large base of middle-class tourists who can travel overseas due to increase in their disposable income. Many countries such as South Africa, New Zealand, and Australia are working relentlessly to attract newer sections of tourists from Asia. According to experts, the economic growth in Asia is far ahead of that of the rest of the world and is instrumental in driving the business demand globally. Asia Pacific (excluding Japan) will be the fastest growing economy in the world by 2010. As per the WTO, tourist arrivals to Asia Pacific reached an all-time high, recording 156.7 million tourist arrivals in 2005. As compared to the world average increase of 5.6 per cent visitor arrivals, that of Asia Pacific increased by 7.8 per cent. An Economic Intelligence Unit report reveals that China features in the list of the world's preferred destination for the fourth time in a row after France, Spain, and the US.

Growth in the tourism sector has also contributed to the growth of hotel industry in the region. Hotels in Asia have shown an increase in performance levels. The revenue per available room (RevPar) has registered an increase of 7.5 per cent during the first half of 2006. Hotels in Southeast Asia witnessed an increase of 16.9 per cent in the RevPar. Strong average room rates have been active in driving performance across the region. The performance of markets in Northeast Asia, except in China, was not encouraging in the first half of 2006. The Indian economy recorded a growth of 8.4 per cent in the year 2005–06. The demand for rooms in the National Capital Region and other cities including Bangalore, Chennai, Kolkata, and Pune is increasing, and this boom is likely to fuel growth in secondary cities too. It is expected that over the next few years too, India's economic growth would be largely fuelled by services and international trade. Most Indian cities have shown an impressive demand for hotel rooms, and without any increase in supply over the next few years, the room tariffs are expected to swell by 20–25 per cent.

STRUCTURE OF BUSINESS ORGANIZATIONS

The choice of a business organization is an important consideration while establishing a hotel or a restaurant business. There are some aspects typical to each kind of business organization, in terms of the ability of the owners to control operations, the quantum of risk assumed by the owners and the creditors, and many other factors. This section will provide a basic understanding of the forms of organizations. Although we will focus on the corporate form of organization throughout the book, it is also necessary to familiarize readers with other forms of organizations.

Sole Proprietorship

A sole proprietorship is an unincorporated business that belongs to a single person. This is the oldest form of organization, and as the title suggests, a single individual is responsible for the outcome of business affairs. Single owners own most of the stand-alone hotels and restaurants. Simplicity in formation and operation is the greatest virtue of a sole proprietorship organization. There are very few regulations that govern this type of an organization. A sole proprietorship organization is not taxed separately.

While this form of organization is common, there are also some principal shortcomings. The foremost drawback is that the owner is personally liable for the affairs of the business. If the business is legally challenged for some reason, the owner is also sued. The owner has *unlimited personal liability* for business debts, which means that a loss in the business will have to be compensated by the owner. The sole proprietor is at a serious disadvantage when business calls for raising huge capital. Ultimately, the scope of business is restricted. Moreover, the life of business is limited to the life of the person responsible for its creation. The proprietorship organization cannot be transferred easily and no portion of the business can be transferred to the family members during the lifetime of the proprietor. For these reasons, this form of organization does not offer the amount of flexibility that other forms of business organizations do.

Partnership

When two or more persons associate to conduct a business venture, it is said to be a partnership. It may be regarded as an extension of the sole proprietorship. The partners share the profits and bear all the risks associated with the business. Partnerships may range from informal agreements involving oral understandings to formal partnership deeds executed under the Indian Partnership Act 1932. A partnership organization enjoys the benefit of ease in formation. In addition, the capital-raising capacity of the partnership organization is higher than that of the sole proprietorship, and the partners bring their individual expertise, which enhances the overall efficiency of the organization.

Partnerships can be classified as *general partnerships*, in which all the partners have unlimited liability, and *limited partnerships*, which calls for unlimited liability of only one partner whereas the others enjoy the privilege of limited liability. This means that the other partners need not contribute more that the amount agreed (promised) during inception of the organization. In India, all partnerships are general in nature. Limited partnerships are common in the US and UK. However, the Parliament of India is also considering the implementation of limited partnership concept in the country.

Unlimited personal liability of the partners, limited life of the business, and difficulty of transferring the ownership are some of the principal drawbacks of the partnership organization. Furthermore, each partner can bind the partnership and other partners with legal obligations, and therefore partners have to be selected with utmost care to avoid possible conflicts and disagreement that can be a threat to the business. Most business ventures begin as partnerships, but at some point, for various reasons, owners find it necessary to form corporations.

Private and Public Corporations

The term 'company' is derived from Latin (*com* means together and *panis* means bread) and refers to an association of people who eat together. The genesis of the term can be traced into the past when business dealings were discussed at length during informal gatherings and festive celebrations. In modern times, the company has assumed great importance, denoting a joint stock enterprise formed with the association of like-minded people. A company can be formed for profit or any other objective. Therefore, a company in a broad sense may refer to an association of people formed for some purpose.

A company may be incorporated or may remain unincorporated. (We shall use the term 'company' for all registered corporations for the purpose of discussion throughout this chapter and the book.) The earlier forms of business organization are illustrations of unincorporated entities. Incorporation guarantees the company a legal status distinct from the owners, unlike a partnership, which is just a collection and association of individuals. The Latin term *corpus*, which means a body, is the source of the term *corporation*. Hence, corporation is a legal entity created by law. As a legal person, this corporate entity enjoys many of the rights and incurs many of the liabilities of a human being.

The advantages of forming an incorporated company are manifold. Some of the characteristic features are mentioned below:

1. *Independent corporate existence* The outstanding feature of any corporation is its distinct independent existence. The principal advantage is that the ownership is distinct from the management. The shareholders are treated as a separate body and are altogether different. Moreover, the law recognises the existence of the company as separate from the objectives, intentions, and conduct of individual shareholders.

2. *Limited liability* The company is the owner and is solely responsible for the assets and the position of liabilities. Members, even collectively, are not the owners of the company's assets, nor are they answerable for the liabilities. In case of a registered company, the liability of the members is restricted to the nominal value of the shares subscribed to by them. No member is liable to contribute more than the nominal value of shares held by

him. As far as other forms of unregistered organizations are concerned, the liability of the owners towards business debts is unlimited. They must meet all the obligations of the business without any limit. The whole fortune of the owners is at stake and the creditors can levy execution on the private property of the owner/partner. Limited liability has enhanced commercial prosperity, contributed to the increase in investor wealth, and enabled pooling of enormous amounts of capital to be employed in projects and undertakings of immense public utility[*] without exposing the owners to unlimited liability.

3. *Perpetual succession*   Corporations have successfully found what human beings have always wanted to possess— immortality! Since the life of the corporation does not depend upon the owners, the corporation may continue even if the owners die or sell their stock. Therefore, perpetual succession draws attention to the fact that neither the continuity of the company nor the commercial and contractual relation is affected by the change in sponsorship, insolvency, or death of the members. In other words, members may change, but the company exists forever.

4. *Separate property*   Being a legal entity, the company enjoys the right to own and dispose of property in its own name to the extent that the shareholders have no claim on the assets of the company. The distinction between the assets of the company and the shareholders is very clear in case of a registered company. A company is free to sell, assign, and mortgage assets as required. Only when fraud is detected will a competent authority investigate the details of the transactions.

5. *Transferability of shares*   The shares or debentures of the company are treated as moveable property and can be transferred at will by the owner. This provision of the law enables a shareholder to sell securities and withdraw money from the company. This provides flexibility to the investing community at large to invest in companies of

---

* Buckley J, citied in Singh A. (2004), *Company Law*, Eastern Book Company, Lucknow.

their choice and preference. Other associations of people are rigid by nature; for example, in a partnership, a partner cannot transfer his contribution in the capital of the firm without the consent of other partners.

6. *Professional management* The corporate sector has the ability to attract professional managers. The managers also enjoy a higher degree of autonomy, as they are not working for a human employer, and the shareholders exercise only formative control. This helps in nurturing and developing extraordinary managerial talent.

7. *Finance* The company is the only organization that can raise money through public subscription either by shares or debentures. Moreover, financial institutions do not hesitate in lending money to companies in comparison to doing so to other forms of business organizations. Therefore, a company can consider implementing projects that require substantial capital investment.

A possible disadvantage of the company is related to taxation policy. Corporate profits are taxed doubly—the company has to pay taxes on the profit it earns and the shareholder is also taxed on the receipt of cash dividends. Other problems associated with the formation of a company are the length of time and the red tapism involved in the process of incorporation. In other words, formation of a company is a cumbersome process and takes a longer time than other forms of organizations.

FINANCIAL ENVIRONMENT

The primary goal of any financial system is to facilitate a process of transformation of savings of individuals, firms, or the government into purchase of assets to produce goods and services. In other words, the function of the financial system is to channelize savings (income minus consumption) to government, individuals, and business. A financial asset is created when savings exceed the investment, and the surplus is either borrowed or raised by way of issuing shares. Therefore, suppliers of funds create financial assets, though there must be a section willing to lend (refer Fig. 2.1).

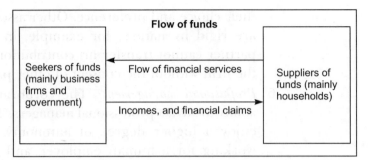

Fig. 2.1   The financial system

In a nutshell, the suppliers of funds create financial assets, and the borrowers create financial liabilities. The whole purpose of the financial system is to match the demand and supply of capital. Apart from people who supply and demand capital, there are intermediaries, such as the financial intermediaries, and financial markets that form a part of the entire system.

Financial Markets

Financial markets are not be a viewed as mere places but as mechanisms to channelize savings into creation of real assets. The components of financial markets can be understood as follows (refer Fig. 2.2):

1. *Money and capital markets*   Financial markets can be classified as money market, which is primarily concerned with buying and selling short term (maturity period of less than a year), and capital market, which deals with instruments (debt and equity) of relatively longer periods of maturity.

2. *Primary and secondary markets*   Primary markets help companies in raising funds by sale of securities to the investors directly. Therefore, a primary market is a new issues market. A secondary market, on the other hand, facilitates buying and selling of securities. The secondary market has no direct connection with the investment sector, but it encourages the buying of securities in the primary market. The secondary market assures investors with marketability for the financial securities. A strong secondary market enhances the performance of primary markets.

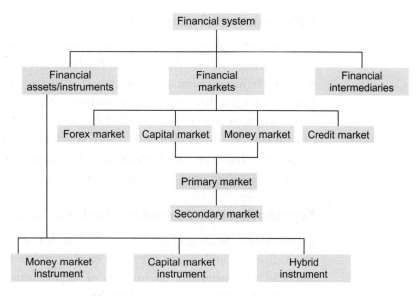

Fig. 2.2 Components of financial markets

We shall discuss the financial markets and financial system in greater detail in Chapter 15.

TAX ENVIRONMENT

Tax is an important aspect of any business, including hotels and restaurants. The quantum of taxes is normally decided by the code of taxation, which is, in turn, decided by political intervention. Tax can be divided into two categories: direct and indirect. Tax levied directly on an individual is known as direct tax. Income tax and property tax are examples of direct taxes. Tax levied on goods and services but paid by the ultimate consumer is referred to as indirect tax. Luxury tax and sales tax are examples of indirect tax.

In this section, we shall highlight some of the important aspects of the Income Tax Act 1961.

Company's Taxable Income

A company's income is taxed according to the income and expenses, after making some permissible adjustments. Domestic companies are taxed at the rate of 30 per cent and foreign companies are charged income tax to the extent of 40 per cent.

Deductions and Exemptions

An array of deductions and exemptions are available under the Act. A proposal in the Union Budget 2007 is the five-year holiday from income tax for two-star, three-star, or four-star hotels as well as for convention centres with a seating capacity of not less than 3000, provided they are completed and begin operations in the National Capital Territory of Delhi or in the adjacent districts of Faridabad, Gurgaon, Ghaziabad, or Gautam Budh Nagar between 1 April 2007 and 31 March 2010.

Depreciation and Unabsorbed Business Loss

Depreciation is an accounting term that denotes the decrease in the value of fixed assets over a period of time. The Income Tax Act 1961 permits the deduction of depreciation before ascertaining the amount of tax liability. Thus, an increase in the amount of depreciation would reduce the tax liability. Depreciation can be claimed when (a) the asset is owned by the person who is being assessed for tax liability (assessee), (b) the asset is used for business or profession, and (c) the asset is used in the period relevant for the purpose of calculating income tax.

If in a particular year there are losses or inadequate profits, depreciation amount may not be fully deductible. Such 'unabsorbed depreciation' can be carried forward and adjusted against income from any head in the future years.

Carry Forward and Set-off

The Income Tax Act 1961 provides for set-off and carry forward of losses and unabsorbed depreciation, and this benefit has been available to hotel companies since 2003. The loss/depreciation of the amalgamating company shall be deemed to be the loss/depreciation of the amalgamated company under certain conditions. For instance, the Ansal Hotels and the ITC Hotels were merged with ITC Ltd. All assets and liabilities of the two merging companies were vested with ITC and the merging companies were dissolved. The losses and unabsorbed depreciation of the merging companies were also transferred to ITC Ltd.

Luxury Tax

Luxury tax is one of the most important sources of revenue for the government. Tax on luxury, though within the powers of the state government, may differ according to the state laws. For instance, the Government of New Delhi introduced luxury tax from November 1996.

Rate of Taxes

Luxury tax is levied on the turnover of receipts of a hotelier at the notified rate not exceeding 15 per cent. The government may notify different rates from time to time and for different classes of hotels. The rate notified from time to time by the government are as under:

- 10% from 1.11.1996 on declared tariff
- 10% from 1.10.1999 on actual/charged tariff
- 12.5% from 10.8.2000 on actual/charged tariff
- 10% from 2.11.2001 on actual/charged tariff till 30.09.2002
- 12.5% from 1.10.2002 on actual/charged tariff
- 10% from 1.12.2002 to 31.03.2003 on actual/charged tariff
- 12.5% from 01.04.2003 on actual/charged tariff

CONCLUSION

The hotel business is bound by many cultural factors to an extent that culturally insensitive hotels and restaurants do not stand a chance to succeed. It is also influenced by the legal and regulatory framework prevalent in any country. Hotel industry is a subset of the tourism scenario as a whole. The growth in tourism creates a demand for hotels and restaurants.

The organisational structure defines the operational ability of the business. The structure plays a vital role in issues such as raising capital and applicability of other regulations. Hotel managers should also be well versed with the changes in the financial and tax environment to optimise business opportunities and gains.

SUMMARY

- Cultural factors, legislation, financial environment, and the tax framework influence financial decisions in the hotel industry.
- It is absolutely essential to understand the cultural preferences of the customers. Failure to do so will have an adverse impact on the business.
- Laws pertaining to food and labour govern the hotel industry in India.
- International Hotel Regulations were framed with a view to facilitate the contractual relationship between a customer and the hotel.
- Growth in the tourism sector has increased the demand for hotel rooms. Asia has experienced a high inflow of tourists. China has emerged as the most-preferred destination of the world.
- Sole proprietorships, partnerships, and companies (private and public) are important forms of ownership structures. Each form has its relative merits and demerits.
- The company has emerged as the most important form of organization due to certain advantages over other forms. The major benefits include limited liability, perpetual existence, ease of transferability, and ability to raise large sums of money.
- The financial system consists of people who want to invest in assets and people who are ready to invest in those assets.
- The purpose of financial markets in an economy is to allocate savings efficiently to the ultimate users.
- Financial markets can be classified as the money markets and the capital markets.
- Tax is a major source of outflow for hotels. Taxes can be classified as direct and indirect taxes. Income tax and property tax are examples of direct tax. Luxury tax is an example of indirect tax.

KEY TERMS

Average room rate It is the total rooms revenues divided by the total number of rooms sold.

Company An association of people acknowledged by law as an entity distinct from its owners.

Culture The set of basic values, perceptions, wants, and behaviour learned by a member of society from family and other important institutions.

Depreciation An accounting term used to denote wear and tear of tangible assets like buildings, equipment, and the like.

Financial intermediaries Individuals and associations facilitating smooth operations of the financial system.

Financial markets An integral component of the financial system that aids trading of securities and instruments.

Invitees People who are allowed to enter into hotels and restaurants—regular guests, patrons, etc.

Licensees People who are allowed to enter the hotel but restricted only to certain areas. Newsboys and visitors are examples of licensees.

Lien A security interest granted by law over an item of property to recover dues from a guest.

Luxury tax A tax levied on the luxury services of five-star hotels. The state government has the right to alter luxury tax as per requirements.

Michelin star The star categorization in the restaurant business.

Partnership An association of people with a common business goal.

Personal disposable income The amount available with an individual after paying all taxes.

Primary market The segment of capital market dealing with the issue of securities to investors for the very first time.

Revenue per available room Also known as the RevPar, this amount is obtained by dividing the total room's revenue by the number of rooms available for sale.

Secondary market The segment of financial market for trading of securities that have already been issued in an initial private or public offering.

Sole proprietorship A form of business organization that is owned and managed by a single person.

Trespassing Entering into an area without the permission of the owner.

Unlimited personal liability A feature of unregistered organizations, wherein the owner has to compensate for the loss in his business.

REVIEW QUESTIONS

1. Write a note on the influence of cultural factors on hotel and restaurant operations, stating relevant illustrations and examples.
2. Elucidate the importance of tourism as an important factor for development of hotels.
3. Explain the following terms:
   - Financial intermediary
   - Sole proprietorship
   - Unlimited personal liability
   - Right to lien
   - International Hotel Regulations
   - Luxury tax
4. State the kinds of taxes levied, along with examples.

CRITICAL THINKING QUESTIONS

1. Compare and contrast partnership to the company form of organization.
2. Discuss the salient features of the financial system.
3. Discuss the advantages and disadvantages of the various forms of business organizations.
4. Discuss the tax framework as a major influence on the hotel business.
5. Mark Brown wants to start a restaurant that would serve global cuisine. He approaches you for advice on the important aspects that he has to bear in mind as regards the cultural and the behavioural pattern of the Indian market. He also wants to understand the legal and the financial environment in India.

    Write a report encompassing the essential information that will enable Mark to understand the Indian market.

PROJECT WORK

Collect information on the licenses and legal procedures required to commence hotel operations in any one of the metropolitan cities of India.

Time Value of Money

> *Money is like a sixth sense without which you cannot make a complete use of the other five.*
>
> **W. Somerset Maugham in** *Of Human Bondage*

Learning Objectives

After studying this chapter, you will be able to

➤ Understand the concept of time value of money, and its importance in financial management
➤ Understand the calculations of future and present value of money
➤ Comprehend calculations as regards annuities
➤ Understand the process of amortising a loan amount

INTRODUCTION

Would you prefer Rs 1000 today or Rs 2000 a year from now? The answer will be very simple. If you are rational, you will prefer Rs 1000 because there is a *time value to money*. Individuals would always prefer current consumption to future consumption. A rupee today is more valuable than a rupee received at any time in the future. The immediate receipt of Rs 1000 would provide an opportunity to invest in some other alternative and to earn interest. *Rate of interest* is the term used to denote the time value of money in the context of cash flows.

In Chapter 1, we saw that the goal of management should be maximization of shareholder wealth, and that depends on the timing of cash flows. Most financial decisions involve comparing and understanding cash flows that occur during different time frames. These cash flows must be brought to the same point for purposes of comparison and aggregation. This chapter would form the basis of most of the topics in financial management. It is necessary for you to understand the concept of time value of money, which is the basis of whatever we do as far as financial management is concerned.

It is impossible to understand finance without understanding the time value of money. Though, the chapter is mathematical in nature, it will focus on a handful of formulae that will help you understand the calculations easily. We shall begin by using the simple interest (SI) formula and use the same to develop all other formulae required to grasp concepts for calculating time value of money.

TIMELINE

It is easy to understand the concept of time value of money through a timeline, which helps to visualize a particular problem chronologically and find a solution for the same. Let us look at Fig. 3.1.

Fig. 3.1 Diagrammatic representation of timeline

Time 0 is today (right now); Time 1 is one period from today, or end of period 1; Time 2 is two periods from today, or end of two periods. Generally the periods are years, but other time intervals such as semi-annual periods, quarters, months, or even days may be used in certain cases. If each period on the timeline represents a year, then the point between 0 and 1 would be year 1, the point between 1 and 2 would be year 2, and so on. Note that each tick mark signifies the end of one period and the beginning of another time period; for instance, time period 1 represents the end of year 1 and the beginning of year 2.

Timelines are extremely essential to understand the underpinnings of time value of money, and even experts use the timeline to analyse complex problems in finance. This and some of the chapters in the book will make extensive use of the timeline and you must form a habit of using them while working out problems.

SIMPLE INTEREST

SI is the interest paid or received on the original or the principal amount borrowed or lent. There are three variables in the calculation of the amount of SI, that is, the original or the principal amount, the rate of interest per time period, and the number of time periods for which the principal is borrowed or lent. The formula for calculating the SI is expressed as follows:

$$SI = P_0 \, (i) \, (n) \tag{3.1}$$

where, SI = simple interest in rupees

P_0 = principal or the original amount borrowed or lent

i = interest per time period

n = number of years

Suppose you deposit Rs 1000 at 10 per cent interest for a period of 10 years, you will get an interest of

$$SI = 1000 \times .10 \times 10 = \text{Rs } 1000$$

While solving for *future value* or *terminal value* of the account at the end of 10 years (FV_{10}), the only interest earned on the principal is added. The future value would be calculated as follows:

$$FV_{10} = 1000 + [1000 \, (.10) \, (10)] = \text{Rs } 2000$$

Thus, we may say that the future value for any SI rate at the end of n period is

$$FV_n = P_0 + SI$$
$$= P_0 + P_0 \, (i) \, (n)$$

The above formula can be represented as

$$FV_n = P_0 \, [1 + (i) \, (n)] \tag{3.2}$$

Practical situations do not always call for calculation of future value only. Sometimes, we need to proceed in the opposite direction or inclination. Instead of calculating the future value, we may require the computation of the principal amount. In other words, we may know the future value of an investment, but not the amount invested originally at i rate of interest for n period. This calls for a simple rearrangement of the formula in

Equation 3.2 to arrive at the desired result. For the purpose of understanding, we shall assume $P_0 = PV_0$

where, PV_0 = value of money at time zero

Now,

$$PV_0 = FV_n/[1 + (i)(n)] \qquad (3.3)$$

Future value or *compounding* involves determining the value of money sometime in the future if it earns a return of i per cent per year. Sometimes there is a reversal of process. You would be interested in knowing the worth of money or cash flow receivable after a year today. This is referred to as *present value*. In other words, present value or *discounting* involves finding the value today of an amount to be received in the future discounted at i per cent per year. Here, the interest rate i is the compound rate when we discuss compounding, whereas i is the discount rate in the context of discounting.

COMPOUND INTEREST

The contrast between SI and compound interest (CI) can be best understood with an illustration. Table 3.1 illustrates the dramatic difference in the future value due to the CI phenomenon.

It is clear from the table as to why some people call CI as one of the greatest inventions. The understanding of the notion of CI is very crucial to the understanding the mathematics of finance. This helps in solving a wide variety of problems in finance. *Compounding* implies that interest paid (earned) on a loan is periodically added to the principal. Consequently, interest is earned on the principal and the interest components. It is this interest-earned-on-interest effect that results in such dramatic difference between SI and CI.

Table 3.1 Contrast between SI and CI

Years	Simple interest (Rs)	Compound interest (Rs)
2	1.16	1.17
20	2.60	4.46
200	17.00	48,38,949.59

Note: This example shows the future value of Re 1 invested for various time periods at 8% simple and compound annual interest rate.

The concept of CI can be explained by the following illustration.

Suppose you have Rs 10,000 today and you deposit it in a bank that pays 9 per cent interest compounded annually for a period of 4 years. The deposit would grow as shown in Table 3.2.

Table 3.2 The process of compounding

Year		Rs
First	Principal amount at start	10,000.00
	Interest for the year (Rs 10,000 * .09)	900.00
	Principal amount at the end of year 1	10,900.00
Second	Principal amount at the start of year 2	10,900.00
	Interest for the year (Rs 10,900 * .09)	981.00
	Principal amount at the end of year 2	11,881.00
Third	Principal amount at the start of year 3	11,881.00
	Interest for the period (Rs 11,881 * .09)	1,069.29
	Principal at the end of 3 year	12,950.29
Fourth	Principal amount at the start of 4 year	12,950.29
	Interest for the period (Rs 12,950.29 * .09)	1,165.53
	Total amount at the end of years 4	14,115.82

In general, the following formula may be applied to calculate the future value of a single amount:

$$FV_n = P_0 (1 + i)^n \qquad (3.4)$$

Where, FV_n = future value n years hence

P_0 = principal amount or cash today

i = interest rate

n = number of years for which compounding is carried out

In the formula, $(1 + i)^n$ denotes the compounding factor or the *future value interest factor* at i per cent for n periods, which can be abbreviated as $(FVIF_{i,n})$. Table 3.3 provides an illustration of the future value interest factor (FVIF) table, while a detailed table is provided in the annexure. While a calculator may simplify the calculations involved, the FVIF table provided in Appendix 1 is another way to quickly solve a problem related to calculating future value. The table provides $(1 + i)^n$ value for

Table 3.3   Future value interest factor

Period (n)	Interest rates (i)				
	6%	7%	8%	9%	10%
1	1.060	1.070	1.080	1.090	1.100
2	1.124	1.145	1.166	1.188	1.210
3	1.191	1.225	1.260	1.295	1.331
4	1.262	1.311	1.360	**1.412**	1.464
5	1.338	1.403	1.469	1.539	1.611

various combinations of i and n. The interest rate (i) headings and the period (n) help us locate the correct interest factors.

For example, the FVIF at 9 per cent for 4 years ($FVIF_{9\%, 4}$) is located at the intersection of the 9 per cent column with the 4-period row and equals 1.412. This means that Re 1 invested at 9 per cent CI for 4 years will return Rs 1.412, which consists of the principal amount plus accumulated interest. Note that if we multiply the FVIF at 9 per cent for 4 years (1.412) with Rs 10,000, we get a value of Rs 14,120, which is an approximation or rounding off of Rs 14,115.82—the final amount in Table 3.2. Also note that with the increase in interest rate and/or increase

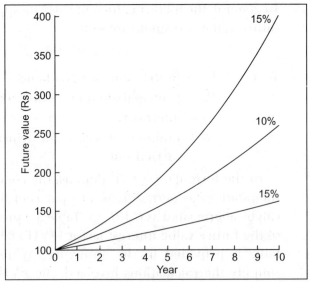

Note: Future values of the initial deposit of Rs 100 compounded annually at 5%, 10%, and 15%.

Fig. 3.2   Future value

> **The power of compounding**
>
> In the early 1600s, the American Indians sold an island, now called Manhattan, in New York for various beads and trinkets worth about $16. Since the real estate of Manhattan is now among the most expensive in the world, it would seem at first glance that the American Indians made a terrible deal. Had the American Indians, however, invested their $16, and received 8 per cent compounded annual interest, not only would they have had enough money to buy back all of Manhattan, but also several hundred million dollars left over. That is the power of CI over time.

in the number of years, the future value increases (refer Fig. 3.2).

FINDING THE GROWTH RATE

Although we are concerned with the interest rates, it is interesting to note that this concept can be applied to compound growth of any nature. To calculate the compound growth of sales or profit series of a large five-star hotel chain, we may employ the FVIF table.

Years	2001	2002	2003	2004	2005	2006	2007
Sales (Rs in millions)	50	57	68	79	86	92	99

The growth rate may be computed in the following two steps:

Step 1 Find the ratio of sales of 2007 to 2002. This would be 99/50 = 1.98.

Step 2 Check with the FVIF table and look at the row for 6 years (we begin our calculations at the end of 2001 or start of 2002) till you find a value close to 1.98, and look for the interest rate corresponding to that value. In this case, the value closest to 1.98 is 1.974 and the corresponding interest rate is 12 per cent. Hence the compound rate of growth is approximately 12 per cent.

PRESENT VALUE OF A SINGLE AMOUNT

We know that a rupee received today is worth more than a rupee receivable one, two, or three years hence. Calculating the present value of future cash flows enables us to compare the worth of a rupee receivable in the future with the worth of a rupee today.

Assume that someone promises to give you Rs 10,000 three years from now. What would be the value of this amount today? We may answer this question by asking what amount should be invested today to yield Rs 10,000 in a period of 3 years at a given rate. Let us also assume that the prevalent interest rate is 10 per cent per annum. This amount is called the present value of Rs 10,000 payable in 3 years, discounted at 10 per cent.

The process of discounting is the reciprocal of compounding, and thus finding the present value is simply the reverse of compounding. We can calculate the present value by rearranging the formula for compounding. Let us recall Equation 3.4.

$$FV_n = P_0 (1 + i)^n$$

By rearranging the terms, we can solve for present value:

$$PV_0 = P_0 = FV_n / (1 + i)^n$$
$$= FV_n [1/(1 + i)^n] \qquad (3.5)$$

Notice that the term $[1/(1 + i)^n]$ is the reciprocal of the FVIF at i per cent for n periods ($FVIF_{i,n}$). This reciprocal is known as the present value interest factor (PVIF) at i per cent for n periods ($PVIF_{i, n}$). We can rewrite Equation 3.5 as

$$PV_0 = FV_n (PVIF_{i, n}) \qquad (3.6)$$

A present value table comprising PVIFs for a combination of interest rates and time periods reduces the calculations involved in Equation 3.5. We can make use of the table to compute the present value of Rs 10,000 receivable after 3 years at a discounted at 10 per cent per annum. Table 3.4 provides some of the values for various combinations of i and n. (A detailed table is provided in Appendix 2.) The intersection point is

$$PV_0 = FV_3 (PVIF_{10, 3})$$
$$= \text{Rs } 10,000 \ (.751)$$
$$= \text{Rs } 7510$$

Table 3.4 Present value interest factor

Period (*n*)	Interest rates (*i*)				
	6%	7%	8%	9%	10%
1	0.943	0.935	0.926	0.917	0.909
2	0.890	0.873	0.857	0.842	0.826
3	0.840	0.816	0.794	0.772	**0.751**
4	0.792	0.763	0.735	0.708	0.683
5	0.747	0.713	0.681	0.650	0.621

Figure 3.3 shows how the present value of a rupee or any other amount to be received in the future diminishes as the time period increases. Note that (1) the present value of a sum to be received at some future date decreases and approaches zero as the date of receipt is further extended into the future and (2) the higher the interest (discount) rate, the greater is the decrease in the present value. At relatively high interest rates, funds due in the future are of very little worth today and even at a relatively low discount rate, the present value of a sum due in a very distant future is again very small. For example, at a 20 per cent discount rate, Rs 10,00,000 due in 100 years is approximately worth 1 paisa today.

COMPOUNDING MORE THAN ONCE A YEAR

So far we have assumed that interest is paid annually. This is a necessary assumption to get a good grasp of the concept of time

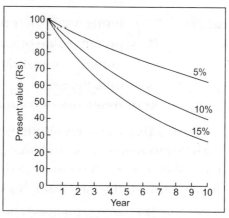

Fig. 3.3 Present values of Rs 100 cash flow at discount rates of 5%, 10%, and 15%

value of money. It is, however, important to understand the relationship between future value and interest rates for different compounding periods. To begin with, suppose interest is paid twice in a year, that is, semi-annually. If you then deposit Rs 1000 in a savings account that pays a nominal or stated 8 per cent annual interest, the future value at the end of 6 months (provided interest is not withdrawn) would be

First 6 months: Principal at the start = Rs 1000

Interest for 6 months = Rs 40

Principal at the end = Rs 1000 × .08/2 = Rs 1040

In other words, at the end of 6 months you would receive 4 per cent in interest, not 8 per cent. At the end of the remaining 6 months, the deposit would grow as follows:

Second 6 months: Principal at the start = Rs 1040

Interest for 6 months = Rs 42.4

Amount at the end = Rs 1082.4

Notice that if compounding is done annually the total amount towards the end of the period would be Rs 1080, whereas in the case of semi-annual compounding, the amount is Rs 1082.40. The difference of 2.4 is actually due to the interest on interest earned during the second 6 months.

This can be expressed in the following formula:

$$FV_n = P_0 (1 + i/m)^{n \times m} \tag{3.7}$$

where, FV = future value after n years

P_0 = present value or cash today

i = nominal annual rate of interest

n = time period

m = frequency of compounding

Assume that the compounding is carried out on a quarterly basis. Suppose you want to know the future value of Rs 1000 at the end of 1 year, where the stated annual rate is 8 per cent. The future value in this case, using Equation 3.5, would be

$$FV_n = P_0 (1 + i/m)^{n \times m}$$
$$= 1000 (1 + .02/4)^{1 \times 4} = \text{Rs } 1082.4322$$

Thus, with the increase in the frequency of the interest paid, the future value will increase.

Present or discounted value

When interest is compounded more than once a year, the formula for calculating the present value must be revised along the same lines as the present value. The formula in the case of present value is represented as follows:

$$PV_0 = FV_n/(1 + [i/m])^{mn} \tag{3.8}$$

where, as always, FV_n is the future value to be received at the end of the period n, m is the number of times a year interest is compounded, and i is the discount rate. This formula can be used to calculate the present value of Rs 1000 to be received at the end of 1 year for a nominal discount rate of 12 per cent compounded quarterly:

$$PV_0 = 1000/(1 + [.12/4])^{1 \times 4}$$
$$= 1000/(1 + [.03])^4 = \text{Rs } 862.60$$

If the discount rate is compounded only annually, then

$$PV_0 = 1000/(1 + .12)^1$$
$$= 1000/1.12 = \text{Rs } 892.85$$

Thus, as the number of frequency of discounting decreases, the present value increases.

CONTINUOUS COMPOUNDING

Sometimes interest is also compounded continuously. When m approaches infinity, we achieve *continuous compounding*. Consider the general formula for solving the future value at the end of the year:

$$FV_n = PV_0 (1 + [i/m])^{mn}$$

As the number of times a year that interest is compounded approaches infinity (∞), we get continuous compounding and the term $(1 + [i/m])^{mn}$ approaches e^{in}, where e is approximately 2.71828. Therefore, the future value at the end of n periods of initial deposit of PV_0, where interest is compounded continuously at a rate of i per cent, is

$$FV_n = PV_0 (e)^{in} \tag{3.9}$$

Recall the previous example of the calculation of present value for Rs 1000. With a continuous compounding at 12 per cent would be

$$FV_1 = 1000 \, (e)^{(.12)\,(1)}$$
$$= 1000 \, (2.71828)^{(.12)\,(1)}$$
$$= 1000 \, (1.127) = \text{Rs } 1127.225$$

Compare this with future value with annual compounding, which would be

$$FV_1 = \text{Rs } 1000 \, (1 + .12)^1 = \text{Rs } 1120$$

It is evident that continuous compounding provides maximum possible future value at the end of n period at a given nominal rate of interest.

Similarly, when interest is compounded continuously, the formula for the present value of a cash flow received at the end of the year n can be written as

$$PV_0 = \frac{FV_n}{(e)^{in}} \tag{3.10}$$

ANNUITY

An annuity is a series of equal payments or receipts occurring over a specified period of time. In an ordinary annuity, receipts or payments occur at the end of each period.

Future Value of an Annuity

In our stated example of Rs 1000, let us assume that you deposit Rs 1000 every year for 3 years in a savings account that pays 10 per cent interest. How much would the deposit accrue to? Using the tools discussed earlier, we can answer the question:

$$FVA_n = R \, (1 + i) \, n - 1 + R \, (1 + i) \, n - 2 +$$
$$\cdots + R \, (1 + i) \, 1 + R \, (1 + i)^0$$

Or

$$FVA_n = A \left(\frac{(1 + r)^{n-1}}{r} \right) r \tag{3.11}$$

$$FVA_n = R \, [FVIF_{i,\,n-1} + FVIF_{i,\,n-2}$$
$$+ \cdots + .FVIF_{i,\,1} + FVIF_{i,\,0}]$$

where, R is the initial amount you deposit.

Alternatively, we may also use the future value interest factor annuity (FVIFA) tables, shown in Table 3.5 (also refer Appendix 3), for various combinations of i and n in order to arrive at the future value:

$$FV_n = R \ (FVIFA_{i, \, n}) \tag{3.12}$$

To illustrate the use of the formula, we will consider the same problem of calculating the future value of an annual deposit of Rs 1000 for 3 years at an annual compounding of 10 per cent.

Table 3.5 Future value interest factor for annuity

Period (n)	Interest rates (i)			
	3	**5**	**8**	**10**
1	1.000	1.000	1.000	1.020
2	2.030	2.050	2.080	2.100
3	3.091	3.153	3.246	**3.310**
4	4.060	4.184	4.310	4.506
5	5.309	5.526	5.867	6.105

Therefore,

$$FVA_3 = \text{Rs } 1000 \ (FVIFA_{10\%, \, 3})$$
$$= 1000 \ (3.310)$$
$$= \text{Rs } 3310$$

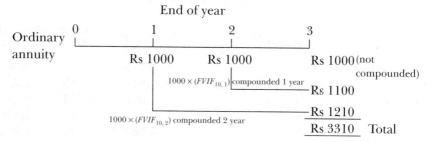

Future value of an (ordinary) annuity at 10 per cent for 3 years (FVA_3) = Rs 3310.

Sinking Fund Factor

Suppose you wish to know what amount is required periodically to accumulate a certain amount at the end of a given period at a specific annual interest rate, use the inverse of the $FVIFA_{r, \, n}$. The inverse of FVIFA is called the sinking fund factor.

Illustration

If you have to accumulate Rs 2,00,000 by the end of 10 years, how much should you start depositing in an account that pays 12 per cent interest per annum?

Let R be the annual amount you deposit.

$$FVA = R \, (FVIFA_{12\%, \, 10})$$

$$\text{Rs } 2,00,000 = R \, (17.548^*)$$

$$R = 2,00,000 \times \frac{1^{**}}{17.548} = \text{Rs } 11,397.31$$

Present Value of an Annuity

Let us suppose that you will receive Rs 1000 every year for the next 3 years. Assuming an annual interest rate of 10 per cent, what would be the present value of the cash flow stream?

In order to solve for the present value, we can make use of the present value interest factor for annuity ($PVIFA_{i, \, n}$):

$$PVA_3 = 1000 \, (PVIFA_{10, \, 3})$$

By referring to the PVIFA table, in Table 3.6 (also refer Appendix 4), we can easily solve the above problem.

Table 3.6 Present value interest factor for annuity

| Period (n) | Interest rates (i) | | | |
	3%	5%	8%	10%
1	0.971	0.952	0.943	0.917
2	1.913	1.859	1.783	1.736
3	2.829	2.723	2.577	**2.487**
4	3.717	3.526	3.312	3.170
5	4.580	4.329	3.993	3.791

By substituting the values, we have

$$PVA_3 = 1000 \, (2.487) = \text{Rs } 2487$$

Present value of an (ordinary) annuity at 8 per cent for 3 years (PVA_3)

---

* Value from the FVIFA table.

** Inverse of the FVIFA.

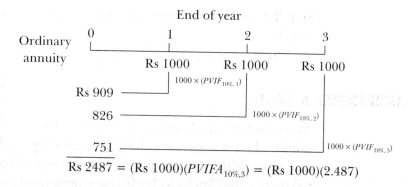

$$\text{Rs } 2487 = (\text{Rs } 1000)(PVIFA_{10\%, 3}) = (\text{Rs } 1000)(2.487)$$

Capital Recovery Factor

Just as the sinking fund factor is the reciprocal of FVIFA, the capital recovery factor is the reciprocal of PVIFA.

Illustration

A person deposits Rs 1,00,000 in a bank that pays 10 per cent interest per annum. How much can she withdraw annually for a period of 10 years?

Let R be the amount that she can withdraw annually.

$$PV_0 = R \ (PVIFA_{10\%, \ 10 \ years})$$
$$1,00,000 = R \ (6.145)$$
$$R = 1,00,000 \times \frac{1}{6.145^*}$$
$$R = \text{Rs } 16,273$$

Combining Single Cash Flow with Annuity

Many a times we come across annuity in combination with single cash flows. This preposition can be best explained through an illustration.

A 10-payment annuity of Rs 5000 will begin 7 years hence. (The first payment occurs at the end of 7 years.) What is the value of this annuity now if the discount rate is 12 per cent?

This problem may be solved in two steps:

Step 1 Determine the value of this annuity a year before the first payment begins, that is, 6 years from now. This should be equal to

$$\text{Rs } 5000 \ (PVIFA_{12\%, \ 10}) = \text{Rs } 5000 \ (5.650) = \text{Rs } 28,250$$

---

* Value from the PVIFA table corresponding to 10 per cent and 10 years.

Step 2 Compute the present value of the amount obtained in step 1.

$$\text{Rs } 28,250 \ (PVIF_{12\%,\ 6}) = \text{Rs } 28,250 \ (0.507) = \text{Rs } 14,323$$

AMORTISING A LOAN

An important application of present value concept is in determining the payments required for an instalment-type loan. The distinctive feature of this loan is that it is repaid in equal periodic payments that include both the components of interest and principal. The payments can be made monthly, quarterly, semi-annually, or annually. Typical examples include home loans, auto loans, insurance premium, and business or consumer loan.

To illustrate the point, let us consider an amount of Rs 1,00,000 borrowed at 15 per cent interest to be repaid at the end of 4 years. The annual instalment payment R is obtained by solving the following equation:

$$\text{Loan amount} = (R \times PVIFA_{15\%,\ 4})$$
$$1,00,000 = (R \times PVIFA_{15\%,\ 4})$$

Looking at the PVIFA table for 15 per cent and 4 years, we get

$$1,00,000 = R \ (2.855)$$
$$R = 1,00,000/2.855 = \text{Rs } 35,026.26$$

The amortization is shown in Table 3.7.

Table 3.7 Amortization calculation

Year (A)	Initial amount (B)	Annual instalment (C)	Interest (D)	Principal repayment (E) C – D	Outstanding amount (F) A – E
1	1,00,000.00	35,026.54	15,000.00	20,026.54	79,973.46
2	79,973.46	35,026.54	11,996.02	23,030.52	56,942.95
3	56,942.95	35,026.54	8,541.44	26,485.09	30,457.86
4	30,457.86	35,026.54	4,568.68	25,889.18	

Note: 1. Interest is calculated by multiplying the initial amount by the interest rate.

2. Principal is the total instalment amount minus interest.

CONCLUSION

It is necessary to have a grasp of the fundamental valuation concepts in finance. Time value of money is one such basic concept in valuation. It plays a pivotal role in determining the future value and the present value of the cash flows. This helps in comparing the future value and the present value of cash flows to make the study of cash flows meaningful.

Solved Problems

1. If you invest Rs 15,000 today at a compound interest of 9 per cent, what will be its future value after 75 years?

    Solution: The future value of Rs 15,000 after 75 years, when it earns a compound interest of 9 per cent, is Rs 15,000 $(1.09)^{75}$.

    Since the FVIF table given in Appendix A has a maximum period of 30, the future value expression may be stated as

    $$Rs\ 15,000\ (1.09)^{30}(1.09)^{30}(1.09)^{15}$$

    The above product is equal to

    $$Rs\ 15,000\ (13.268)(13.268)(3.642) = Rs\ 96,17,055.58$$

2. A borrower offers 16 per cent nominal rate of interest with quarterly compounding. What is the effective rate of interest?

    Solution: The effective rate of interest is

    $$\left(\frac{1+0.16}{(4)^4}\right)^4 - 1 = (1.04)^4 - 1$$

    $$= 1.17 - 1 = 0.17 = 17 \text{ per cent}$$

3. Ten annual payments of Rs 5000 are made into a deposit account that pays 14 per cent interest per year. What is the future value of this annuity at the end of 10 years?

    Solution: The future value of this annuity will be

    $$Rs\ 5000\ (FVIFA_{14\%,\ 10\ years}) = Rs\ 5000\ (19.337) = Rs\ 96,685$$

4. A mutual fund company advertises that it will pay a lump sum of Rs 30,000 at the end of 5 years to investors who deposit annually Rs 5000 for 5 years. What is the interest rate implicit in this offer?

Solution: The interest rate may be calculated in two steps.

(a) Find the *FVIFA* for this contract as follows:

$$\text{Rs } 5000 \; (FVIFA_{x\%, \, 5 \, years}) = \text{Rs } 44,650$$

So, $$FVIFA_{x\%, \, 5 \, years} = \frac{\text{Rs } 30,000}{\text{Rs } 5000} = 6$$

(b) See the *FVIFA* table and read the row corresponding to 5 years until 6 or a value close to it is reached. Doing so, we find that

$$FVIFA_{9\%, \, 5 \, years} \text{ is } 5.985$$

So, we conclude that the interest rate is 9 per cent.

5. What is the present value of Rs 1,000,000 receivable 60 years from now, if the discount rate is 12 per cent?

Solution: The present value is Rs 10,00,000 $\dfrac{(1)^{60}}{(1.12)^{60}}$

This may be expressed as

$$\text{Rs } 10,00,000 \; \frac{(1)^{30}}{(1.12)^{30}} \; \frac{(1)^{30}}{(1.12)^{30}} = \text{Rs } 10,00,000 \; (0.03378) \; (0.03378)$$

$$= \text{Rs } 1114.086$$

6. A 12-payment annuity of Rs 1,00,000 will begin 8 years hence. (The first payment occurs at the end of 8 years.) What is the present value of this annuity if the discount rate is 14 per cent?

Solution: The problem may be solved in two steps.

Step 1   Determine the value of this annuity a year before the first payment begins, i.e., 7 years from now. This is equal to

$$\text{Rs } 1,00,000 \; (PVIFA_{14\%, \, 12 \, years}) = \text{Rs } 1,00,000 \; (5.660)$$
$$= \text{Rs } 5,66,000$$

Step 2   Compute the present value of the amount obtained in step 1 as

$$\text{Rs } 56,600 \; (PVIF_{14\%, \, 7 \, years}) = \text{Rs } 5,66,000 \; (0.400)$$
$$= \text{Rs } 2,26,400$$

7. Kailas deposits Rs 2,00,000 in a bank account that pays 8 per cent interest. How much can he withdraw a constant amount annually for a period of 10 years?

Solution: The annual withdrawal is equal to

$$\frac{\text{Rs } 2,00,200}{PVIFA_{8\%, 10 \text{ yrs}}} = \frac{\text{Rs } 2,00,000}{6.710} = \text{Rs } 29,806$$

8. Shyam borrows Rs 20,00,000 for a restaurant at a monthly interest of 1.25 per cent. The loan is to be repaid in 12 equal monthly instalments, payable at the end of each month. Prepare the loan amortization schedule.

Solution: The monthly instalment A is obtained by solving the equation

$$20,00,000 = A * PVIFA_{n = 12, r = 1.25\%}$$

$$20,00,000 = A * \frac{1 - \frac{1}{(1 + r)^n}}{r}$$

$$20,00,000 = A * \frac{1 - \frac{1}{(1.0125)^{12}}}{.0125} = A * 11.0786$$

$$A = 20,00,000/11.0786 = \text{Rs } 18052.82$$

SUMMARY

- Most financial decisions, whether personal or business, involve calculations pertaining to the time value of money.
- Rate of interest is used to express the time value of money
- Simple interest denotes interest paid (earned) on only the principal amount borrowed (lent).
- Compound interest denotes the interest paid (earned) on the principal amount as well as interest earned in the previous period.
- Two important concepts—future value and present value —are the underpinnings for all CI problems.
- Future value is the value at some future time of a present amount of money or a series of payments, evaluated at a given interest rate.
- Present value is the current value of a future amount of money or a series of payments, evaluated at a given interest rate.

- An annuity is a series of equal payments or receipts occurring over a specified number of periods.
- Effective annual interest rate is the interest rate compounded annually that provides the same annual interest rate as the nominal interest rate does when compounded *m* times per year.
- Amortising a loan involves ensuring a periodic payment necessary to reduce the principal amount to zero at maturity, while also providing for the unpaid interest on the unpaid principal amount.

KEY TERMS

Amortization The process of decreasing or accounting for an amount over a period of time.

Annuity In finance theory, any terminating stream of fixed payments over a specified period of time.

Compound interest The concept that whenever interest is calculated, it is based not only on the original principal, but also on any unpaid interest that has been added to the principal. The more frequently interest is compounded, the faster the balance grows.

Discounting The process of finding the present value of an amount of cash at some future date and, along with compounding cash forms, the basis of time value of money calculations.

Future value The measure of the nominal future sum of money that a given sum of money is 'worth' at a specified time in the future, assuming a certain interest rate. This value does not include corrections for inflation or other factors that affect the true value of money in the future.

Present value In single or multiple future payments (known as cash flows), the nominal amounts of money to change hands at some future date, discounted to account for the time value of money, and other factors such as investment risk.

REVIEW QUESTIONS

1. What do you understand by the term simple interest?

2. Explain the term compound interest.
3. Explain the following terms:
   (a) Future value
   (b) Present value
   (c) Annuity
4. State the general formula to calculate the present value of a single cash flow stream.
5. What is a sinking fund and capital recovery factor? Illustrate it with an example.
6. State the formula and the procedure to amortize a loan.

CRITICAL THINKING QUESTIONS

1. Discuss the kind of personal financial decisions that involve CI calculations.
2. Present value and future value are mirror images or inverse of each other. Comment. Demonstrate how the present value and future value interest factor relate to each other.
3. Discuss the concept of an annuity.
4. Compare and contrast the calculation of future (terminal) value with the calculation of present value.
5. Assess the advantages of using present or future values table instead of using formulas.
6. Ashok graduated from a hotel school of repute and joined a leading hotel company in Southeast Asia as a front office executive. As per the terms of the employment, Ashok has to undergo a 24-week cross-functional exposure in the area of finance. The training programme expects him to prepare the following questions on time value of money before the next session. Ashok seeks your help in answering the following questions:
   (a) What is the future value of the initial Rs 100 after 3 years if it is invested in an account paying 10 per cent annual compounding?
   (b) What is the present value of Rs 100 to be received in 3 years if the appropriate interest rate is 10 per cent annual compounding?
   (c) What is the future value of a 3-year ordinary annuity of the Rs 1000 if the appropriate interest rate is 10 per cent annual compounding?

(d) What is the present value of the following uneven cash flow stream? The appropriate interest rate is 10 per cent, compounded annually.

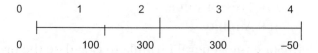

(e) What annual interest rate will cause Rs 100 to grow to Rs 125.97 in 3 years?

(f) Construct an amortization schedule for Rs 10,000 at 10 per cent annual compounding loan with 3 equal instalments?

(g) What is the annual interest expense for the borrower and the annual interest income for the lender during the second year?

REVIEW PROBLEMS

1. Calculate the following future values:

    (a) Rs 10,000 compounded annually for 5 years at 8 per cent.
    (b) Rs 50,000 compounded annually for 10 years at 10 per cent.
    (c) Rs 500 per year for 6 years compounded at 6 per cent annually.
    (d) Rs 1500 per year for 12 years compounded at 12 per cent annually.

2. Find the present value of the following:

    (a) Rs 5000 received 8 years from now discounted at 8 per cent.
    (b) Rs 10,000 received 5 years from now discounted at 6 per cent.
    (c) Rs 8000 per year for 4 years discounted at 12 per cent.
    (d) Rs 4000 per year for 6 years discounted at 10 per cent
    (e) Rs 4000 per year for 3 years followed by Rs 3000 per year for 5 years, all discounted at 8 per cent.

3. Which amount is worth more today at a discounted rate of 8 per cent? Show your working.

    (a) Rs 20,000 received today.
    (b) Rs 25,000 received 2 years from now.
    (c) Rs 5000 per year for 6 years.

4. A bank is willing to lend a developer Rs 2,00,000 to build a restaurant. The bank expects to be paid back Rs 3,94,788.79 in 6 years. Calculate the annual rate of interest on the loan.

5. Your employer would like to set aside a sum of money today so that you are able to spend Rs 5000 at the end of each year for the next 5 years on room refurbishment. Your employer is able to earn 8 per cent per year on the invested money. Calculate the amount the employer needs to invest today.

6. A restaurant purchased a new pizza oven and borrowed Rs 15,000 of the purchase price from a local bank. The loan will be paid back over 4 years in equal annual installments. The bank charges an interest rate of 12 per cent. Calculate the annual loan payments.

7. A hotel has purchased new exercise equipment, which it has partly financed by borrowing Rs. 60,000 from a bank at 10 per cent interest. The bank expects the loan to be paid back in 3 equal annual installments. You are required to

   (a) Calculate the annual payment on the loan.
   (b) Construct an amortization table for the loan.

PROJECT WORK

Collect data on products offered by various insurance companies in India from their websites. Prepare a detailed report highlighting the returns, based on the techniques discussed in this chapter.

Financial Statements of Hospitality Business

> *Financial statements are like fine perfume; to be sniffed but not swallowed.*
>
> **Abraham Briloff**

Learning Objectives

After studying this chapter, you will be able to

➤ Understand the basic financial statements pertaining to the hospitality business
➤ Understand the foundations and the components of the income statements
➤ Understand the underpinnings and the structure of the balance sheet

INTRODUCTION

In the hotel business, as in every other business, managers require financial information to arrive at rational decisions about the financial performance. This chapter seeks to lay the foundation for an understanding of financial analysis and planning. Financial analysis requires understanding of financial information. This information is useful to both the internal managers) and external (trade creditors, shareholders, banks, government, etc.) users. The managers are concerned with the internal control and performance of the firm. For example, they would be interested in assessing and evaluating opportunities available to the business in the current financial conditions. The external users, however, may have diverse reasons to seek financial information.

All stakeholders associated with the hospitality firm are primarily interested in knowing the following:

1. What is the financial performance over a given period of time?
2. What is the financial condition of the firm at a given period of time?

The answers to the above questions lie in understanding two major financial statements that are used across the globe—the income statement and the balance sheet. The income statement (referred to as profit and loss statement or 'account' in India) provides an insight into the financial performance of the firm during a particular period, whereas the balance sheet provides information regarding the financial position at a given point of time. The modern business environment demands a competent financial recording and communicating system to fulfil the requirements of various stakeholders. This chapter discusses the financial statements and the rationale of the concepts in ensuring uniformity in the reporting system all across the world.

UNDERPINNINGS OF INCOME STATEMENTS

The income statement is based on the following accounting concepts and guidelines.

Accounting period concept In order to determine the financial position of the business, time span is divided into accounting periods. The accounting period for external users is one year and is referred to as financial year. This year is chosen on the basis of business characteristics of the firm and tax considerations. This helps in determining the difference between income and expenses for a particular period of time.

Realization concept This concept implies that revenue is deemed earned only when it is realized. We will consider revenue earned only when a guest checks into his room or when he is served on the table, and not at the time of reservation or at the time of placing an order. This accounting concept suggests that profit should be considered only if there is adequate objective evidence.

Matching concept This concept implies that expenses incurred must be matched with the revenue generated. This ensures that the revenue earned from room or food sales and the corresponding expenses refer to the same products. It is important to note that expenses are matched to the revenues, and not vice versa. Expenses that cannot be identified or traced to the products, such as the remuneration paid to an external auditor, are charged to the accounting period for which they are incurred.

Materiality concept While maintaining accounts it is expected that we consider events that are material, since record keeping requires both time as well as money. Therefore, the accountant may record some minor purchases as consumption rather than considering them as assets at the end of the year. For instance, purchase of stationary material is recorded as expenses rather than recorded as assets due to judgment on the basis of materiality. In other words, the concept of materiality allows us to discriminate between assets and expenses.

Accrual concept The accrual concept is one of the cornerstones of the modern science of accounting. This concept states that income is measured by increase or decrease in the owner's contribution to the business operations. This can be illustrated with the following example. A restaurateur sells food and beverage costing Rs 12,000 for Rs 15,000. This transaction would result in an increase in the owner's contribution, as the excess income would always belong to the owner. Simply put, an increase in the owner's equity as a consequence of business operations is called revenue, whereas a decrease is called expense.

INCOME STATEMENT: BASIC CONCEPTS

The income statement, also called the profit and loss account, is the accounting report that provides a summary of the total revenue (income) and expenses and the difference between them for an accounting period. Hospitality operations prepare income statements for both external and internal users, which contain the following (refer Exhibit 4.1):

- Sales by segment
- Operating expenses by segment
- Operating profits by segment
- Corporate expenses
- Interest expense
- Income before taxes
- Provision for taxes
- Net income
- Earnings per share

Although the information and the frequency provided in the income statement may be sufficient from the external reporting aspect, internal users would require more information on a regular basis. Generally, the higher the frequency of decision making, the higher would be the need for financial information. Many firms in the hospitality industry revise their budgets and show current forecasts of results if they expect a major difference between the year-to-date numbers and the originally

Exhibit 4.1   Income statement of Lakeview Hotel Company

Particulars	Year ended 31 March	
	2006	2005
	(Rs in millions)	
Net sales	399	372
Other income	10	08
Total sales	409	380
Cost of goods sold	268	250
Gross profit	141	130
Selling, administrative, general expenses	91	84
Earnings before interest and taxes	50	46
Interest	8	7
Earnings before taxes	42	39
Income taxes	12	11
Earnings after taxes	30	28
Dividends	14	13
Retained earnings	16	15

budgeted figures. This aids the management in comparing actual results against the more recent forecasts. In addition to the monthly operating statement, a daily report of the operations or business is also circulated to the concerned departmental heads.

In order to understand the income statement, we need to know its components. The income statement is a culmination of the revenues and expenses of the firm as a whole and shows the profitability (ability to generate profit) over a period of time. Exhibit 4.1 shows the revenue and expenses over two financial years. Let us now see the components of the income statement in a greater detail.

- *Sale of goods and services* occurs between the seller (hotel) and the buyer (guest). It is the total amount of room sales plus food and beverage sales. The revenue from concierge services, telephone, and the like is shown as other income.
- *Cost of goods sold* is the sum of the cost incurred on production of goods and services during the particular period. It consists of direct material cost (food cost), direct labour cost, and overheads.
- *Gross profit* is the difference between net sales, revenue, and the cost of goods sold. Since there is no particular format, some companies may choose to report the gross profit separately as shown in the table above, while some others may show all expenses together without a separate mention of the gross profit.
- *Selling, general, and administrative expenses* is the sum total of all operating expenses, including depreciation, recorded under this category.
- *Earnings before Interest and Taxes (EBIT)* is the difference between the gross profit and the selling, administrative, and general expenses. It is also referred to as *profit before interest and taxes*. This represents the profit earning capacity of the hotel and is useful to compare hotel operations since earnings before interest and taxes remain unaffected by the interest and the tax factors.
- *Interest expense* is the expense incurred on borrowed funds such as term loans, debentures, working capital advance from the banks, and other financial institutions.

- *Earnings after taxes* is calculated by deducting interest, from profits before interest, and taxes.
- *Income tax* represents the total income tax payable on the taxable profits for the year.
- *Dividend* is the total amount earmarked for distribution to equity shareholders. Note that the dividends are paid after debt obligations have been settled. Hence, the shareholders are said to have a residual claim on the profits of the company.
- *Retained earnings* are calculated by deducting the dividends from earnings after tax.

FOUNDATIONS OF BALANCE SHEET

The preceding section discussed the basic principles that underlie the preparation of the income statement. This section discusses the fundamental principles and foundations of a balance sheet.

Entity concept   For accounting purposes, the business is regarded as an entity distinct from the owners. Recall from Chapter 2 that we have regarded the company as a separate entity, distinct from owners (shareholders). While this distinction may not be valid for other organizational structures from a legal viewpoint, it is absolutely valid from an accounting perspective. Due to this distinction, accounts are maintained for the business and not for the owner. The accountant is expected to record transactions that affect the entity and regard owners, creditors, suppliers, employees, customers, and the government as parties transacting with this entity.

Money measurement concept   Accounting is concerned with those aspects that can be represented in terms of money and money alone. The use of money as a common denomination can help ascertain the value of different categories of assets such land, buildings, equipment, inventories, and the like. It will be very difficult to read the balance sheets of hotels that show inventories of chicken in quantity and not in terms of money. While currency may vary across countries, it is necessary that accounting transactions be recorded in monetary terms only.

This principle ensures that there is uniformity in recording transactions, but there are some inherent problems like inability to record non-monetary facts that are equally important in the operations of a business. The relationship between the chefs and the restaurant manager is an important factor for serving the guest, but this cannot be expressed in the books of accounts.

Going concern concept   Accounting is based on the premise that a business entity will remain a going concern perpetually and is unlikely to be wound up in a short period of time. This is an important principle when it comes to the valuation of assets. Assets are shown as the cost of acquisition minus depreciation. Similarly, liabilities are shown at the values reflected for what the business owes and not the values that the creditors will settle for during the winding up of the business.

Cost concept   The assets acquired by a hotel are generally recorded at cost, that is, price paid during the acquisition. This cost is used for all subsequent accounting purposes. For example, depreciation is charged on the basis of original cost.

Conservatism concept   The concept of conservatism is a modification of the cost concept. This concept follows the principle that anticipated profits should not be recorded but all expected losses must be provided for. Accordingly, currents assets (refer to next section on balance sheet for meaning) are valued at cost or market price, whichever is lower.

Dual aspect concept   This is the most distinctive and fundamental concept of accounting and provides a conceptual basis for accounting mechanics, and there is a universal agreement on this concept. It brings to light the fundamental accounting equation:

$$\text{Assets} = \text{Equity}$$

Let us try and understand both the aspects of the equation. Assets are resources owned by a hotel. Equities represent claims of various stakeholders against the claim of the assets. Equities can be further divided into liabilities towards the owners and liabilities towards the outsiders. In other words, the equation can be stated as 'the resources of a business are equal to the claims or liabilities'.

BALANCE SHEET: COMPONENTS AND CONTENTS

The balance sheet depicts the financial position of the business at a particular time. The Companies Act 1956 prescribes a format for contents of a balance sheet. Let us view the balance sheet in Exhibit 4.2 in the light of the above discussed principles.

Assets

In a very broad sense, assets are resources that are of some value to the firm. They have been acquired at a specific cost to carry out operations. Assets pertaining to hotel operations can be classified as follows.

Fixed assets

Fixed assets have two characteristic features. They are acquired for use over relatively longer time frames to carry out operations of the hotels. Examples of fixed assets include land, buildings, equipment, and the like. It is noteworthy that hotels have a large amount of investments in fixed assets as compared to any other category of assets. Depreciation amounts to the value of the wear and tear of the asset, and the amount is shown against every category of the asset.

Investments

These represent the securities owned by the hotel. Some investments represent long-term commitment of funds. According to law, companies must show all investments (short term or long term) in this category.

Current assets

This category consists of cash and other resources that are converted into cash during the course of a business operation. Hotels usually do not have large investments in current assets. In Chapter 7, we take a closer look at the factors that influence the requirement of current assets in hotels. The major components of current assets are cash, accounts receivable, and inventory. Cash represents resources that are available for disbursements. Inventory is the stock of raw material, supplies (amenities), and the like. Accounts receivable denotes the amount that is not recovered from credit. Sometimes items like loans and advances also feature in the balance sheet. Loans and

Exhibit 4.2 Balance sheet of Lakeview Hotel Company

Liabilies and Shareholders Equity		31 March	
		2006	2005
		(Rs in millions)	
Shareholders equity			
Capital		421	421
Reserves and surplus (retained earnings)		121	105
	Total	**542**	**526**
Long-term debt (secured and unsecured loans)		151	111
Current liabilities			
Bank loans and notes payable		44	35
Accounts payable		14	13
Accrued taxes		36	27
Other accrued liabilities		91	64
Total current liabilities		**185**	**139**
Total liabilities and shareholders equity		**878**	**776**

Liabilies and Shareholders Equity	31 March	
	2006	2005
Fixed assets at cost	596	513
Less: accumulated depreciation	(64)	(45)
Net fixed assets	**532**	**468**
Investment—long term	65	55
Current assets		
Cash and equivalents	19	17
Accounts receivable	74	67
Inventory	132	123
Prepaid expenses	21	17
Accumulated tax prepayments	35	29
Total assets	**878**	**776**

advances are the amount extended to employees, suppliers, and other agencies. Deposits for various services also are included in this category.

Liabilities

Liabilities are a set of financial obligations that a business owes to (i) owners and (ii) outsiders such as creditors, banks, and other financial agencies. Liabilities are generally classified into the following categories.

Share capital

Share capital can be further categorized into equity and preference share capital. Equity share capital represents the contribution of the equity shareholders who are theoretically the owners of the business. Equity shareholders enjoy certain rights of ownership but are not entitled to a fixed amount of dividends. Preference capital represents the contribution of preference shareholders and carries a fixed rate of dividends.

Long-term debt

These denote borrowings of the firm against some securities. The important components of long-term debt are debentures, loans from financial institutions, and other commercial banks. The long-term debt consists of secured and unsecured loans. Loans that are obtained against some asset (security) are referred to as secured loans.

Current liabilities

Current liabilities consist of the amount due to suppliers for the supplies purchased on credit. For managerial purposes, current liabilities are defined as obligations that will mature in the next 12 months. By virtue of the definition, it would include accounts payable, bank overdrafts, and any other liability to be paid within a period of 12 periods.

CONCLUSION

Financial statements are of great importance to the managers, investors, and all other stakeholders. The balance sheet and the income statements are the basic financial statements that communicate the financial health of any organisation to the rest of the world.

SUMMARY

- Income statement and the balance sheet are the two important financial statements generated by any business enterprise, including hotels.

- Fundamental principles govern the income statements. Important principles associated with the income statement are (i) accounting period concept, (ii) accrual concept, (iii) realization concept, and (iv) materiality concept.
- It is important to note that an income statement shows the summary of income and expenses for a particular period of time, usually a year.
- The balance sheet depicts the financial position (state) as on a particular time, normally the last day of the financial year.
- The important principles associated with the balance sheet are (i) entity concept, (ii) money measurement concept, (iii) going concern concept, (iv) cost concept, and (v) conservatism concept.
- The important components of the income statement are (i) net sales, (ii) cost of goods sold, (iii) gross profit, (iv) earnings before interest and taxes, (v) interest, (vi) earnings before taxes, (vii) tax, (viii) earnings after taxes, (ix) dividends, and (x) retained earnings.
- The important components of the balance sheet on the liabilities side are (i) share capital, (ii) long-term debt, and (iii) current liabilities. The important components on the assets side are (i) fixed assets, (ii) investments, and (iii) current assets.

KEY TERMS

Balance sheet A sheet of balances showing the resources owned by an enterprise and the claims on the resources.

Current liabilities The financial obligations that need to be paid within one year or 12 months.

Equity shares Also referred to as common or ordinary shares, are, as the name implies, the most usual and commonly held form of stock in a corporation.

Income statement A statement showing the income and expense earned over a period of time.

Preference shares Shares in a listed company that pay the holder a fixed rate of interest rather than a dividend. Preference shareholders are also paid out first if a company is liquidated.

Secured loans The amount of money borrowed by providing some securities against loans.

Share capital The part of a company's total capital obtained by a shareholder.

REVIEW QUESTIONS

1. Explain the answers provided by the financial statements.
2. Explain the concepts of entity, money measurement, going concern, cost, money measurement, matching, realization, and materiality.
3. Describe the various components of the income statement
4. Describe the various components of the balance sheet.

CRITICAL THINKING QUESTIONS

1. Discuss the purpose and aims of preparing the income statement and the balance sheet.
2. Discuss the various components of the income statement.
3. Discuss the various assets and liabilities account in the balance sheet.
4. Shyam, a student of a hotel management programme, has approached you with his problem with respect to accounting concepts. He is at a loss to understand the business entity concept. According to him the business and the owner are one and the same and there is absolutely no necessity to treat them separately.

    Can you help him?

PROJECT WORK

Collect financial statements of hotel companies operating in different countries. Note down the similarities and differences in the method of reporting financial information.

Analysis and Interpretation of Financial Statements

A probing analysis of the problems of evolution forms the basis of my prose.

Johannes Vilhelm Jensen

Learning Objectives

After studying this chapter, you will be able to

➢ Understand the meaning and importance of financial statement analysis
➢ Comprehend various ratios in the hotel industry
➢ Use ratios to ascertain the financial position of a hotel company
➢ Appreciate the use of common size statements
➢ Appreciate trends analysis

INTRODUCTION

The hotel financial statements of a provide a lot of information to the users. It is necessary that the users of financial statements be able to 'read between the lines' to have a better understanding of the financial position of the hotel. This chapter seeks to explain the methods used to analyze the financial statements and to obtain a better view of the financial performance.

Financial analysts depend on financial statements to assess the financial performance of the firm for the following reasons:

• Momentous inference can be drawn by examining trends in raw data and financial ratios.

- Comparison between various firms in similar industry can provide conclusive results.

Therefore, analysis of financial statements is of interest to lenders of funds (short and long term), investors (existing and potential), security analysts, managers, and others. Analysis of financial statements may be carried out for a variety of reasons, ranging from simple assessment of the firm's ability to meet short-term obligations to a comprehensive assessment of fundamental strengths and weaknesses on various parameters. It is also helpful in assessing corporate excellence, judging creditworthiness, valuing equity shares, assessing market risk, and for similar purposes.

The process of analysis is discussed in the following sections:

1. Financial ratios
2. Some caveats pertaining to ratios
3. Common size and index analysis

FINANCIAL RATIOS

A ratio expresses a numerical relationship between two numbers. The study of the relation between various items or groups, expressed as a ratio, is called financial ratio analysis. A meaningful analysis must satisfy two requirements. First, it should be able to track progress over a period of time, say three to five years. Second, it should be able to benchmark against the most recent result with appropriate competitors. Finding a perfect benchmark may be difficult due to many factors, like variation in scale of operations, product mix, brand image, and financial structure.

Purpose of Financial Ratios

Why are ratios used to evaluate financial position instead of raw numbers? Calculation of ratio allows a comparison that may prove more useful than that allowed by the absolute or raw numbers provided by the financial statements. For example, a hotel earns a revenue of Rs 1,00,00,000. This is a simple piece of information. But it is of no use unless it is compared to some other aspect of the operations. It has to be compared with the total investment in assets or sales revenue of the competition to be meaningful. You also need to be careful in selecting the components for the ratios. However, ratios at all times may not be significant. For example, taking accounts receivable and dividing it by food costs will certainly give a ratio, but arriving at a wise conclusion is impossible.

Ratio analysis can facilitate two types of comparison. The first is internal comparison, where the comparison can be carried out within all departments of a unit or the different units of the company, or the performance of the unit or company over a period of time. A comparison over a period of time enables an analyst to determine if the financial condition has improved or worsened over the period of comparison.

The second type of comparison involves comparison between the firm and other such firms in the industry. This is referred to as external comparison. External comparison provides an insight into the relative performance of the firm as regards other firms. It also helps in identifying any deviation from the applicable industry average. External comparison can also be applied to benchmark the hotel's performance against competition. For example, RevPar or RevPar premium of a city is a benchmark to compare the performance of a hotel. It may be noted that the industry averages must be considered as guidelines, rather than being looked upon as the absolute truth.

Types of Ratios

There are two types of ratios that are used widely in financial analysis. The first kind, the *balance sheet ratios*, summarize and highlight the financial performance of the hotel company at a point in time—the point at which the balance sheet is prepared. Balance sheet ratios imply that the numerator and the denominator in each ratio come directly from the balance sheet. The second kind, *income statement* or the income statement/ balance sheet ratio, compares two items from the income statement, or one item from the income statement and the other from the balance sheet.

Further, for the sake of better understanding, we can sub-divide our financial ratios into five distinct types: liquidity, financial leverage, activity, profitability, and operating ratios. *Liquidity ratios* highlight the ability of a firm to fulfil short-term obligations. *Financial leverage or solvency ratios* measure the degree of dependence on borrowed funds and the ability to fulfil long-term commitments. *Activity ratios* measure the management's ability to use assets, while *profitability ratios* depict the operational efficiency in terms of return on investment. Finally, *operating ratios* provide help in analysing operations of the firm. It is not possible to assess the financial position of the firm by referring to one ratio, or even to one class of ratios. Reasonable assessment can only be made after referring to several ratios and the economic, business, and other environmental factors that will affect the financial performance of a hotel.

After having known the meaning, purpose, and kinds of ratios, we now turn to a discussion on the calculation, formula, and the purpose of individual ratios. To facilitate discussion on various ratios, we shall refer to the balance sheet of the Prime Hotels, shown in Exhibit 5.1.

Liquidity ratios

Liquidity ratios are used to measure the ability of a hospitality establishment to meet its current obligations. Liquidity means the ability of a firm to meet short-term obligations. Liquidity ratios are based on the relationship between current (short term) assets and current (short term) liabilities. For example, will the Prime Hotels Co. face any problem in meeting financial obligations as and when they are due? While a complete liquidity analysis involving complex tools is required, a simple analysis of cash and other current assets in relation to obligations can provide a quick answer. The most widely used liquidity ratios are discussed in this section.

Current ratio   Current ratio, which is computed by dividing total current assets by the current liabilities, is a widely used indicator of liquidity. Using the figures from the Exhibits 5.1 and 5.2, we calculate all the ratios, beginning with the current ratio:

$$\text{Current ratio} = \frac{\text{Current assets}}{\text{Current liabilities}} \qquad (5.1)$$

Exhibit 5.1 Balance sheet of Prime Hotels

Liabilities	2004	2005
Capital		
Equity shares	2,50,000	2,50,000
Reserves and surplus	90,250	1,30,750
Current liabilities		
Accounts payable	30,000	32,500
Short-term loans	30,000	40,000
Accrued expenses	3,000	3,500
Tax accrued	2,250	2,500
Long-term loan	6,90,000	6,50,000
	10,95,500	11,09,250
Assets		
Fixed assets		
Land and buildings	8,50,000	8,50,000
Furniture and equipment	3,00,000	4,00,000
Less depreciation	(1,50,000)	(2,50,000)
Total fixed assets	10,00,000	10,00,000
Other assets	21,000	20,000
Current assets		
Cash	5,000	11,250
Marketable securities	10,000	12,500
Accounts receivable	50,000	55,000
Inventory—Food	3,000	4,250
—Others	1,500	2,000
Prepaid expenses	5,000	4,250
	11,95,500	11,09,250

$$= \frac{89,250}{78,500}$$

$$= 1.14 \text{ or } 1.14{:}1$$

The result indicates that for every Re 1 of current liabilities, there are Rs 1.14 of current assets. In other words, current assets are in excess of current liabilities to the extent of Rs 0.14. Generally, a higher current ratio indicates a greater ability to meet short-term obligations. This ratio is a raw estimate as it

Exhibit 5.2   Income statement of Prime Hotels

	Year ended 31 March	
	2004	2005
Sales revenue		
Rooms	11,00,000	12,00,000
Food and beverage	3,00,000	3,15,000
Others	50,000	52,500
	14,50,000	15,67,500
Cost of food sold	81,354	88,750
Salaries and wages	2,20,000	1,84,500
Energy and fuel cost	72,500	77,500
Other direct expenses	1,53,000	1,64,000
Administrative expenses	1,16,000	1,20,000
Marketing	65,000	58,000
Maintenance	1,45,000	1,56,000
Rent, property tax, and insurance	1,45,000	1,05,000
Interest	2,00,000	1,95,000
Depreciation	1,01,000	1,01,000
Total expenses	9,87,854	11,49,750
Profit or income before tax	3,62,146	3,17,750
Income taxes	2,14,146	1,39,075
Net income	1,48,000	1,78,675

does not consider the individual components of current assets. Then, how would the current ratio matter to different stakeholders?

Since stockholders consider current assets to be less productive than investments in non-current assets, they would favour a lower current ratio as compared to a higher one. Creditors would generally prefer a higher current ratio as this would provide an assurance of receiving payments on time. Sometimes, lenders incorporate a minimum current ratio in the contracts of borrowing and lending. Contravention of this provision leads to the lender demanding full payment of the loan. Management has to maintain an adequate level of current assets without compromising on the profitability of the firm.

In a nutshell, a high current ratio may be an outcome of a large inventory, excess balance of overdue receivables due to slow collection or liberal credit policies, or holding of too much cash than is actually required.

Acid test (quick) ratio   We now turn our attention to a critical measure of analysing liquidity, the acid test ratio. This ratio serves as a supplement to the current ratio. The acid test ratio measures liquidity by considering only 'quick assets'. Quick assets are typically cash and equivalents. Inventories and expenses paid in advance are excluded from the calculations. The level of inventories would be different across industries. Hotels and restaurants show an extreme variation in the context of inventory usage or consumption pattern. In the case of quick service restaurants, food inventory may be replenished twice a week, or even more frequently. On the contrary, some restaurants may choose to replenish their inventory only once in two months.

The amount of inventory and prepaid expenses is a factor that determines the difference between the current ratio and the acid test ratio. Depending on the amount of inventory and prepaid expenses, there may be minor to significant differences between the current ratio and acid test ratio in some operations. Using relevant figures, the acid test ratio for our operations is calculated below:

Acid test ratio

$$= \frac{\text{Cash} + \text{Marketable securities} + \text{Accounts receivable}}{\text{Current liabilities}} \quad (5.2)$$

$$= \frac{78{,}750}{78{,}750}$$

$$= 1.00 \text{ or } 1{:}1$$

So far, we have successfully computed the current and the acid test ratio. Even though we compare these ratios to the industry average and conclude that the firm enjoys an adequate amount of liquidity, we shall comment on the liquidity position after ascertaining the amount of inventory and receivables position. Both the ratios calculated above, are silent on the accounts receivable and inventory position, which may be a cause of concern as far as the liquidity position is concerned.

Solvency or financial leverage ratios

Solvency ratios measure the degree of debt that is used to finance operations of the hotel and indicate, in part, its ability to meet long-term financial obligations. The lenders are primarily interested in this ratio as they always prefer low risk over high risk while lending funds to any enterprise. High solvency ratio would indicate a higher ability of the enterprise to tide over financial crisis.

Debt-to-equity ratio   To assess the extent to which a firm relies on debt to finance operations, we may use several categories of debt ratios. The debt-to-equity ratio is computed by dividing the total debt of the firm (inclusive of current liabilities) by its shareholders' equity.

$$\text{Debt-to-equity ratio} = \frac{\text{Total liabilities}}{\text{Total owners equity}} \qquad (5.3)$$

$$= \frac{7,28,500}{3,80,750}$$

$$= 1.91 \text{ or } 1.91{:}1$$

The ratio reveals that for every Re 1 of owners' net worth, the enterprise owed its long-term creditors Rs 1.91. Creditors would generally like this ratio to be low as this would indicate that a large amount of funds is provided by the shareholders. A comparison of debt-to-equity ratio of a given hotel company with those of other hotel companies provides a general indication of creditworthiness and financial risk of the hospitality enterprise.

A high debt/equity ratio generally means that a company has been aggressive in financing its growth with debt. This can result in volatile earnings as a result of the additional interest expense. If a lot of debt is used to finance increased operations (high debt-to-equity ratio), the company could potentially generate more earnings than it would have without outside financing. If this were to increase earnings by a greater amount than the debt cost (interest), then the shareholders benefit, as more earnings are being spread among the same number of shareholders. However, the cost of this debt financing may outweigh the return that the company generates on the debt through investment and business activities, and may become too much for the company to handle. This can lead to bankruptcy, which would leave shareholders with nothing.

Long-term debt to total capitalization ratio Calculation of long-term debt as a percentage of the sum of long-term debt and owner's equity is another indicator of long-term solvency. The sum of long-term debt and owner's equity is known as total capitalization. The only difference between this ratio and the debt-to-equity ratio is that current liabilities are excluded from the numerator whereas long-term debt is added to the denominator. Current liabilities are not considered as current assets are generally adequate to cover the liabilities, and also, current liabilities are not a long-term concern.

Long-term debt-to-total capitalization

$$= \frac{\text{Long-term debt}}{\text{Long-term debt} + \text{Total owner's equity}} \quad (5.4)$$

$$= \frac{6,50,000}{10,30,750}$$

$$= 0.6306 \text{ or } 63.06\%$$

Long-term debt of the Prime Hotels Company Ltd at the end of 2005 is 63.06 per cent of its total capitalization.

Activity ratios

In the earlier sections, we have discussed the balance sheet ratios. In all the ratios we have seen so far, both the numerator and denominator were available from the balance sheet. We now shift our attention to the income statement and the income statement/balance sheet ratios. This section commences with activity ratios. Ratios that highlight the effectiveness in using the available resources are called activity ratios. Hotels rely on a large amount of fixed assets and therefore, it is essential that the resources are used efficiently.

Inventory turnover Inventory turnover ratio is an indicator of the speed of the use of the inventory. More often, it is better to turnover inventory faster because maintaining inventory can be expensive. Inventory must be carefully controlled as there is always a danger of theft and other possible proliferation. It is always advisable to calculate inventory turnover separately for food supplies and beverages.

The inventory turnover for Prime Hotels Company is calculated as (refer Exhibit 5.2)

$$\text{Food inventory turnover} = \frac{\text{Cost of food used}}{\text{Average food inventory}} \qquad (5.5)$$

$$= \frac{88,750}{3625}$$

$$= 24.5 \text{ times}$$

* Average food inventory = Beginning plus ending inventory/2

The food inventory for Prime Hotels Co. is turned over 24.5 times or approximately two times a month. The inventory turnover, however, depends upon the kind of food service operations. For instance, a fast food or a quick-service restaurant will have a higher inventory turnover as compared to a fine dining restaurant. While it is desirable that the inventory turnover be high as this indicates that the restaurant is able to operate with a limited investment in inventory, but, at the same time, too high a turnover indicates problems associated with *stock outs*. Frequent stock outs will lead to disappointed guests, which is undesirable for any restaurant. Too low level of inventory turnover suggests that there is a possibility of overstocking of food. Maintaining more inventory than required adds to the maintenance costs, including expenses for storage space, freezers, insurance, record keeping, and spoilage.

Asset turnover Another ratio to measure the management's use of assets is asset turnover. It is calculated by dividing total revenue by average total assets. This ratio examines the use of total assets in relation to total revenues. Asset turnover ratio is calculated by using the following formula:

$$\text{Asset turnover ratio} = \frac{\text{Total revenue}}{\text{Average total assets}} \qquad (5.6)$$

$$= \frac{15,67,500}{11,02,375}$$

$$= 1.42 \text{ times}$$

Average total assets = Total assets at beginning plus end of year/2

The asset turnover of 1.42 times indicates that each Re 1 of assets generated Rs 1.42 of revenue in 20X5. As compared to other industries, asset turnover ratio is usually lower in the hotel industry due to their inability to increase output to meet demand. It is not unusual for many hotels to turn away guests on some days of the week, and operate at an extremely low level of output on other days of the week.

Paid occupancy percentage   Paid occupancy percentage indicates the percentage of rooms sold as compared to the number of rooms available for sale. In the context of restaurants, this is referred to as the seat turnover and is calculated by dividing the number of people served by the number of seats available. The annual paid occupancy can be calculated as follows:

Assuming that the Prime Hotels Company has 200 rooms and the number of rooms sold during the year amounts to 50,000 rooms:

$$\text{Paid occupancy percentage} = \frac{\text{Paid rooms occupied}}{\text{Available rooms}} \qquad (5.7)$$

$$= \frac{50,000}{73,000}$$

$$= 0.6849 \text{ or } 68.49\%$$

$$\text{Available rooms} = \text{Rooms available per day} \times 365$$

$$= 150 \times 365 = 73,000 \text{ rooms}$$

The Prime Hotels Company's annual paid occupancy percentage is 68.49 per cent. This implies that 68.49 per cent of the rooms were sold on an average, and not daily. Paid occupancy percentage is an average of the total number of rooms occupied during the year.

Average occupancy per room   Average occupancy per room is another ratio that measures the management's ability to use the available resources. This ratio is calculated by dividing the number of guests by the number of rooms occupied.

Profitability ratios

Profitability ratios highlight the efficiency of the management. Profitability ratios are of two kinds. The first type of profitability ratios depict profitability ratio in relation to sales, whereas the second kind reflect profitability in relation to investment.

Profit margin   The first ratio that we consider in relation to sales is the profit margin. Profit margin is determined by dividing net income by total revenue. The net profit margin is a measure of the firm's profitability after considering all expenses and income tax.

The profit margin for the Prime Hotels Company for the year 2005 is calculated as follows:

$$\text{Profit margin} = \frac{\text{Net income}}{\text{Total revenue}} \qquad (5.8)$$

$$= \frac{1,78,675}{15,67,500}$$

$$= 0.1140 \text{ or } 11.40\%$$

The profit margin for the Prime Hotels Company for the year 2005 is 11.4 per cent which implies that for every Re 1 sale, there is a profit of 11 paise. A high profit margin not only ensures adequate returns to the owners, but also enables a hotel to hold-up against adverse conditions like, a price rise, escalating costs, and declining demand. A low net profit has reverse implications during unfavourable conditions. Does this mean that hotels with lower profitability ratios will face a financial crisis? Not necessarily. Hotels with low profit margin can earn a high rate of return with higher inventory turnover. The profit margin must be considered along with the turnover ratios.

Return on investment   Profitability ratios also relate to profits on investment. One such measure is the rate of return on investment.

$$\text{Return on investment} = \frac{\text{Net profit after taxes}}{\text{Total investment}} \qquad (5.9)$$

$$= \frac{1,78,675}{15,67,500}$$

$$= 0.1140 \text{ or } 11.40\%$$

Return on assets   Return on assets (RoA) is a variation that uses the average of assets as denominator:

$$\text{Return on assets} = \frac{\text{Net profit after taxes}}{\text{Average assets}} \qquad (5.10)$$

$$= \frac{1,78,675}{11,02,375}$$

$$= 0.16 \text{ or } 16\%$$

A very low ROA may be the result of inadequate profits or excessive assets. A very high ROA may indicate supplementing the existing assets. High or low ratios can be ascertained by benchmarking against industry average.

Return on equity A major profitability ratio that compares profits of the enterprise to the owner's investment is called return on equity (ROE). The ROE is calculated as follows:

$$\text{Return on owner's equity} = \frac{\text{Net income}}{\text{Average owner's equity}} \qquad (5.11)$$

$$= \frac{1,78,675}{3,60,500}$$

$$= 0.49 \text{ or } 49.6\%$$

Average owner's equity = Owner's equity at the beginning plus end/2

This ratio reflects the management's ability to produce returns for the owner.

Operating ratios

Operating ratios help managers to analyse and evaluate the hotel operations. Operating ratios express expenses as a percentage of sales. These ratios are extremely useful in planning and controlling operations as the ratios are related to some resource, like time, money, etc. Managers can develop productivity standards based on the operating ratios like the number of employees per room, or the number of rooms serviced by an attendant, or the average check-in and check-out time.

There are some factors that do not allow uniformity in the process of establishing a standard. Every department has unique and distinct requirements. For instance, the productivity standard applicable to the housekeeping department may not be useful in judging the performance of the restaurants.

The requirements of every department make it extremely difficult to spell out a set of productivity standards across the hotel. It is important that quality is not compromised while establishing standards. This section discusses a few ratios critical to hotel operations.

Average daily rate Average daily rate is an important rooms department ratio and is calculated as follows:

$$\text{Average daily rate} = \frac{\text{Rooms revenue}}{\text{Number of rooms sold}} \quad (5.12)$$

Average owner's equity = Owner's equity at the beginning and End/2

Let us consider antohter example:

Number of rooms	60
Rooms revenue	4,00,00,000
Occupancy percentage	75

$$\text{Average daily rate} = \frac{4,00,00,000}{16,475} = \text{Rs } 2428$$

Revenue per available room (RevPar) The ADR combined with the paid occupied percentage gives a powerful tool for comparison and is referred to as RevPar. Hoteliers have traditionally relied on the occupancy percentage or the average daily rate as indicators of activity and performance. These indicators may not be meaningful at all times. It would be difficult to differentiate between a hotel with Rs 5000 ADR and 80 per cent occupancy and a hotel with Rs 6000 ADR and only 60 per cent occupancy. Hence, the RevPar considers the average daily rate and the paid occupancy percentage.

$$\text{RevPar} = \frac{\text{Rooms revenue}}{\text{Available rooms}} \quad (5.13)$$

$$= \frac{4,00,00,000}{21,900} = \text{Rs } 1826$$

Alternatively,

RevPar = Paid occupancy percentage x ADR

Most hotel managers, operators, investing community, and analysts use RevPar as a measure to assess and analyse performance.

In the preceding section, we have seen the mechanics of calculating RevPar. While this is a significant tool to review operational performance, there are some drawbacks associated with RevPar. The following points have to be kept in mind while using the RevPar:

1. *Mix of revenue* Rooms revenue in India typically accounts for 60 per cent of the total revenue. These include hotels with a considerable amount of food and beverage operations, meetings, conferences, etc. The use of RevPar in such cases would reflect the performance of the accommodation department only and would disregard all other sources of incremental revenue. Consequently, this would provide inaccurate analysis when comparing the hotel's performance. Hotels with higher revenue from other sources as compared to room revenue would earn more money in contrast to hotels with higher room revenue and low revenue from other sources.

2. *Size* The RevPar for larger hotels would be lower as compared to smaller properties, given the same market conditions. Smaller properties will have a higher occupancy percentage as compared to large hotels. Due to this phenomenon, RevPar deals severely with larger hotels.

3. *Value implications* RevPar does not have adequate correlation to the income capitalization[*] value of the property as hotel values are typically based on free cash flows, and not total revenues.

In conclusion, it can be said that RevPar indicates the performance of hotels in terms of room inventory management but does not provide an indication of the corresponding costs, and therefore, the profitability of the hotel.

GOPPAR (Goh-Par) GOPPAR, or the gross operating profit per available room, tries to highlight the profit (total revenue *less* total departmental and operating expenses) earned by selling a room every day. Exhibit 5.3 and the following example show the calculation of GOPPAR.

---

[*] Refer to Chapter 13 for a detailed discussion on hotel valuation techniques.

Exhibit 5.3   Calculating GOPPAR

		Amount (Rs)	Total	Percentage of total
1	Rooms revenue	2,55,50,000		64.19
2	Food and beverage	1,00,00,000		25.12
3	Others	42,50,000		10.69
4	Total revenue		3,98,00,000	100.00
5	Departmental expenses			
6	Rooms	51,10,000		20.00
7	Food and beverage	60,00,000		60.00
8	Other departments	20,00,000		47.00
9	Undistributed expenses	80,00,000		30.00
10	Total expenses		2,11,10,000	20.00
11	Gross operating profit (4–10)		1,86,90,000	47.00
12	GOPPAR		512	

GOPPAR = Gross operating profit/number of rooms
= 1,8,6,90,000/36,500 = Rs 512

In the above example, we have assumed the following:

Number of rooms	100
Number of days in a historic period	365
Number or rooms available per year	36,500
Occupancy	60%
Average rate	Rs 1,000
RevPar	600

From the above illustration it is evident that GOPPAR does not provide for the evaluation of the rooms division but reflects the profitability, efficiency of the management, and the underlying value of the hotel as a whole. Using GOPPAR has the following advantages:

1. *Mix of revenue* GOPPAR reflects the operating profit of a hotel. It also reflects the cash flow generating potential of the hotel. This helps the hotel company's investors and developers to evaluate the hotel management's effectiveness, based on the total revenue and the operating profit per year.

2. *Size of hotels and operations* GOPPAR includes revenue and also the costs, both fixed and variable. Fixed costs are associated with the size and requirements of the hotel while the variable components are related to the volume of business attributed to the hotel. A larger hotel would benefit from the economies of scale in contrast to a smaller hotel and therefore, a smaller hotel is likely to have higher expenses. A smaller hotel can benefit from a higher RevPar due to limited room inventory, but the operating expenses *per room* are prone to be higher. Thus, GOPPAR provides a perfect judgement of the performance of the hotels irrespective of the size of operations.

3. *Value implications* The value of the hotel is based on the net cash flow. In contrast to RevPar, GOPPAR has a greater and more reliable relationship with a hotel's value. In other words, a high RevPar does not necessarily indicate a high level of profit whereas a high GOPPAR reflects a high level of profitability and consequently, is a better indicator of value.

Food cost percentage   Food cost percentage is a key food service ratio that compares the total food cost to the sales revenue. Most food service managers, chefs, and general managers tend to rely on this ratio to determine if the cost levels are under control.

$$\text{Food cost percentage} = \frac{\text{Cost of food sold}}{\text{Total food sales}} \qquad (5.14)$$

$$= \frac{88,750}{3,15,000}$$

$$= 0.28 \text{ or } 28\%$$

The ratio indicates that for every Re 1 of food sales, Rs 0.39 is the cost incurred on the food sold. The best method again is to compare the budgeted percentage for the period. An increase or decrease should be dealt with in an investigatory manner. Managers and executive chefs should be equally concerned about both the low food cost and the high food cost percentage. Poor quality and incorrect food portioning may result in lower levels of food cost. On the other hand, thefts, wastage, spoilage, and poor portion control may result in a high food cost percentage.

Profitability of hotels

Occupancy of hotels affects profitability more than the average daily rate (ADR). Keeping all other factors as constant, hotels with higher occupancy are more profitable as the operating costs are lower. The phenomena of 'more heads in beds' will yield a higher profit margin across all categories of hotels. This does necessarily mean that hotels cannot have a higher ADR with a low occupancy. Hotels with higher occupancy can always trade-off ADR in order to enhance profitability during recessionary phases or purely to manage revenues efficiently. During a growth in the economy, there is an affinity to increase the room rates whereas increasing occupancy is an appropriate strategy to remain profitable.

We have seen that occupancy is a major factor that affects the revenue generation capacity of a hotel. This is true to the extent that food, beverage, and other ancillary facilities like spas facilitate additional revenue. Therefore, by attracting and accommodating the market segments that demand such facilities, hotels can earn higher revenues and can be more profitable.

SOME CAVEATS

Ratios are extremely beneficial to everyone including owners, creditors, and management in ascertaining the financial position and to plan the future course of action. However, there are some problems associated with the use of ratios for financial analysis:

1. *Indicators* Ratios must be looked upon as indicators only. Ratios do not solve problems, nor do they reveal the exact nature of the problem. At the most, a major deviation from the standard, budget, or industry average can indicate that there could be a problem. Therefore, specific areas of the problem require a thorough investigation before arriving at any conclusion.

2. *Complexities in comparison* Ratios are meaningful only when compared to some other related figure or average. Net profit percentage of 15 per cent has little relevance unless compared to a benchmark, such as the profit per cent in the past, the industry average, or the budgeted performance. While dealing with inter-firm comparisons, it is

necessary that both the hotels should be comparable. Comparisons as regards some ratios, such as the operating ratios, may not be conclusive if one hotel belongs to the luxury segment and the other to the economy segment. Furthermore, accounting practices of two hotels may be dissimilar and may not allow an easy comparison.

3. *Seasonal factors* Seasonal factors also distort ratio analysis. For instance, the inventory turnover ratio of a restaurant is significantly different from other times immediately after a busy season like the New Year celebration. This problem can be solved by looking at the monthly inventory when calculating turnover ratios.

4. *Window dressing techniques* Techniques employed by hotels to ensure that the financial statements look stronger are referred to as window dressing techniques. For example, a hotelier in Mumbai postponed some purchases in order to pay-off the creditors. This ensured that the current ratio looked better and therefore, the balance sheet looked better, but after some time the balance sheet slipped back to the original level. Analysts must be wary of the consequences of window dressing as far as ratio analysis is concerned.

5. *Inflation* Ratio analysis is based on historical cost data and therefore, does not reflect the impact of inflation on assets purchased at different time periods. Consequently, ratio analysis will not be able to provide a comparable result.

6. *Lacks in providing generic result* Ratio analysis also fails to provide a common result across hotels. Though the industry average does serve as a guidepost, it is still very difficult to ascertain the intensity of the ratios. It very difficult to judge how good or bad a ratio is. Moreover, some ratios are favourable and the others are unfavourable. In such a situation, passing a verdict on the overall financial position is a challenge.

COMMON SIZE ANALYSIS AND INDEX ANALYSIS

It is often beneficial to express the balance sheet and the income statement as percentages. The percentages can be related to totals such as total assets, or total sales, or to some base year.

Relating to total assets, or total sales, is called common size analysis, whereas relating to some base year is referred to as index analysis. Common size analysis expresses all the balance sheet items as a percentage of total assets and all the income statement items as a percentage of net sales or revenues. Common size analysis helps in comparing two hotels of different sizes because each item on the financial statement is expressed as a percentage, or as a standard.

Common size analysis expresses the components of the balance sheet as a percentage of total assets of the hotel. The items can be expressed as a percentage of total sales in the case of income statement. The method of calculating the gross and the net margin can be extended to all the items in the income statement. By expressing items as a percentage, it is possible to track trends and changes in items over a period of time. An illustration is provided in Table 5.1. On examining the common size balance sheet, it can be ascertained that

1. The proportion of secured loans has declined, while the proportion of unsecured loans has increased.
2. While the proportion of fixed assets (net) has decreased, the proportion of current assets, loans and advances has increased.

Table 5.1   Balance sheet

	2004	2005	2006
		(Rs in millions)	
Assets			
Fixed assets	64	63	64
Investment	3	2	2
Current assets, loans, and advances	31	33	32
Miscellaneous expenditure	2	2	1
Total	100	100	100
Liabilities			
Share capital	26	22	32
Reserves and surplus	17	23	19
Secured loans	33	30	28
Unsecured loans	6	6	5
Current liabilities and provisions	19	19	16

Table 5.2 Income statement

	2004	2005	2006
	(Rs in millions)		
Net sales	100.0	100.0	100.0
Cost of goods sold	45.8	49.2	46.7
Gross profit	54.2	50.8	53.3
Selling, general, and administrative expense.	40.7	37.6	37.7
Depreciation	2.4	2.5	2.3
Interest expense	0.5	0.4	0.4
Earnings before taxes	10.6	10.3	12.9
Taxes	3.9	3.9	4.9
Earnings after taxes	6.7	6.4	8.0

The common size income statement as shown in Table 5.2 shows a fluctuation in the gross profit margin in the period under consideration. A control over the cost of goods sold and selling, general, and administrative expense has increased the overall profitability of the hotel.

Solved Problems

1. The Mahal hotel has a capital of Rs 10,00,000: its turnover is three times the capital and the net profit margin on sales is 6%. Calculate the return on investment.

Total gross sales	Rs 15,00,000
Cash sales (included in above)	2,00,000
Employee consumption	7,000
Total debtors at the end	90,000
Bills receivable	20,000
Provision for doubtful debts at the end of the year	1,000
Total creditors at the end	10,00,000

Calculate the average collection period.

Solution:

$$\text{Total credit sales} = \text{Gross sales} - \text{cash sales}$$
$$- \text{employee consumption}$$

$$= \text{Rs } 15,00,000 - \text{Rs } 2,00,000 - \text{Rs } 7000$$

$$= \text{Rs } 12,93,000$$

$$\text{Debtors turnover} = \frac{\text{Credit sales}}{\text{Debtors} + \text{Bills receivable}}$$

$$= \frac{\text{Rs } 12,93,000}{\text{Rs } 1,10,000}$$

$$= 11.75 \text{ times}$$

$$\text{Average collection period} = \frac{365 \text{ days}}{\text{Debtor's turnover}}$$

$$= 31.06 \text{ days}$$

2. The following are the ratios relating to the activities of a service apartment division of a large hotel chain in South Asia.

Debtors velocity (months)	3
Stock velocity (months)	8
Creditors velocity (months)	2
Gross profit ratio (%)	25

Gross profit for the current year ended 31st December amounts to Rs 8,00,000. Closing stock of the year is Rs 1,00,000 above the opening stock. Bills receivable amounts to Rs 25,000 and bills payable to Rs 10,000. Find out (a) cash sales and credit sales (assume that the division sells on 80% credit and 20% cash and (b) sundry debtors.

Solution:

(a) Determination of sales: Sales $= \dfrac{8,00,000 * 100}{25}$

$$= \text{Rs } 32,00,000$$

Therefore, Credit sales $= \text{Rs } 25,60,000$

Cash sales $= \text{Rs } 6,40,000$

(b) Determination of sundry debtors: Debtors velocity is 3 months. In other words, debtors' collection period 3 months, or debtors' turnover ratio is 4. Assuming credit sales at 80% and debtors turnover ratio being calculated on the basis of year-end figures,

$$\text{Debtors turnover ratio} = \frac{\text{Credit sales}}{\text{Closing debtors} + \text{Bills receivable}}$$

$$= \frac{\text{credit sales}}{\text{debtors' turnover ratio}}$$

$$= \frac{25,60,000}{X + 25,000}$$

$$X + 25,000 = 6,40,000$$
$$X = 6,40,000 - 25,000$$
$$= \text{Rs } 6,15,000$$

3. The following are details pertaining to the financial performance of the Intercon Hotel Corporation, a 400-room hotel operating in the city of Calcutta, and the corresponding industry averages:

Balance Sheet as at 31 March 2006

Liabilities		Assets	Amount
			(Rs in million)
Equity share capital	240	Net fixed assets	1210
5% Debentures	460	Cash	20
Sundry creditors	330	Accounts receivable	50
Notes payable	242	Inventory	65
Other current liabilities	73		
	1345		1345

Statement of profit for the year ending 31 March 2006

	(Rs in million)	
Sales		
Rooms	2475	
Food and beverage	1650	4125
Less:		
Food cost	1568	
Labour	660	
Heat, light, and power	486	
Gross profit		1411
Less: Selling and distribution expenses	275	
Less: Administrative and general expenses	307	582
Earnings before interest and taxes		829
Less: Interest		380
Earnings before taxes		449
Less: Income taxes (@ 40%)		180
Net profit		269

Ratios

Ratios	Industry
Current assets/current liabilities	2.0
Sales/total assets	3.0
Net profit/sales (per cent)	10.00
Average daily rate	Rs 20,000
RevPar	Rs 15,000
Return on assets (ROA)	12.00

1. Determine the indicated ratios for the hotel.
2. Indicate the company's strengths and weaknesses as shown by your analysis.

Assume that the hotel has 75 per cent occupancy throughout the year.

Solution:

1. Calculation of ratios

Ratios		Computation result	Indicated	Industry
Current ratio	$\dfrac{\text{Current assets}}{\text{Current liabilities}}$	$\dfrac{135}{73}$	1.84	2.0
Asset turnover ratio	$\dfrac{\text{Sales}}{\text{Total assets}}$	$\dfrac{4125}{1210}$	3.4	3.0
Net profit ratio	$\dfrac{\text{Net profit}}{\text{Sales}}$	$\dfrac{269}{4125}$	6.5	10.00
Average daily rate	$\dfrac{\text{Room revenue}}{\text{Number of rooms sold}}$	$\dfrac{2475}{0.1095}$	Rs 22,602	Rs 20,000
RevPar	$\dfrac{\text{Room revenue}}{\text{Number of rooms available}}$	$\dfrac{2475}{0.146}$	Rs 16,952	Rs 15,000
Return on assets	$\dfrac{\text{Net profit}}{\text{Total assets}}$	$\dfrac{269}{1210}$	22.22	25.00

2. While all ratios conform to the industry standards, the net profit ratio is significantly lower when compared to the industry averages. There is a possibility that the hotel is operating at high cost levels because the average daily rate (ADR) and the revenue available per room (RevPar) are better than the industry average. Hence, the hotel must find out the reasons for lower profitability either by checking the operational or the administrative and other costs.

Note that the number of rooms is calculated as 400 * 365 = 1,46,000 or 0.146 million rooms.

Similarly, number of rooms sold is calculated as 400 * 365 * .75 = 1,09,500 rooms or 0.1095 million rooms.

SUMMARY

- Irrespective of the requirements of the users, financial analysis involves the use of financial statements and if interpreted correctly, can provide valuable insight into the hotel's performance and position.
- The main tool of financial analysis is ratio analysis that essentially involves analysis of ratios which summarize the relationship between two items in the financial statements.
- Financial ratios can be divided into five categories: liquidity, leverage, coverage, activity, and profitability ratios.
- Additional information can be drawn by common size and index analysis.

KEY TERMS

Balance sheet A financial statement that reflects the position of a business enterprise as on a particular date.

Income statement A statement that reflects the profitability of the firm for a particular period.

Liquidity ratios Ratios that reflect the ability of the hotel to pay dues on time.

Profitability ratios Ratios that depict the ability of the hotel to generate profits.

Ratio analysis The analysis of financial statements using ratios.

REVIEW QUESTIONS

1. Explain the different types of financial ratios.
2. What are important liquidity ratios?
3. What are the limitations of ratio analysis?
4. What do you understand by common size analysis?

CRITICAL THINKING QUESTIONS

1. Discuss the importance of profitability ratios for the managers of a hotel.
2. Critically review the importance of GOPPAR as against RevPar as a measure of the operational performance of a hotel.
3. Compare and contrast return on assets to return on equity.
4. Discuss the importance of common size analysis.
5. Mr Ajay Sharma has recently received a good amount of money as his performance bonus for the current financial year. He feels that investing in shares of hotel companies would be a wise decision because the industry is on the rise. He has also read analysts' and other experts' reports that have spelt a great future for hotels globally.

   Mr Sujit Kapoor is also an investor but, unlike Sharma, Sujit wants to invest in debt and not equity, as he is very conservative and does not want to be exposed to a high level of risk.

   Mr Rohan Das operates a business of supplying materials to hotels and is contemplating extending credit to some new hotels in his list. He wants to ensure that the customers have a good credit rating.

   Mr Shankar Rao, general manager of a large hotel, is setting up goals for the next financial year. He wants to be very objective and is contemplating basing his targets on the financial performance of the previous year.

   You are required to help all of them with your knowledge of ratio analysis and advise them as to the category of ratio they must focus on.

PROJECT WORK

Collect the financial statements of leading hotel companies of the world. Carry out a common size analysis for a minimum of three years. Write a report on the trends in your analysis.

Funds Analysis, Cash Flow Analysis

Isn't it interesting that the same people who laugh at science fiction listen to weather forecasts and economists?

Kelvin Throop III

Learning Objectives

After studying this chapter, you will be able to

➢ Understand the importance of funds flow analysis
➢ Carry out a funds flow analysis of a hotel company
➢ Appreciate the significance of a cash flow statement in ascertaining the cash position of a hotel
➢ Gain competence to prepare a cash flow statement
➢ Comprehend the various methods used to forecast a financial statement

McDonalds' Growth

The fast food giant McDonalds is benefiting from the global business boom.[*] The overseas business has shown a higher rate of growth as compared to business in the US. The company operates over 30,000 outlets across the globe.

The company has added new menus and has plans to target the breakfast fast food segment. This will call for all its outlets to open by 5 am by 2009. Apart

---

[*] McDonalds Cooks up Overseas Growth (2007), Dow Theory Forecasts.

from aggressive growth plans, the company has withdrawn from the outlets that have been underperforming or are too expensive on core resources. For instance, the company has sold existing businesses in 18 countries in Latin America and the Caribbean to a licensee, which has facilitated cash flows in the form of royalty from extremely competitive markets without over-reliance on the mother company's own contribution of resources. Furthermore, the company has identified strong growth opportunities in Asia, particularly China.[*] McDonalds has also fulfilled investor expectation by paying dividends regularly, without compromising on the growth front.

THE IMPORTANCE OF TOTAL RESOURCES

In this chapter, we shall focus on the importance of total resources, and cash in particular. Furthermore, the chapter also deals with the methods of forecasting financial outcomes.

An income statement provides a summary of the income and expenses over an accounting period whereas a balance sheet presents a static view of the financial position of a hotel on a particular date. In addition to the financial statements, managers require additional tools for the purpose of better decision making. One such tool is the *funds flow statement* that shows the source and application of funds during a particular period. *Funds flow analysis* helps to track the movement of funds

---

[*] McDonalds opened the first drive-through restaurant in China in 2005, and plans to establish 120 of these by the year 2008.

and also helps to understand the changes in the structure of assets and liabilities and owners' equity. We shall understand the other aspects of our tool-kit that will help us to analyse the financial performance of hotels. This section discusses the funds flow analysis, and the next section talks about the cash flow analysis, which aims at reporting the cash flow trifurcated into categories, such as operating, investing, and financing activities. Funds flow analysis helps in answering questions that cannot be provided by the basic financial statements. Funds flow analysis is directed at obtaining answers to the following critical questions:

- What is the quantum of funds generated by operations?
- What is the amount of capital expenditure during the year and what is the corresponding source? Are short-term funds employed for long-term use?
- What is the mix of external (outsider contribution) and internal financing?
- What have been the major uses of funds during the year?
- Has the liquidity position of the firm improved as compared to the previous year?

FUNDS FLOW STATEMENT

The funds flow statement draws a lot of information from the basic financial statements and shows the source and application of funds during the period. Before proceeding any further, let us understand the definition of the term *funds*. In common parlance, funds are referred to as cash (and near cash) items. This definition, however, restricts the analysis to transactions that affect the cash accounts only. This approach would not provide a critical evaluation of the business as transactions may not necessarily involve cash at all times. For example, purchase and sale on credit and acquiring property and assets by issuing shares are some transactions that do not necessarily involve cash. Therefore, it is necessary to extend our definition of funds to include all the assets and liabilities (claims on assets). By doing so, it is possible for us to include all the cash and credit transactions. At this moment, we will turn our attention to the balance sheet, which is a statement of 'funds' position. The assets side depicts all the assets (property and investment), and the liabilities, the claim on the assets. A hotel's fund flow statement, therefore, consists of tracking changes in individual items between two points in time. These time points are the beginning and end of the relevant period of examination, normally a year. The changes in the individual balance sheet account item represent net funds flow as a consequence of total transactions of the hotel. In other words, the balance sheet represents stock of funds on a particular date, whereas following the changes in the balance sheet item refers to finding the net flow of funds. It must be noted that the funds flow statement portrays net changes between two comparable balance sheets of the hotel. Gross changes would include all changes that occur between the two statement dates. While the analysis of gross changes would reveal far more detailed results than the analysis of net funds position, the emphasis is on the cash flow or the net working capital (current assets minus current liabilities) in the funds flow analysis.

SOURCES AND USES EXPLAINED

The preceding section has talked about the sources and the application or use of funds. This section would talk more about the sources and application of funds. The examples of sources of funds can be stated as follows:

- Funds from business operations
- Income from any other source. In the context of hotel operations, income from laundry, telephone, etc. would be considered as other income
- Sale of non-current assets. Sale of hotel property would be regarded as a source of funds in the statement
- Long-term borrowings
- Issue of additional equity or preference share capital

On the other hand, the following would be called the application of funds:

- Loss from business operations
- Purchase of non-current assets
- Redemption (paying back) of debentures and/or preference shares
- Payment of dividends to shareholders

Implications of Sources and Application

Let us now familiarize ourselves with the mechanics of the funds flow statement. In the context of working capital, the rules shown in Table 6.1 can be applied.

Table 6.1

Source of funds	Application of funds
Any decrease (-) in an asset	Any increase (+) in an asset
Any increase (+) in a liability	Any decrease (-) in a liability

Thus, we see that

- Increase in current assets increases working capital
- Decrease in current assets decreases working capital
- Increase in current liability decreases working capital
- Decrease in current liability increases working capital

Let us consider the balance sheet of the Sample Hotel Company Ltd for the last two years, shown in Exhibit 6.1, and the income statement in Exhibit 6.2.

The first step is to ascertain the change in the current assets and current liabilities. Table 6.2 shows the changes in working capital.

Exhibit 6.1 Balance sheet of Sample Hotel Company Ltd

Liabilities	2005	2006	Assets	2005	2006
	(Rs in millions)			(Rs in millions)	
Equity capital	1,000	1,098	Property and equipment		
Reserves and surplus	768	1268	Land and buildings	10,200	10,200
Secured loans	4,500	3,750	Equipment	1,000	1,100
Current liabilities			Less: Accumulated depreciation	(5,000)	(5,500)
Accounts payable	6	7	Investments	50	300
Accrued liabilities	4	5	**Current assets**		
Income tax payable	17	20	Cash	5	10
			Accounts receivable	30	26
			Inventory	10	12
	6,295	6,148		6,295	6,148

Exhibit 6.2 Income statement of Sample Hotel Company Ltd for the year ended 31 March 2006

	(Rs in millions)
Sales	7,000
Cost of goods sold	1,000
Payroll expenses	2,450
Other operating expenses	2,400
Income taxes	250
Depreciation	500
Gain on sale of investments	100
Net income	500
Additional information	

- No property and equipment was sold during the year.
- Investments costing Rs 5,00,00,000 were sold for Rs 15,00,00,000, resulting in a Rs 10,00,00,000 gain on the sale of investments during 2006.

Table 6.2

Particulars	31 March 2005	31 March 2006	Increase	Decrease
	(Rs in millions)			
Current assets				
Cash	5	10	5	
Accounts receivable	30	26		4
Inventory	10	12	2	
Current liabilities				
Accounts payable	6	7		1
Accrued payroll	4	5		1
Income taxes payable	7	6	1	
Dividends payable	10	14		4
Net working capital (CA - CL)	18			

FUNDS FROM BUSINESS OPERATIONS

The profit/loss figure from the income statement of the Sample Hotel Company Ltd in Table 6.2 does not reflect the quantum working capital provided by business operations, as the revenue and the expenses are not in tandem to the flow of working capital. The income statement contains a variety of *write-offs*, adjustments that do not involve any corresponding outflow of funds. Hence, appropriate adjustments have to be made in order to arrive at the correct amount of funds from business operations. The adjustments have to be made in the following manner:

1. All expenses that do not reduce the working capital but have been deducted from revenue must be added back to the profit. In the example of Sample Hotel Company Ltd, depreciation is one such expense that must be added back to the net income.

2. Income that has not been added to the working capital but has been added to the revenue must be subtracted from the net income. In the example of Sample Hotel Company Ltd, gain on sale of investment must be subtracted from the net income.

3. Revenues that are not the direct fall-out of the business operations should also be deducted and shown distinctly in the statement.

The adjustment to the profit is depicted in Table 6.3.

Table 6.3

Particulars	Amount (Rs in millions)
Net income (loss) as shown in the Income Statement	500
Add: Depreciation expense	500
Less: Gain on sale of investments	(100)
Funds from operations	900

CHANGES IN NON-CURRENT ASSETS

In the section on funds flow statement, we have seen the changes in current assets. This section will help in understanding the changes in non-current assets. The tangible assets balance increases due to appreciation or further addition to the category of assets. Consider the case of investment in the example of Sample Hotel Company Ltd. The account balance shows an increase of Rs 25,00,00,000. In Table 6.4, further analysis of the account reveals that the investment of Rs 50,000 has been sold and there has been a purchase of investment to the extent of Rs 3,00,000.

Table 6.4

Date	Particulars	Amount (Rs in millions)	Date	Particulars	Amount (Rs in millions)
31/03/05	Opening balance	50		Sale of investment	50
	Purchase of investment (balancing figure)	300	31/03/06	Closing balance	300
		350			350

Let us also take a look at the journal entry to record the sale of investment, shown in Table 6.5.

Table 6.5

Particulars	Debit	Credit
Cash	1,50,000	
Investments		50,000
Gain on sale of investment		1,00,000

Sale of investment would be a source for the income of Rs 15,00,00,000. Note that the actual cash received would be considered in case the non-current assets are being sold at a loss. There are no changes in land and buildings as there are no purchases or sales during 2005–06. There will be no change in the funds position. Let us take a look at the equipment account. Refer to Exhibit 6.2 additional information 1 that says that no equipment was sold and therefore we shall consider the increase of 100 million rupees in the equipment account as additional purchase. Purchase of the equipment will be an application of funds. The final non-current account in the example is the accumulated depreciation. The increase of Rs 50,00,00,000 will not affect the working capital and, therefore, will be added to the net income as discussed in the preceding section.

CHANGES IN THE NON-CURRENT LIABILITIES

In the illustration, the share capital shows an increase of Rs 9,80,00,000 in 2006. This amount can be treated as a source of funds to the business as the hotel has raised funds by issuing shares. On the other hand, the long-term debt shows a decrease of Rs 75,00,00,000, signifying that liability has been paid-off to the extent of the said amount. The final account that remains to be analysed is the retained earnings accounts, which is nothing but the profit for the current year. A closer look at the difference between the balances of both the years is the profit of the current year. The account is illustrated in Table 6.6.

Table 6.6

Date	Particulars	Amount	Date	Particulars	Amount
			31/03/01	Opening balance	768
				Profit for the year	500
31/03/02	Closing balance	1,268			
		1,268			1,268

PRESENTING FUNDS FLOW BY ACTIVITY ON A STATEMENT

Recall from the earlier discussion that the funds flow statement is a summary of all the source and application of funds during a particular period. The following table is the culmination of the impact of the transaction we have discussed so far.

Table 6.7

Source	Amount (Rs in millions)	Application	Amount (Rs in millions)
Issue of equity shares	98	Purchase of equipment	100
Sale of investment	150	Payment of secured loans	750
Funds from operations	900	Purchase of investment	300
Decrease in working capital	2		
	1,150		1,150

CASH FLOW STATEMENT

The funds flow statement on cash basis is hereafter referred to as the statement of cash flows shows. The cash flow statement is an important tool to understand the cash receipts and disbursements of a hospitality firm. The flow of cash helps creditors, investors, managers, and others to

- Understand the pattern of cash flows and the ability of the organization to generate positive net cash flows in the future. A review of the cash flow statement will help potential investors evaluate the firm's ability to pay dividends in the future.
- Review the firm's ability to meet its obligations. Suppliers, vendors, and other creditors would be interested in determining the firm's ability to pay bills on the due date. If the cash flow statement reflects a poor ability to pay bills on time, then the suppliers would not be interested in selling their goods and services under such conditions.
- Assess the difference between the firm's net income and the cash inflows and outflows. The cash flow statement captures the major net sources of cash and their relation to operations.
- Assess the effect of both cash and non-cash investing and financing during the accounting period. Investing activities refer to the acquisition and disposal of non-current assets like land, buildings, etc. Borrowing and repayment of long-term loans constitutes the financing activities. The cash flow statement also provides a view of whether the firm is able to fulfil its long-term commitment in addition to the short-term liabilities.

We can broadly classify three major groups of users who would be interested in the cash flow statement—managers, creditors (short term and long term), and shareholders. The first group constitutes the managers who would be interested in the liquidity position of the organization, the degree of financial flexibility, determining a suitable dividend policy based on the present cash flow position of the organization, and most important, planning future investing and the corresponding future financing requirements. On the other hand, short-term creditors would be interested in judging the ability to pay bills on the due date. Long-term creditors would pay attention to the security of the principal amount and would also be expecting some return. Shareholders would want to know the future dividend paying capacity of the organization.

Classification of Cash Flows

The cash flow statement classifies cash inflows and outflows as operating, investing, and financing activities. We will discuss these three categories in brief:

Operating activities   This category includes cash transactions, related to revenues and expenses. The major source of cash inflow for hotel operations is food and beverage and/or room sales. Cash outflow in this category includes payment of salaries, wages, supplies, etc.

Investing activities   As mentioned in the earlier section, inflow and outflow on account of purchase and sale of non-current assets are a part of the investing activities, including purchase and sale of short-term assets.

Financing activities   The organization has to raise finance by borrowing on a long-term basis. Companies also raise finance by issuing equity or preference shares. All these activities constitute financing activities. Cash outflow includes repayment of long-term loans and dividends[*] and repurchase of shares. It must be noted that accounts payable, taxes payable, and other short-term liabilities are not to be considered as cash outflow on account of financing activities, but such outflow is considered while ascertaining cash flow from operating activities. Exhibit 6.3 explains the basic format of the cash flow statement.

Methods of Ascertaining Cash Flow from Operations

Cash flows from operations can be ascertained in two ways, the direct and the indirect methods. The *direct method* shows cash receipts from sales and cash payments for expenses. This method requires the conversion of accrual basis to cash basis. The accrual basis suggests that revenues are recorded as and when they are earned and not when cash is received from guests. Similarly, expenses are recorded as and when they are incurred and not when they are paid in cash. Recall from the Sample Hotel Company Ltd's example that the sales are

---

[*] Interest on long-term debt is considered as cash outflow on account of operating activity.

Exhibit 6.3 Basic format of the cash flow statement

Cash flow from operating activities

Includes cash inflows on account of sale and purchase of goods and services and includes cash outflows such as • Payment to suppliers • Payment to employees and staff • Payment to lenders (interest) • Payment to government as taxes • Payment to other vendors and suppliers for operating expenses	This section captures the impact of transactions that affect the net income. Therefore, some items, such as interest, are considered in this segment.

Cash flow from investing activities

Includes cash inflows from sale of assets and other short-term and long-term assets, and includes cash outflow on account of purchase of long-term and short-term assets like equipment, buildings, marketable securities, and other short-term assets	This section captures the implications of purchase and sale of short-term and long-term assets.

Cash flow from financing activities

Includes cash inflows from borrowings and sale of the firm's own equity shares, and includes cash outflows on account of repayment of borrowings, repurchase of the firm's own shares, and payment of dividends to the shareholders	This section shows the impact of all cash transactions with shareholders and long-term creditors of the company.

7,00,00,00,000 and the accounts receivables (AR) from guests, at the beginning of the year, are 3,00,00,000 as compared to the balance of Rs 2,60,00,000 at the end of the year.

Cash receipts for sales

$$= \text{Sales} - \text{Increase in AR } (or + \text{Decrease in AR})$$
$$= 700 - 4 = \text{Rs } 69,40,00,000$$

Thus, an amount of Rs 69,40,00,000 would be reported as sales on the cash flow statement, even though the income statement reports a sale of Rs 70,00,00,000. Some expenses shown on the income statement do not involve any direct expense and therefore are ignored when the direct method is used.

The *indirect method* for determining net cash flows from operations commences with the net income. Net income is then adjusted for non-cash items included on the income statement. The most common non-cash item is depreciation. Since depreciation is subtracted from net income, it is added back to net income to compute net cash flows from operating activities. Other items that are to be added or subtracted would include amortization expenses and gains and losses on the sale of non-current assets and short-term assets. Let us consider our Sample Hotel Company Ltd example and focus on the aspect of sale of investment for a gain of Rs 10,00,00,000. In this transaction, the sum of Rs 15,00,00,000 would be recorded as an inflow in the investing activity, whereas the gain of Rs 10,00,00,000, that was included in the computation of net income, would be subtracted while calculating net cash flows from operating activities. Several other adjustments, with regard to current assets and liabilities, are carried out to further ascertain cash flows from operating activities. The adjustments are discussed in the succeeding sections.

Irrespective of the method used, the result will show the same amount of net cash provided by operations. However, we shall discuss only the indirect method to draft the statement of cash flows (refer Exhibit 6.4).

Variations of the Cash Flow Statements: Discretionary and Non-discretionary Cash Flows

The classification of cash flows as operating, investing, and financing is very effective for internal purposes. Firms can also classify cash flows based on whether they can control them or if the cash flows are beyond their control. These two variations of cash flows are discussed in this section.

Consider a hotel company that wishes to finance the acquisition of another property. Is it possible to finance this acquisition without any external borrowing or any selling of existing assets? In other words, can the hotel firm generate the entire requirement from operations? The firm will have obligations like paying interest on debt or repaying an existing

Exhibit 6.4   Cash flow statement of Sample Hotel Company Ltd   for the year ended 31 March 2006 (direct method)

Cash Flow from Operating Activities	
Net Income for the period	500
Add: Depreciation	500
Decrease in accounts receivable	4
Increase in accounts payable	1
Increase in accrued liabilities	1
Increase in income tax payable	3
Less: Increase in Inventory	(2)
Gain on sale of investment	(100)
Net cash flows from operating activity	907
Cash Flow from Investing Activities	
Add: Sale of investment	150
Less: Purchase of equipment	(100)
Purchase of investment	(300)
Net cash flow from investing activity	(250)
Cash Flow from Financing Activities	
Add: Issue of equity shares	98
Less: Payment of secured loan	(750)
Net cash flow from financing activity	(652)
Total cash flow from investing operating and financing activities	5
Add: Opening balance of cash	5
Equals closing balance of cash	10

loan. The cash flow that the firm is legally obliged to pay is called *non-discretionary cash flow*. The cash flow available to a firm after deducting the non-discretionary cash flow from the net operating cash flows is referred to as *discretionary cash flow*. Discretionary cash flow is the cash flow available for capital expenditure like acquisitions and other strategic purposes.

FINANCIAL PLANNING

The globalized environment has provided enormous business opportunities to hotel companies in India. Strategic planning in the hospitality industry has become the order of the day due to the intense competition and other factors like rapidly changing market conditions. Therefore, if a hospitality firm has to grow, assets must also increase. The expansion would also require additional investments in current assets and additional capacity to be added to the existing facilities. Consequently, there will be need for additional capital to finance the requirement of procuring more assets or the creation of additional facilities. The earlier section explains that while some of the additional requirements can be raised through operations, a large part will have to be arranged from external sources. There is a need for an accurate forecast of estimated capital requirements as it takes time to raise capital. A plan is required well in advance to obtain the right amount of funds at an appropriate time. The planning process is an integral aspect of any hospitality firm that wants to grow and expand. It is essential to know what has happened in the past, the cause and the future implications, and the ways to improve performance. In the chapters that follow, you will see that raising long-term finance involves a cost and is, therefore, not a frequently carried out exercise. It becomes necessary for a firm to consider the next few years, and not the immediate future, when it comes to utilizing long-term funds for optimum benefit. We have seen in Chapter 1 that managers and investors would be interested in future cash flows and the repercussions of alternative growth and financing plans on the cash flow. The genesis of forecasting cash flows is to project financial outcomes. Hence, this chapter discusses forecasting financial outcomes through projected financial statements. We shall see how projected financial statements are constructed and how they are useful in preparing for a future course and plan of action. The important elements in financial planning can be summarized as follows:

- *Economic factors*   Financial plans of all hotel companies are affected by domestic and global economic conditions. Factors such as exchange rate, inflation, and the state of the economy play an important role in determining the sales revenue for a hotel. Furthermore, the Internet has facilitated reserving a room well in advance, and last-minute guests have to pay an inflated price for the room. A recent survey indicates that there has been an increase in hotel room rates all across the globe due to the demand and supply conditions. It is necessary that hotel companies should focus on business strategies for success and survival.

- *Sales forecast* Sales forecast is the start of the financial planning exercise. This is a plan for the target sales revenue to be achieved during the period. Sales forecast helps in communicating the objectives to every person in the organization. Moreover, sales forecast is the basis for determining all other financial variables.

- *Pro forma financial statements* Forecasting sales revenue may spell out the expected income of the company. However, it is also necessary to estimate the corresponding expenses to earn the target net income. Pro Forma income statements help in determining the net income to be achieved in the given time frame. Similarly, pro forma balance sheet will help in assessing the assets and liabilities position corresponding to the level of sales revenue to be achieved.

- *Requirement of assets* Determining sales revenue also calls for additional investment in either fixed or current assets. According to a recent report, India is targeting for around 10 million tourists to visit the country in the next few years. In order to meet the demand, an additional inventory of 1,50,000 rooms is required. A further investment in fixed assets would be incurred if the hotels decide to add to the existing capacity. With the increase in the number of guests, there would be additional working capital requirement.[*] It is necessary to estimate the additional requirements of current and non-current assets to obtain optimum operating outcomes.

- *Financing plan* Recall that it is not possible for the operations to finance expansion and other non-current asset requirements. Hence, a comprehensive plan must be drawn that encompasses sources of finance.

Functional heads and managers at all levels of operations spend enormous amount of time and resources in financial planning. The managers have to provide departmental revenue and expense details at the start of the financial year and ensure

---

[*] Refer to Chapter 7 for a detailed discussion on working capital.

success of the plan by the end of the year. The benefits of financial planning can be summarized as follows:

- Financial planning pre-empts action to be taken at various levels.
- Evaluation of various available alternatives in different spheres is possible in the light of an all-inclusive financial plan.
- A systematic review of the financing and investment interface can be carried out, provided there is a financial plan.
- Financial planning, though not a corporate crystal ball, helps in providing a back-up plan in case of an exigency.
- Financial planning provides a benchmark for individual, unit, and corporate performance appraisal and measurement.
- Financial planning helps in clarifying present and future links.

SALES FORECAST

Sales forecast generally commences with a review of sales during the past five to ten years. Quintessentially, sales forecast is the beginning of the financial planning exercise. Hence, sales forecast is a critical factor in estimating future rooms or food and beverage revenue. Sales forecast can be spread over short and long periods, and for varied reasons. Sales forecast for a short period of time can be directed at ascertaining working capital and cash requirements. Long-term sales forecast is developed to facilitate long-term investment planning.

Forecast Financial Statements or Pro Forma Financial Statements

A summary of the anticipated revenues and expenses over some future time period, highlighting the net income (or loss) for the period, is called the forecast income statement. The restaurant sales forecast ensures that food, beverage, and other materials are scheduled appropriately. The forecast of the requirements will, in turn, help in estimating the corresponding cost associated with a particular level of turnover. We shall discuss the most commonly used method to forecast financial outcomes.

Per cent of sales method

The per cent of sales method for drafting the projected income statement is very simple. This method assumes that the future relationship between various elements remains constant to the level of sales and that the current levels of all assets are optimal for the present sales level. Put differently, this method assumes that the relationship of costs to sales will remain unaltered. It needs to be decided here whether we consider the percentage of the last year or the average of the past two or three years. The pro forma income statement for the Sample Hotel Company Ltd is depicted in Exhibit 6.5.

Exhibit 6.5 Income statement of Sample Hotel Company Ltd (based on the per cent sales method)

Sr. No.	Particulars	Historical 2006	Per cent of sales revenue	Projected (assuming a sales revenue of 1500) 2007
1	Sales revenue	1200	100.00	1500.00
2	Direct expenses	700	0.58*	875.00**
3	**Gross profit**	**500**	0.42	625.00
4	Administrative and general expenses	70	0.06	87.50
5	Selling expenses	30	0.03	37.50
6	Depreciation	50	0.04	62.50
7	Operating profit	350	0.29	437.50
8	**Earnings before interest and tax**	**350**	0.29	**437.50**
9	Interest on bank borrowings	75	0.06	93.75
10	Interest on bonds and debentures	60	0.05	75.00
11	**Earnings before tax**	**215**	0.18	**268.75**
12	Tax	83	0.07	103.75
13	**Earnings after tax**	**132**	0.11	**165.00**
14	Dividends	75		
15	**Retained earnings**	**57**		

* $700 \div 1200 = 0.58$ and every item is divided by the sales revenue (1200) to obtain the consequent percentages.

** $0.58 * 1500 = 875$ and every item is calculated in a similar manner.

For the purpose of projection, the ratio of cost to sales for every element is taken into account. For example, the relationship of 58 per cent of direct expenses is assumed for the projected statement (refer to Exhibit 6.6). All items have been expressed in terms of sales except for dividend, which is an outcome of managerial policy and hence cannot be determined in a

Exhibit 6.6   Pro forma balance sheet of Sample Hotel Company Ltd as on 31 March 2006 and projected outcomes as of 31 March 2007

Sr. No.	Particulars	Historical		Projected basis	
		31 March 2006	Per cent of sales	31 March 2007	Target level of sales
1	Sales revenue	1200		1500	Revenue
	Assets				
2	Fixed assets	800	0.67*	1000.00	
3	Investments	30		30.00	Remains unaltered
4	Current assets				
	Loans and advances				
	Cash	25	0.02	31.25	
	Receivables	212	0.18	265.00	
	Inventory	425	0.35	531.25	
	Total assets	**1492**		1857.50	
5	Liabilities and equity share capital	300			
6	Reserves and surplus	350		100.75	
7	Secured loan	400		400.00	Remains unaltered
	Long-term loan	100	0.08	125.00	
8	**Unsecured loans**				
	Bank borrowings	125	0.10	156.25	
9	Current liabilities and provisions				
	Trade creditors	138	0.12	172.5	
	Accrued expenses	79	0.07	98.75	
		1492		1053.25	
10	Additional fund requirement (balancing figure)			**804.25**	Balancing figure (total assets *minus* liabilities)

---

* Using the per cent sales method, calculated as 800/1200.

mechanical manner. For the sake of simplicity, the illustration considers only the preceding year as a base. If the balances are available for the two or three years, an average of all the past figures can be considered as a base for all calculations to even-out inconsistencies.

Use of Budgets in Financial Planning

One of the drawbacks of using the per cent of sales method is that it is too mechanical. We have assumed that all the expenses are directly influenced by sales, and a change in sales revenue will automatically affect the corresponding level of expenses. This may not be true at all times. The other option is to estimate the value of each and every item on the basis of certain expected developments and to use a budgeted number rather than using plain arithmetic. This method calls for a detailed exercise and involves a lot of effort.

Using Both Methods

It is necessary to mention here that no one method used in isolation can be successful in forecasting the financial outcomes. Hence, we shall use both methods in combination because there are some expenses that vary directly with the sales revenue, while others can be budgeted. Exhibit 6.7 takes into account a combination of both methods in order to arrive at a fruitful decision.

Pro Forma Balance Sheet

Once the pro forma income statement is drafted, the balance sheet can also be summarized using the guidelines provided below:

1. Using the per cent of sales method, determine the balance of current assets. We shall assume an increase in capacity as far as occupancy is concerned and, therefore, increase the balance of fixed assets with the increase in sales turnover.
2. Calculate the estimated values of 'investments' and other non-current assets, based on some specific information available.

Exhibit 6.7 Income statement of Sample Hotel Company Ltd (based on a combination of per cent sales method and budgeted expenses)

Sr. No.	Particulars	Historical 2006	Per cent of sales revenue	Projected (assuming a sales revenue of 1500) 2007	Basis of calculation
1	Sales revenue	1200	100.00	1500	
2	Direct expenses	700	0.58	875	
3	**Gross profit**	**500**	0.42	625	
4	Administrative and general expenses	70	0.06	87.5	
5	Selling expenses	30	0.03	32	Budgeted
6	Depreciation	50	0.04	62.5	Budgeted
7	Operating profit	350	0.29	443	
8	**Earnings before interest and tax**	**350**	0.29	443	
9	Interest on bank borrowings	75	0.06	93.75	
10	Interest on bonds and debentures	60	0.05	75	Budgeted
11	Earnings before tax	215	0.18	268.75	
12	Tax	83	0.07	83	Budgeted
13	**Earnings after tax**	**132**	0.11	**185.75**	
14	Dividends	75	0.06	85	Budgeted
15	**Retained earnings**	**57**	0.05	**100.75**	

3. Since the current liabilities would also be an outcome of sales turnover, use the per cent of sales method to calculate the balance of current liabilities wherever applicable (for example, change in bank borrowings for working capital).

4. Carry over the amount of projected retained earnings calculated from the pro forma income statement to the balance of retained earnings.

5. Set the projected values for non-current liabilities, such as equity and preference capital, at approximately the same level if there is no major deviation. In the same way, the

debentures can also be assumed at the same level provided there is no reduction. Bank loans can be considered after the regular payment of the principal amount.

6. Finally, compare the total of the assets to the liabilities and determine the balancing amount.[*] The excess of assets over liabilities represents additional requirement of funds (more borrowings) whereas excess liabilities over assets would mean availability of surplus funds.

Solved Problems

1. The following are the condensed balance sheets of the Retreat Hotel Ltd.

Particulars	2005	2006
Assets		
Fixed assets		
Property	2,97,000	2,88,500
Equipment	2,25,900	2,52,400
Goodwill		20,000
Current assets		
Inventory	2,20,000	1,84,000
Accounts receivable	1,72,320	1,38,860
Cash and bank	3,000	22,000
Prepayments	6,740	2,000
	9,24,960	**9,07,760**
Liabilities		
Shareholders funds		
Paid up capital	4,40,000	5,40,000
Reserves and surplus	1,39,380	1,62,240
Current liabilities		
Accounts payable	78,000	83,320
Notes payable	67,580	22,000
Bank overdraft	1,20,000	
Provision for tax	80,000	1,00,000
	9,24,960	**9,07,760**

---

[*] The balance sheet will not agree by itself in such cases.

Prepare a statement showing changes in working capital, considering the following information:

1. During the year ended 31 March 2006, dividend of Rs 52,000 was paid to equity shareholders.
2. During the year ended 31 March 2006, The Retreat Hotel Company Ltd acquired assets of another hotel for Rs 1,00,000 and the amount was settled in fully paid shares. The assets are inventory Rs 43,280, equipment Rs 36,720, and goodwill Rs 20,000.
3. Additionally, food and beverage equipment costing Rs 11,300 was also purchased during the year.
4. Depreciation charged on property and equipment amounted to Rs 8500 and Rs 21,520, respectively.
5. The net profit reported by the company for the year ended 31 March 2006 was Rs 23,060.

Prepare a schedule showing sources and application of funds for the year ended 31 March 2006.

Solution:

Sources	Amount	Application	Amount
Funds from business operations	1,05,080	Purchase of Non-current Assets:	
Issue of equity shares (for purchase of assets of another company)	1,00,000	Food and beverage equipment (for cash)	11,300
		Equipment (in exchange for equity shares)	36,720
		Goodwill (in exchange for equity shares)	20,000
		Dividends paid	52,000
		Increase in working capital	85,060
	2,05,080		2,05,080

Notes

Calculation of funds from operations:

Net profit for the year (given)		23,060
Add Depreciation		
Property	8,500	
Equipment	21,520	30,020
Payment of dividends		52,000
		1,05,080

Schedule showing changes in working capital

Particulars	2005	2006	Increase	Decrease
Current assets				
Inventory	2,20,000	1,84,000		36,000
Accounts receivable	1,72,320	1,38,860		33,460
Cash and bank	3,000	22,000	19,000	
Prepayments	6,740	2,000		4,740
Current liabilities				
Accounts payable	78,000	83,320		5,320
Notes payable	67,580	22,000	45,580	
Bank overdraft	1,20,000	0	1,20,000	
Provision for taxation	80,000	1,00,000		20,000
Net increase or decrease in working capital				**85,060**
			1,84,580	1,84,580

2. The following balance sheets pertain to the Imperial Hotels Ltd for the year ended 31 March 2005 and 2006.

	2005	2006
	(Rs in million)	
Liabilities		
Equity capital	291	291
Reserves and surplus	228	166
Long-term borrowings		
Banks and other financial institutions	136	194
	655	651
Assets		
Net fixed assets	572	583
Current assets	83	68
	655	651

Prepare a schedule showing sources and application of funds considering the following information:

- The Imperial Hotels Ltd incurred a loss of Rs 6,20,00,000 in the year ended 31 March 2006.
- Depreciation to the extent of Rs 5,20,00,000 was charged in the year 31 March 2006.

Solution:

Schedule showing sources and application of funds for the year ended 31 March 2006

Sources	Amount	Application	Amount
Borrowings from banks	58	Purchase of fixed assets	63
Decrease in working capital	15	Funds lost in operations	10
	73		73

Notes

1. Purchase of fixed assets is calculated as follows:

Opening balance	572	Depreciation	52
Additions (balancing figure)	63	Closing balance	583
	635		635

2. Funds lost in operations is calculated as follows:

Net loss	(62)
Add Depreciation	52
Funds lost in operations	10

3. From the balance sheet of the ABC Hotels Ltd, prepare a statement of sources and application of funds.

	2005	2006
	(Rs in million)	
Liabilities		
Share capital	7	9
Reserve and surplus	1	6
Secured loans	7	6
Current liabilities		
Accounts payable	4	3
Bank overdraft	4	3
Accrued expenses	3	3
Total	26	30
Assets		
Fixed assets	5	5
Investments	0	3
Current assets		
Cash and bank	1	4
Inventory	14	11
Sundry debtors	6	7
Total	26	30

• Net profit for the year ended 31 March 2006 is Rs 50,00,000.

Solution:

Sources		Applications	
Share capital issue	2	Payment of secured loans	1
Funds from operations	5	Purchase of investment	3
		Net increase in working capital	3
Total	7		7

Particulars	2005	2006	Increase	Decrease
Current assets				
Cash and bank	1	4	3	
Inventory	14	11		3
Sundry debtors	6	7	1	
Total	**21**	**22**	**4**	**3**
Current liabilities				
Accrued expenses	3	3		
Accounts payable	4	3	1	
Bank overdraft	4	3	1	
Total	**11**	**9**	**2**	
Net increase in w/c				3
Total w/c			**6**	**6**

4. From the condensed balance sheets of the West India Hotel Company prepare schedule of sources and application of funds for the year ended 31 March 2006.

Balance sheet for XYZ company as year ended 2006

	2005	2006
	(Rs in million)	
Share capital	1000	1000
Reserve and surplus	850	1000
Long-term debt	600	660
Short-term bank borrowing	400	450
Accounts payable	200	190
Provisions	150	160
	3200	3460
Fixed assets (net)	1200	2000
Inventory	1180	700
Debtors	720	660
Cash	60	70
Other assets	40	30
	3200	3460

Income statement for XYZ company for year ended 2006

	2005	2006
		(Rs in millions)
Room sales		4080
Cost of goods sold		
Food inventory	2020	
Wages and salaries	420	
Heat, light, and power	<u>280</u>	<u>2720</u>
		1360
Gross profit		
Operating expenses		
Depreciation	220	
Selling admin and general	460	680
Operating profit		680
Non-operating surplus		50
Profit before interest and tax		730
Interest		140
Profit before interest and tax		590
Tax		260
Profit after tax		330
Dividends		180
Retained earnings		150

Solution:

Schedule showing source and application of funds for the year ended 31 March 2006

Source	Amount	Application	Amount
Long-term debt	60	Fixed assets	1020
Reserves and surplus	550	Payment of dividends	180
Decrease in working capital	590		
	1200		1200

Schedule showing changes in working capital

Particulars	2005	2006	Increase	Decrease
Current assets				
Inventory	1180	700		480
Cash	60	70	10	
Debtors	720	660		60
Other assets	40	30		10

Current liabilities

Short-term bank borrowings	400	450		50
Accounts payable	200	190	10	
Provision	150	160		10
Net decrease in working capital		590		
			610	610

5. From the condensed balance sheets of the Sea Princess Hotel Ltd. Prepare a statement showing application and sources of funds during the year 2006.

Particulars	31 March 2005	31 March 2006
Assets		
Fixed assets (net)	255	310
Investment	15	40
Current assets	65	78
Pre opening Expenses	10	5
	345	433
Liabilities and Capital		
Share capital (equity)	150	200
Share capital (preference)	65	50
Debentures	45	65
Reserves	50	72
Provision for tax	5	6
Current liabilities	30	40
	345	433

Additional information:

1. The net profit reported by the income statement was Rs 22 million.
2. Depreciation charged during the year was Rs 7 million.
3. An equipment costing Rs 7 million (book value Rs 4 million), was sold for Rs 2 million.
4. Preference shares were redeemed at a premium of Rs 5 million.
5. Dividend @ 10% was paid on equity shares of the previous year.
6. The provision for depreciation stood at the beginning of the current year at Rs 15 million and Rs 19 million at the end of the year.

7. Some of the current assets valued at Rs 4 million at the beginning of the year were written up to cost (Rs 5 million) for preparing the income statement for the current year.

Solution:

Schedule showing sources and application of funds for the year ended 31 March 2006

Sources	Amount (Rs in million)	Application	Amount (Rs in million)
Funds from operations	52	Purchase of fixed assets	63
Issue of equity shares	50	Increase in working capital	1
Issue of debentures	20	Purchase of investments	25
Sale of equipment	2	Redemption of Preference Shares	20
Payment of dividends	15		
	124		124

Statement of changes in working capital

Particulars	31 March 2005	31 March 2006	Working capital Increase	Decrease
Current assets (65 + 1 million of the valuation of current assets)	66	78	12	
Current Liabilities	30	40		10
Provision for tax	5	6		1
Total Current Liabilities	40	55		
Net Working Capital				
Increase in Working capital				1
			12	12

Calculation of funds from operations:

Net income	22
Add Reduction in pre-opening expenses	2
Depreciation	7
Premium on redemption of preference shares	5
Loss on sale of equipment	2
Dividends	15
Less Overvaluation of current assets	(1)
Funds from operation	52

Note
1. Profit on sale of asset = Selling price – Book value
2. Loss on sale of asset = Book value – Selling price
3. Book value = Cost of the asset – Depreciation

SUMMARY

- The sources and application of funds statement is a summary of changes in the financial position from one period to another. A perfect understanding of this statement provides an insight into the uses of funds and how the requirements of funds are financed over a specific period of time. Funds flow analysis is very valuable in analysing the usage of funds and in planning the hotel's intermediate and long-term funds requirements.
- The balance sheet represents the position of funds whereas the sources and uses statement tracks changes over two balance sheet periods. However, the statement charts the net changes as compared to gross changes while analysing two balance sheets.
- The cash flow statement takes into account only the changes in the position of cash.
- Three main components on the cash flow statement are the operating, investing, and financing activities.
- The per cent sales method or the budgeted sales method can be used to forecast financial statements, or both the methods can be used in conjunction to forecast financial statements.

KEY TERMS

Discretionary cash flows Cash flows that occur at the discretion of the enterprise.

Financial planning The process of drafting the future course of action for the business.

Financing activities Activities pertaining to raising of cash for operations or expansion of operations are referred to as financing activities.

Funds flow analysis An analysis of the changes in the financial position.

Funds flow statement A statement that shows changes in the financial position.

Investing activities All activities pertaining to expansion of operations would be regarded as investing activities. For example, the purchase and sale of hotel property and the purchase/sale of assets such as equipment would be investment activities.

Net working capital Total current assets minus current liabilities.

Non-discretionary cash flows Cash flows that are not subject to the will of the enterprise.

Operating activities Activities on account of operations would be classified as hotel operations. Room sales and food and beverage sales will be considered as operating activities.

Pro forma financial statement Financial statement for the future.

Sales forecast An estimate of the amount of sales revenue to be generated in a given period of time.

REVIEW QUESTIONS

1. How would you classify changes into sources and uses of funds by comparing balance sheets of two different periods?
2. State the sources and uses of the working capital.
3. Which of the following are sources of funds?
   - Sale of land
   - Payment of dividends
   - Depreciation
   - Sale of shares
   - Redemption of debentures
4. Explain the importance of the cash flow statement.
5. Explain the importance of the process of financial planning.
6. Describe the methods to forecast financial statements.

CRITICAL THINKING QUESTIONS

1. Critically evaluate the importance of funds flow analysis and cash flow analysis.
2. Discuss the principal methods for drafting financial statements.
3. Discuss the importance of the sales forecast in the context of financial projections of hotel companies.
4. Depreciation is a source of funds. Comment.

PROJECT WORK

Talk to restaurant managers, executive chefs, or revenue managers of a five-star hotel in your city and gain an insight into the methods they adopt to arrive at projecting financial outcomes.

CASE STUDY

The managing director of a large hotel corporation was surprised to find that though his company had incurred a loss during the year ended 31 March 2007, the cash balance had increased during the period. He was further puzzled on finding that there was an increase in the stock and that the collections from corporate guests were slow.

Income statement for the year ended 31 March 2007

		(Rs in millions)
Sales	560	
Cost of goods sold		385
(including depreciation on equipment		
of Rs 60,00,000)		
Operating expenses		
Office and administrative	170	
Selling and distribution	55	
Amortization of goodwill	25	250
Net profit/loss		(75)

Comparative Balance Sheets as on 31 March 2006 and 31 March 2007 (Rs in lacs)

	2006	2007
Assets		
Cash	95	140
Debtors	35	80
Stock	80	100
Prepaid rent	12	10
Land	150	150
Equipment (net of depreciation)	600	440
Goodwill	100	75
	1092	**995**

Capital and Liabilities

Creditors	90	60
Bills payable	5	10
Interest payable	9	10
Accrued wages	18	20
Long-term loans	245	245
Share capital	600	600
Reserves and surplus	125	50
	1092	**995**

Analyze the financial statements and discuss the probable reasons for the increase in cash balance and why the income statement reports a loss.

Write a report to the managing director on the financial health of the organization.

Working Capital of Hotel Companies

Every action in Nature is voided as it occurs, is repeated as it is voided, and is recorded as it is repeated.

Charles Augustin de Coulomb

Learning Objectives

After studying this chapter, you will be able to

➤ Understand the meaning and importance of working capital management

➤ Understand the various issues surrounding working capital management

➤ Understand the financing mix of working capital—short term and long term

➤ Differentiate between the various working capital policies

➤ Appreciate the cash conversion and operating cycles in context

INTRODUCTION

If asked to list requirements to start a restaurant or a hotel, you will probably start with a building and go on to items such as furniture, equipment, etc. All these requirements would need allocation of funds, which we know as investment. This investment is provided by the owner (capital) and/or through external borrowings. Any business operation would require fixed or permanent capital and fluctuating or working capital for successful operations. Investment in the form of land, buildings, kitchen equipments, or food and beverage equipments, furniture, and similar other assets, procured with the intention of retaining the business, represents fixed capital. On the other hand, investment in working capital involves investment in current assets required to support the daily operations of any business. Current assets consist of assets that would be converted into cash sooner or later. Thus, we can say that current assets represent the source of liquid resources. Like the liabilities to be paid over a longer period of time (non-current liabilities), we also have liabilities to be discharged over a short time period (current liabilities). Current liabilities represent a claim on current assets and, thereby, on liquid resources also. As the chapter unfolds, we shall be able to understand the relationship between current assets and current liabilities.

There are two major concepts of working capital—gross working capital and net working capital. We shall begin our discussion on the concept of working capital by reviewing some of the fundamental concepts:

- *Gross working capital* simply refers to the current assets used in operations.
- *Net working capital* is the difference between current assets and liabilities.
- *Net operating working capital* is defined as current assets minus non-interest bearing liabilities.
- *Working capital policy* refers to the firm's policy regarding target levels for each category of current assets and the source for financing current assets.
- *Working capital management* involves both setting up a working capital policy and implementing it in day-to-day operations.

Working capital management is an important aspect of financial management because investment in current assets represents a substantial portion of total investment of a business operation, and investment in current assets and the level of current liabilities have to be adjusted according to changes in sales. Financial managers spend a considerable amount of time in managing current assets and liabilities. Arranging short-term finance, negotiating favourable credit terms, controlling inflow and outflow of cash, monitoring receivables, and managing appropriate levels of current assets is extremely important. Inventory forms a major part of the financial manager's routine responsibility because excessive levels of current assets can result in a poor return on investment. However, inadequate levels of current assets may impede smooth operations. Working capital management assumes importance because it has a significant impact on the profitability of the business. Research results have been able to indicate that optimum level of working capital potentially maximizes returns. This chapter focuses on the importance of working capital management.

LEVEL OF WORKING CAPITAL

Working capital requirements may vary from industry to industry and from one business to another. Hence, it is practically impossible to have a universal rule applicable to hotel operations. Working capital requirements of any business depend on numerous factors that together determine its level. Some of the important considerations are as follows.

The period of credit extended to guests is important. Usually, a longer credit period extended would mean more working capital requirement. Similar consideration is also applicable to suppliers. If suppliers allow a longer credit period, the working capital requirements would be lower. One of the other important factors to be considered is the 'production cycle', that is, the period from the purchase of raw material to the sale of the finished product. If the production cycle is long, higher levels of inventory would be required and, thereby, working capital requirement would be higher. Seasonality of operations is another factor that determines the quantum of working capital. Business operations that experience a pattern of revenue inflow distinct from the pattern of cash outflow require a relatively higher level of working capital. For instance, where most of inflows occur between April and September and the heaviest of expenses are payable between October and March, a larger amount of working capital is called for. Finally, the sales mix of the business is also an important factor. Room sales are not supported by stocks and food sales necessitate maintaining higher level of inventories.

ISSUES WITH WORKING CAPITAL

While determining the appropriate quantum of current assets, it would be appropriate to consider the trade-off between profitability and risk. To illustrate this point, let us consider the case of a restaurant that has the capacity to serve 200 seats per month. For each of the level of sales turnover, the restaurant can have a combination of the levels of current assets. The level of current assets will depend on the level of operations. The restaurant may choose to have an optimum level of current assets, based on the kind of policies that may be regarded as conservative, moderate, or aggressive working capital policies. The policies are based on the level of current assets. Higher level of current assets call for a higher level of investments, reducing the total risk. Thus, an aggressive working capital policy would call for lesser investment in current assets, while increasing the component of risk. The question is not as important to the room sales as to the restaurant operations, because we have seen that the sales mix is one of the influential factors in deciding the quantum of investments in current assets. Working capital management relates to the source and application of short-term capital. The hospitality business will lose profitable investment opportunities or will suffer from a short-term liquidity crisis if there is too much or too little short-term capital. The exact quantum of investment in working capital that will strike a balance between meeting unforeseen capital requirements and avoiding non-efficient management of working capital depends upon internal and external factors relevant to the business. The internal characteristics include debt ratio, operating cash flow, growth, firm's performance, etc., while the external factors comprise of business and industry factors.[*]

CLASSIFICATION OF CURRENT ASSETS

Current assets can be classified on the basis of components or time. In the first case, they can be classified as cash, marketable securities, etc. and can be classified as permanent or temporary

---

[*] Chiou, J. and Cheng L. (2006), 'The Determinants of Working Capital', *The Journal of American Academy of Business*, Cambridge, 10(1) 149–155.

on the basis of time. It is relevant to seek an explanation for the classification on the basis of time, rather than on the basis of components. The amount of current assets required to meet long-term capital needs is called *permanent working capital*. Investment in current assets that varies with seasonal requirements is called *temporary working capital*. For example, consider a restaurant that serves 40 seats. The amount of investment in current assets required to sustain an average level of operations will be regarded as permanent working capital, while the investment required to sustain the seasonal or high demand period will be referred to as temporary working capital. Permanent working capital should not be misconstrued as current assets staying permanently in the business, but should rather be understood as a minimum level of investment that keeps turning over and facilitates operations. Like permanent working capital, temporary working capital also consists of ever-changing form. The level of temporary working capital would vary with seasonal requirement. Let us now direct our attention to the question of financing current assets. To illustrate this point, let us consider the 40-seat restaurant that serves breakfast, lunch, and dinner. The table turnover would generally vary with the meal period. If we consider the dinner turnover to be high, the requirement of current assets would be higher during dinner as compared to breakfast and lunch. This additional requirement will be regarded as temporary working capital.

FINANCING CURRENT ASSETS

The way in which the assets of operations are financed involves a balance between risk and profitability. Therefore, before deciding on an appropriate level of working capital, the company's management has to evaluate the trade-off between the expected profitability risks involved. Profitability is measured by the rate of operating return on total assets. Current assets may be financed through spontaneous sources of financing, which includes trade credit, other payables, and accruals. Any hotel or restaurant operation would have suppliers and vendors who provide short-term credit and thus finance operations of the business.

WORKING CAPITAL POLICY

Working capital policy involves (i) the appropriate level of current assets and (ii) the financing of current assets. We shall now examine alternative policies regarding the level of investment in current assets and the financing of current assets.

An important decision associated with the level of current assets is known as the *working capital policy*. The flexible or conservative policy provides for higher levels of investment in current assets as compared to the moderate or aggressive policies. This calls for higher inventory levels, huge investments in marketable securities, and generous credit policies. Under a restrictive or aggressive policy, the investment in current assets is low as compared to a flexible policy. This calls for a lower level of investment in short-term securities and smaller cash balances. In other words, it is a lean and mean policy for maintaining investments in current assets.

Consequences of Working Capital Policy

A flexible working capital policy ensures that there is a proper flow of inventory and, thus, no impediment to the hotel or restaurant operations. Maintaining a higher level of cash balance ensures flexibility in operations. This is a regular feature in flight catering operations. If the regular vendor is unable to provide for the requirement beyond a certain time limit, the supplies have to be purchased from the open market by paying cash. On the contrary, a restrictive current assets policy will suffer a lot on account of improper supplies of inventory. Guest satisfaction, to a large extent, depends on the speed of service. Satisfaction level would drop if timely delivery of service is not maintained. This would lead to a negative image of the hotel or restaurant. This is the price that a hotel would pay for following an aggressive or restrictive working capital policy. There is definitely a limit to how lean and mean the hotel operations can be. Maintaining an appropriate level of current assets, without compromising on the quality of service, is an important point to be considered while deciding on the appropriate working capital policy.

Determining an optimal level of current assets involves striking a balance between the costs, with the rise and fall in the level of current assets. The rise in costs are known as *carrying costs* whereas the costs associated with a fall in the level of current assets are called *shortage cost*. Carrying costs basically arise due to the increase in level of current assets. Shortage costs are a consequence of loss of customers, goodwill, failure to provide service to a guest, and other similar costs. In Fig. 7.1, the optimal level of current assets is denoted by the point X. At this point, the total carrying and shortage costs are minimized.

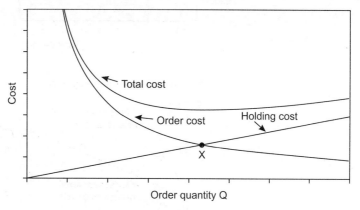

Fig. 7.1 Optimal level of current assets

After establishing the level of current assets, the next step is to determine the method to finance the current assets. What should be the mix of long-term and short-term debt to be employed to fulfil the current assets requirement? Figure 7.2 shows the total assets change over time for a restaurant operation that is in its growth phase. We can divide the assets into two classes, *fixed assets* and *current assets*. The requirement of fixed assets would grow at a steady rate. This is due to the fact that there will be a steady growth in sales. Let us assume a 40-seat restaurant that is open for breakfast, lunch, and dinner. Assuming a meal period of two hours, the capacity of the restaurant would be to serve 240 seats. The requirement of fixed assets will change with the increase in total number of seats. Similarly, the current assets will also increase with the increase in the seat turnover. However, there will be fluctuations around the seasonal sales and purchases. Typically, restaurants

a. Moderate approach (maturity matching)

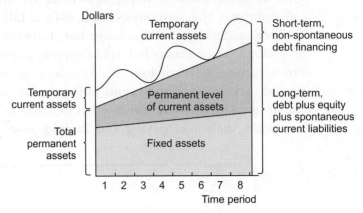

b. Relatively aggressive approach

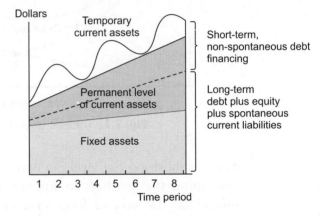

c. Conservative approach

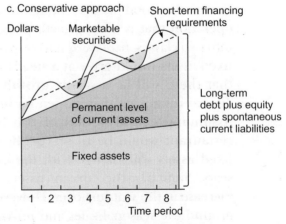

Fig. 7.2 Working capital policy

experience a heavy turnover during New Year and other festive seasons. Similarly, there would be lean periods during the year. This is a common phenomenon experienced by the restaurant business to a large extent. Nonetheless, this is a factor that affects the restaurant business. The requirement of current assets would be high during season time, whereas it may be low during off-season time.

The strategies available for financing capital requirements may be summarized as follows:

Strategy A   Fixed assets and peak working capital requirements are financed by long-term sources. The surplus working capital during the lean period is invested in liquid assets, such as short-term securities, or simply held back as cash.

Strategy B   Fixed assets, permanent working capital requirements, and a portion of fluctuating working capital requirements are financed by long-term sources. Short-term financing, like short-term loan or bank overdraft, is employed to finance short-term requirements during seasonal upswings.

Strategy C   Fixed assets and permanent working capital are financed by long-term sources, whereas short-term financing is employed to meet the fluctuating capital requirements (refer to Fig. 7.3).

Matching Principle

Strategy C above reflects the principle which advocates that the time frame of the sources of financing should match the time

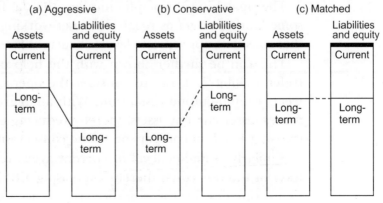

Fig. 7.3   Alternative policies

frame of the corresponding asset. This is known as the *matching principle*. In other words, permanent sources of financing should be employed for permanent assets, while short-term financing must be employed for short-term assets. The rationale here is to match the cash flow generating characteristics of assets with the time frame of financing. A temporary build-up in current assets can be financed with current liabilities that can be paid-off with the reduction in current assets.

An aggressive working capital policy calls for low level of current assets, while a conservative policy would call for a higher level of current assets. Similarly, an aggressive working capital policy would call for a high level of current liabilities whereas a conservative policy would call for a lower level of current liabilities. The following rules apply in case of matching the current assets to the current liabilities:

1. If a firm has an aggressive current assets position, it should match with a corresponding conservative liability position. For instance, if a restaurant has a low level of investments in inventory, cash, and receivables, the level of current liabilities such as payables and other short-term debts has to be low.

2. If a firm has a conservative current assets position, then this should be matched with an aggressive current liabilities position.

3. If a firm has a moderate current assets position, it should match the same by employing a moderate current liabilities position.

The matching principle implies that a firm should set some kind of target as regards the net working capital position that considers appropriate levels of current assets and liabilities.

This can be further shown with the help of an illustration (refer Exhibit 7.1). Let us consider the operations of The Retreat, a multi-cuisine restaurant. With an aggressive approach, it uses lesser current assets, thereby reducing expenses and increasing EBIT in comparison to the conservative approach.

Similarly, a higher level of current assets results in a lower level of interest costs, thereby increasing EBIT. Note that the two strategies in the middle are in accordance with the

Exhibit 7.1

	Lower assets; higher liabilities	Lower assets; lower liabilities	Higher assets; lower liabilities	Higher assets; lower liabilities
Sales turnover	3,75,000	3,75,000	3,75,000	3,75,000
Less: Expenses	3,25,000	3,25,000	3,35,000	3,35,000
EBIT	50,000	50,000	40,000	40,000
Less: Interest	14,200	17,000	14,200	17,000
EBT	35,800	33,000	25,800	23,000
Less: Taxes (40%)	14,320	13,200	10,320	9,200
EAT	21,480	19,800	15,480	13,800
	Aggressive strategy	Moderate strategy		Conservative strategy

matching principle. Considering the risks involved, the aggressive strategy has earnings of Rs 21,480 whereas the conservative strategy has earnings of Rs 13,800.

OPERATING AND CASH CONVERSION CYCLE

The investment in working capital is influenced by four major events in the restaurant or food and beverage operations:

(a) Purchase of supplies
(b) Payment for supplies
(c) Sale
(d) Collection of cash from sales

Figure 7.4 is a representation of cash conversion cycle in the food and beverage operations. The cycle begins with the purchase of raw material that is paid for after a time-lag that represents the accounts payable period. The sales occur sometime after the supplies are ordered. The time-lag between the purchase of raw material and sale of finished goods is called the inventory period. The last step in the process is the sale and collection of cash. We can assume that there is a lag between the sales and the collection from the guest, which is referred to as the accounts receivable period.

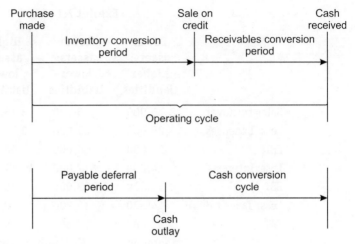

Fig. 7.4 Cash conversion cycle

It is interesting to note that a lower gross operating profit is associated with an increase in the number of days of accounts payable. In other words, less profitable operations will wait longer to pay their bills. Similarly, a negative relationship between accounts receivable and profitability would suggest that less profitable firms would attempt to reduce the cash gap in the cash conversion cycle by tracking accounts receivables. Finally, an increase in the inventory conversion cycle and profitability suggests that improper management of inventory will lead to wedging excess capital at the cost of profitable operations. A proper conduct of the cash conversion cycle and keeping the different components (receivables, payables, and inventory) at optimum levels will ensure profitability in operations.[*]

The time period between the purchase of supplies and the collection of cash from sales is called the *operating cycle*. The length of time between the payment of supplies and the collection of cash is called the *cash cycle*. In other words, the operating cycle is the sum of the inventory period and the accounts receivable period, whereas the cash cycle is equal to the operating cycle minus the accounts payable period. It is possible

---

[*] Lazadiris, I. and Tryfonidis D. (2006), 'Relationship between Working Capital Management and Profitability of Listed Companies in the Athens Stock Exchange', *Journal of Financial Management and Analysis*, 19(1) 26–35.

to calculate the inventory period, the accounts receivable period, and the accounts payable period as follows:

Inventory period

$$= \text{Average inventory}/$$
$$\text{(Annual cost of goods sold}/ 365)$$

Accounts receivable period

$$= \text{Average accounts receivable}/$$
$$\text{(Annual sale}/365)$$

Accounts payable period

$$= \text{Average accounts payable}/$$
$$\text{(Annual cost of goods sold}/365)$$

Income statement data			Balance sheet data	
			2006	**2007**
Sales	800	Inventory	96	102
Cost of goods sold	720	Accounts receivable	86	90
		Accounts payable	56	60

From the above example we can now calculate several aspects:

Inventory period

$$= (96 + 102)/2 \,/(720/365) = 50.1 \text{ days}$$

Accounts receivable period

$$= 86 + 90/(800/365) = 40.2 \text{ days}$$

Accounts payable period

$$= 56 + 60/2 \,/(720/365) = 29.4 \text{ days}$$

Operating cycle

$$= \text{Inventory period} + \text{accounts receivable}$$
$$\text{turnover period}$$
$$= 50.1 + 40.2 = 90.3 \text{ days}$$

Cash Cycle $= \text{Operating cycle} - \text{accounts payable cycle}$
$$= 90.3 - 29.4 = 69.9 \text{ days}$$

In our example, we see that the hotel takes about two months to collect payment from its guests, from the time it pays for its inventories. It is very unlikely that a hotel or restaurant will have a cognizable outstanding balance as receivables towards the end of the year.

This is helpful in monitoring the overall operating cycle and its individual components. A time series analysis may be carried out to understand the variations within the firm, while a cross-section analysis may be carried out to benchmark the hotel operations against competition.

SUMMARY

- The two concepts of working capital are expressed as gross working capital and net working capital. Gross working capital is the investment in total current assets, whereas net working capital is the difference between the total current assets and current liabilities.
- Working capital management is an important aspect of financial management in hotel and restaurant operations.
- The characteristics of current assets are (i) short lifespan and (ii) swift transformation into other assets, which are important aspects of working capital management.
- Working capital management needs are influenced by internal and external factors such as (i) nature of business, (ii) seasonality of operations, (iii) production policy, and (iv) conditions of supply.
- Current assets can be classified as permanent current assets and temporary current assets.
- Working capital policies can be classified as aggressive, moderate, and conservative.
- The matching approach to financing suggests that each asset would be backed by financing instrument of the same maturity. The short term of the seasonal variation in current assets would be financed with short-term debt. The permanent component would be financed with long-term debt or equity.
- Cash conversion cycle and operations cycle are two important factors that influence the profitability of organizations, which include hospitality organizations.
- The key considerations in working capital management are the level of current assets to be maintained and the method of financing the current assets. These aspects are intertwined and, hence, cannot be considered in isolation.

- Operating cycle of a firm begins with acquiring supplies and ends with collection of receivables. Subtracting accounts payable from the operating cycle would result in cash cycle.
- Operating cycle information is helpful in forecasting and controlling working capital.

KEY TERMS

Aggressive working capital policy The policy suggests that some permanent current assets and, perhaps, fixed assets are financed with short-term debt.

Cash conversion cycle The time lag between the payment for supplies and the receipt of cash from the sale.

Conservative working capital policy The policy suggests that long-term debt should be used to finance some of the temporary current assets.

Gross working capital The current assets used in operations.

Net working capital The difference between current assets and liabilities.

Permanent current assets The current assets that operations would hold at all times.

Temporary current assets The additional current assets that are needed during cyclical or seasonal peaks.

REVIEW QUESTIONS

1. Define the term working capital.
2. What are the characteristics of current assets?
3. Define permanent and temporary current assets.
4. What factors influence the working capital requirements of hospitality organizations?
5. What are the various methods used to finance current assets?
6. What do you mean by a cash conversion cycle and an operating cycle?

CRITICAL THINKING QUESTIONS

1. Discuss the importance of working capital management in the context of hospitality organizations.
2. Distinguish between temporary and permanent working capital.
3. Discuss the consequences of adopting various working capital policies on the level of current assets used in operations.
4. Discuss the rationale for adopting the matching principle.
5. A hotel company currently follows an aggressive working capital policy as regards to the level of current assets it maintains (relatively low levels of current assets for each possible level of output). The company has decided to switch to a conservative working capital policy. What will be the effect on the company's profitability and risk?
6. What would be the impact of financing temporary assets with long-term funds on the profitability and risk of the firm?

PROJECT WORK

Talk to financial managers of at least two hotel companies and find out more about the working capital policy they adopt for successful operations.

CASE STUDY

WORKING CAPITAL MANAGEMENT

Romesh Sharma is engaged in the business of food catering for the past several years. He follows a very simple business model, which has been a critical success factor. His customers are extremely happy and his business has flourished dramatically in the past few years. He is back from an entrepreneurship development programme, organized by the local centre for entrepreneurship development on working capital management, and is plagued with many questions.

Before taking a look at his questions, it would be pertinent to understand his business operations. He receives an order from the customer and negotiates the price on the basis of number of packs, items to be served, and some other considerations. He buys from the local suppliers on 15 or 20 days credit period. He collects the receivables in about 7 to 10 days from his customers. Sometimes, he has to reach out for some exotic supplies for which he has to pay immediately.

The speaker at the workshop emphasized the importance of working capital management, operating and cash conversion cycles, and working capital policies. Romesh is exposed to the idea of the negative relationship among the increase in the receivables period, the increase in the accounts payable, and the increase in inventory levels and lower profitability. The questions that have been left unanswered are listed as follows:

1. With regard to catering operations, is working capital an important point to be considered?
2. How does an increase in receivables collection period decrease profitability?
3. What kind of working capital policy should he follow for his catering business?
4. He wants to know more about the matching principle and the benefits that he will derive from adopting such a principle. Can you help him?

Management of Cash

> *Can anybody remember when the times were not hard and money not scarce?*
>
> **Ralph Waldo Emerson**

INTRODUCTION

Cash is the lifeblood of any business enterprise. While cash is the most liquid current asset, all other current assets like inventory and receivables are also converted into cash. Improper management of cash may prove to be fatal for the business. Management of cash refers to management of money to pay bills and debts as and when they are due. Although the requirement of cash may be anywhere between one and three per cent of the total assets, management of cash is extremely crucial for the success of any business operation. Management of cash is one of the key aspects of working capital management. The objective of cash management is to maintain sufficient cash balance to cover daily expenses and maintain a little excess cash. By maintaining excessive cash in the business, the company will lose out on the opportunity to earn interest that can be generated by investing excess cash in some other avenue. On the other hand, if the firm does not maintain adequate cash, then there are chances that the business may face liquidity crisis. This implies that firms must maintain a balance between the cash in the business and investment in short-term securities. Therefore, cash management is concerned with optimizing short-term funding requirements of a firm and, as such, is an important activity of financial managers of hotel companies operating in an international or national environment.

MOTIVES FOR HOLDING CASH

Cash, by itself, does not provide any return unless it is invested. Then why do firms hold cash? There are four primary motives for any company to hold cash—(1) for transactions, (2) as a precaution, (3) for speculation, and (4) as compensation. We shall now understand these motives in greater detail.

Transaction Motive

An important reason for firms to maintain cash is to carry out routine transactions. This refers to holding of cash for meeting routine requirements like purchase of raw materials, paying wages and salaries, operating expenses, etc. The firm experiences inflow and outflow of cash during its regular course of operations. But the inflows (receipts) and outflows (disbursements) do not exactly coincide or synchronise with each other. Sometimes the receipts may be more than the disbursements while at other times the receipts would be inadequate to meet the disbursement requirements. Therefore, an adequate balance of cash is to be maintained to deal with situations where the payments are in excess of receipts.

Precautionary Motive

In addition to daily transactions, the firm should also be prepared for some unforeseen events. The cash balance held in order to tide over such situations is called *precautionary balance*. In other words, precautionary motive of holding cash balance implies the need to hold cash in order to meet unexpected expenses. If the cash inflows are unpredictable, then the need to maintain a higher precautionary balance will arise. Another important factor that influences precautionary balance is the availability of short-term credit. If the firm has access to short-term funds at short notice, then the cash balance will be relatively smaller in size, and vice versa.

Speculative Motive

Speculative motive refers to the desire of any firm to exploit opportunities that are typically beyond the normal course of business. Firms may choose to hold cash balance to benefit from an opportunity to purchase supplies at a discounted or favourable price on paying immediate cash. In other words, firms would like to benefit from the fluctuations in commodity prices, interest rates, foreign exchange rates, etc. by holding some cash balance on account of speculative motives.

Compensating Motive

In the era of anywhere banking and anytime money, it has become necessary for firms to hold cash to compensate banks for providing services. Banks provide clearing facilities, supply of credit information, transfer of funds, and numerous banking facilities to their customers. There are explicit charges for some of these facilities, but most banks carry out these services free of charge. To avail such services, the customers of the bank have to maintain a specified sum, *minimum balance*, with the bank at all times. This balance is unavailable to the customers as far as transactions are concerned. Such balances are referred to as *compensating balances*. Compensating balances can be of two kinds, an absolute minimum, say Rs 3,00,000, below which the absolute cash balance will never fall, or a minimum average balance, say Rs 3,00,000, over a period of a month.

Of the four motives discussed above, hotel and restaurant firms would hold cash for transactions and compensation. There is rarely any need to speculate and the requirement of precautionary balances can be met by borrowing on a short-term basis.

OBJECTIVES OF CASH MANAGEMENT

As mentioned earlier, the basic objectives of cash management are two-fold: (a) to meet the cash disbursement needs and (b) to reduce the balance of cash. These are mutually conflicting and the task of cash management is to reconcile these goals.

Meeting the Disbursement Schedule

In the normal course of business, payment of cash to vendors and employees has to be made on a continuous and regular basis. The fundamental objective of cash management is to meet the payment schedule. In other words, a firm must maintain sufficient cash to meet its disbursement requirements. Maintaining adequate cash balance is beneficial to the firm and helps the business in more than one way. By maintaining sufficient cash balance, the firm can prevent insolvency or bankruptcy arising out of its inability to meet financial obligations, maintain a cordial relationship with banks and other financial institutions by fulfilling commitments on time, sustain a healthy relationship with suppliers and vendors by paying on time, and at times benefit from discount offered by the suppliers. This, however, does not imply keeping a large balance of cash. The benefits of prompt payment of cash can be realized by maintaining adequate and not excessive cash balance.

Minimizing Balance of Cash

The other objective of cash management is to minimize commitment of funds to cash balances. High level of cash balance will help achieve the aforesaid advantages but will also result in cash lying idle. On the other hand, a low level of cash balance will lead to a cash crunch and may even mean failure to meet payment schedules. Therefore, the objective of cash management should be optimum cash balance.

FACTORS INFLUENCING REQUIREMENT OF CASH BALANCE

In the preceding sections, we have discussed the importance of management of cash. In this section, we will try to understand the factors influencing the requirement of cash balance. The major factors that determine the requirement of cash balance are discussed below.

Inflow and Outflow of Cash

The need for maintaining the cash balance arises from the mismatch in the inflow and outflow of cash. If the payments coincide with the receipts, there would be no need for cash balance. The first consideration in determining the cash needs is the extent of misalignment between cash inflows and outflows. It is advisable that a forecast of receipts and payments be worked out well in advance to avoid any adverse effect on the liquidity position of the business.

Short Costs

Another general factor to be considered while determining cash requirements is the cost associated with a shortfall in the requirement of cash. The forecast presented in the cash budget should reflect the period of cash shortfalls. Expenses incurred due to shortfall of cash are referred to as *short costs*. The following costs are associated with shortfall in the cash balance of the business.

- *Transaction costs* Costs incurred while borrowing to cover the cash shortage are referred to as transaction costs. In other words, transaction costs would mean the costs incurred on a transaction related to covering the shortage of cash. For example, brokerage paid on the sale of marketable securities would be termed as transaction costs.

- *Borrowing costs* Costs allied to borrowing in order to tide over a situation of cash shortage are referred to as borrowing costs. This may typically include items such as interest on loans and incidental charges associated with borrowing money.

- *Penalty rates*   Imposed by the banks for failure to meet the shortfall in the compensating balance are also shortfall costs.
- *Some other short costs*   Loss of credit rating leading to higher bank charges on loans, stoppage of supplies, etc.

Opportunity Cost of Excess Cash

An excessive cash balance maintained by the firm indicates that it has lost an opportunity to earn returns by investing the excess cash elsewhere. This would also be considered as excess cash balance cost to the firm.

Uncertainty

Uncertainty plays an important role in determining the requirement of cash flows. If there are violent fluctuations in the cash flow, then there arises a need to hold more cash as compared to dealing with accurate, predictable cash flow. This is a necessary precautionary measure to sustain irregularities in cash flow, unexpected delay in disbursement, defaults, and other similar conditions. The higher the amount of uncertainty in the cash flows, the higher would be the cash requirements.

CASH FLOW

Cash management is not only about ensuring a correct balance at the bank and maintaining adequate cash for expenses. It also encompasses the management of all working capital components such as inventory, accounts receivables, plus the management of payables, loan repayment, and certain payments that are at the discretion of the business, such as cash purchases of assets and payment of dividends in cash. The circular flow of cash is represented in Fig. 8.1 (see Coltman 1994 in Further Reading).

CASH BUDGET: A MANAGEMENT TOOL

A firm must try and maintain adequate cash balance while trying to avoid excessive cash balance. Chronologically, a hotel company would first forecast sales. Next, it would forecast the fixed assets and the level of inventory required to achieve the

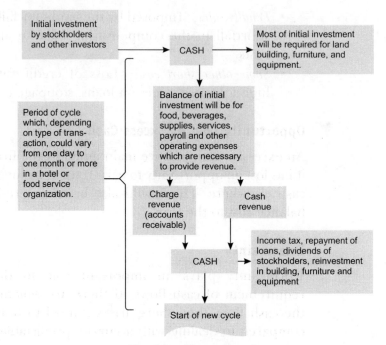

Fig. 8.1 The cash cycle

targeted level of sales, then the time and the amount to be paid to suppliers and towards expenses. This information is summarized in the cash budget, which depicts the hotel firm's projected cash inflows and outflows over some specified period. Cash budget can be prepared for a year and also over short time-frames like a month, a fortnight, a week, or even a day. The yearly/monthly cash budgets are used for planning whereas the weekly or daily cash budgets are used for actual control of cash.

TRANSACTIONS THAT AFFECT CASH BUDGET

As cash investments are recorded as cash disbursements, cash loans from banks or any other source should be recorded as receipts. Apart from these, typical transactions like sale of fixed assets for cash would be recorded as receipts.

Cash budgets prepared for a year aid the management in deciding avenues for investment of surplus cash. A cash budget prepared in advance helps the management to find out the things that it can do or cannot do, depending on the availability of cash.

CASH BUDGET: THE PRACTICE

The basic purpose of the cash budget is to ascertain the likelihood of cash surplus or deficit in the given time period. The first step towards preparing a cash budget is selecting the time-frame for the budget. Also known as *planning horizon*, this step indicates the span of time and the sub-periods for which the cash flows are to be projected. The cash requirements of every individual firm would vary and hence there is no fixed rule. A long time-frame would yield inaccurate results whereas a short time period would call for preparing budgets more frequently. Therefore, the general principle is that the cash budget period should neither be too long nor too short. The planning horizon for a cash budget should be determined in the light of the circumstances and the requirements of a particular case. If a hotel operation experiences a steady cash flow throughout the year, then the cash budgeting exercise can be carried out for the entire year, divided over smaller intervals, say a month. If the cash flows are characterized by seasonal fluctuations, cash budgets may be divided on a weekly or even daily basis. It becomes possible to highlight the movement of cash from one sub-period to another.

The second aspect of the process is identification of the factors that influence the cash flows during the said period. It must be noted that only the cash items are considered. Non-cash items such as amortization and depreciation are not included in the cash budget. The inflows and outflows can be broadly classified into operating and financial categories. Inflows and outflows on account of operations are regarded as operating cash flows whereas cash flows on account of sale or purchase of capital equipment and sale of shares and stocks are referred to as financial flows.

There are various methods for forecasting short-term cash requirements.

RECEIPTS AND PAYMENTS METHOD

This is the principal method for forecasting short-term cash requirements. Cash budget, as per this method, shows the timing quantum of expected cash receipts and disbursements (payments) over the forecasted period. The preparation of the cash budget can be illustrated through the following example.

Consider the following example of a 50-seat restaurant situated in a prominent mall in a metropolitan city. From the details provided, we shall prepare a cash budget for the period from January through March:

- Expected sales for the months of January, February, and March are Rs 5,00,000, Rs 5,50,000, and Rs 6,00,000, respectively. All sales would be in cash.
- The estimated purchases would be Rs 2,00,000, Rs 2,20,000, and Rs 2,50,000. The suppliers for raw material provide a 30-day credit period and, therefore, can be paid after 30 days. Purchases for the previous month (December) amount to Rs 2,20,000.
- Rent per month is Rs 50,000.
- Salaries and wages are expected to be Rs 1,50,000, Rs 1,80,000, and Rs 2,00,000 in the month of January, February, and March, respectively. Salaries and wages are to be paid in cash.
- The owner has a requirement of a calamander and bain-marie and is contemplating purchasing the same in February. This will call for an outflow of Rs 2,50,000.
- The cash balance at the start of the budget period is Rs 10,000. The owner insists on a target balance of Rs 50,000.

See Table 8.1 for a cash budget determining the surplus/deficit of cash in relation to the target cash balance.

Negative Cash Balance

On some occasions, some operations may experience a higher disbursement as compared to the receipts, to an extent that they experience a negative cash balance. Let us consider Table 8.2.

From Table 8.2, it can be ascertained that there is shortage of cash in some month(s). Having prepared a cash budget, the company is able to ascertain the requirement of the shortfall and arrange for a cover by borrowing on a short-term or long-term basis, as may be convenient to the company.

Table 8.1

(Rs in thousands)	January	February	March	April
Opening balance	10,000	2,40,000	2,60,000	4,20,000
Cash receipts				
Cash sales	5,00,000	5,50,000	6,00,000	
Total cash receipts	6,10,000	7,90,000	8,60,000	
Cash disbursements				
Purchases	2,20,000	2,00,000	2,20,000	
Salaries and other expenses	1,50,000	1,80,000	2,00,000	
Capital expenditure	2,50,000			
Total cash disbursements	3,70,000	5,30,000	4,40,000	
Surplus/deficit*	2,40,000	2,60,000	4,20,000	

* Total cash receipts – Total cash expenditure

Table 8.2

(Rs in thousands)	Month 1	Month 2	Month 3
Opening balance	50,000	70,000	(10,000)
Receipts	2,20,000	1,50,000	2,00,000
Total	2,70,000	2,20,000	1,90,000
Disbursements	2,00,000	2,30,000	1,80,000
Closing balance	70,000	(10,000)	10,000

DEVIATIONS FROM EXPECTED CASH FLOWS

The cash budget expresses a precise estimate of cash inflow and outflow in the forecasted period. It is necessary to remember that the actual cash flows may vary from the estimated cash flows. The deviation would depend on the volatility of the cash flows of the business. Given the uncertainties characterizing hotel and restaurant operations, only one set of assumptions may prove inadequate in providing a clear perspective of the future. Therefore, to gain a better insight into the future, the company may use three possible scenarios—pessimistic, normal, and optimistic scenarios—while drafting a cash budget.

LONG-TERM CASH FORECASTING

Arbitrarily, we can divide short-term and long-term cash forecasts as within a year and beyond a year. Long-term cash forecasts are generally prepared for periods ranging from two to five years and above. Preparing this kind of forecast enables a firm to determine its long-term cash requirements and availability of surplus funds, if any, for investment.

The long range cash flow budget is somewhat different from the routine or day-to-day cash budgets. The long range cash flow projections assume that the position of current assets and liabilities remain the same over the long run and, therefore, ignores changes within the working capital of the firm. Theoretically, the receipts and payments method can be used to estimate the long-term cash requirements—the method generally employed is the adjusted net income method. A format for the estimation of long-term cash requirements is shown in Table 8.3.

The long-term cash flow budget has the following advantages:

1. It allows the firm to see whether there will be adequate cash available to meet long-term financial commitments, for example, repayment of loan.

Table 8.3   Format for estimation of long-term cash requirements

Source	Year 1	Year 2	Year 3	Year 4
Net income after tax				
Non-cash charges (depreciation, amortization, etc.)				
Increase in borrowings				
Sale of equity shares				
Uses				
Capital expenditure				
Increase in current assets				
Repayment of borrowings				
Dividend payment				
Miscellaneous				
Surplus/deficit				
Opening cash balance				
Closing cash balance				

2. It identifies the need to arrange for excess cash by borrowing or by issuing shares.

3. It facilitates planning the replacement of, or additional purchase of, long-term assets, given the fact that the cash disbursed or received is included in the cash flow projections.

4. It provides a guideline for planning the dividend policy, which will indicate the availability of surplus cash to pay dividends.

CASH CONTROL REPORTS

Cash reports are extremely beneficial in providing actual developments for a comparison with the forecasted picture and aid in controlling and revising cash forecasts on a continual basis. The important cash reports are outlined as follows:

- *Daily cash report* shows the daily opening balance, receipts, payments, and closing balance.
- *Daily treasury report* provides a comprehensive change in cash, marketable securities, and accounts receivable and payable. This is an extended picture of the daily cash report.
- *Monthly cash report* shows the actual receipts and payments on a monthly basis. This report aids in comparing the actual results to the budgeted figures and the calculation of variance.

CASH MANAGEMENT IN THE HOTEL INDUSTRY

Cash management strategies are basically directed at minimizing operating cash balance requirements. Higher level of cash sales would mean lesser cash requirements. However, a firm must maintain a minimum level of operating cash balance. Some of the points to be considered while managing cash are as follows.

Playing the Float

The cash balance shown in the books is referred to as *book* or *ledger* balance whereas the balance shown by the bank account is known as *available* or *collected* balance. The difference between the available balance and the ledger balance is called a *float*.

There are two kinds of floats, namely, collection float and disbursement float. Cheques issued by the firm would create a disbursement float whereas cheques received by the firm would create a collection float. For example, you have a book balance and an available balance of Rs 4,00,000, as of 31 December, with your bank. On 1 January, you issue a cheque of Rs 1,00,000 to your suppliers. While you would reduce your cash balance, the bank would not do so unless the cheque has been presented for payment. In this case, let us assume that the suppliers present the cheque by 7 January. There is a time lag between the time the cheque is issued and the time it is presented for payment. Hence, between 1 January and 7 January, you will have a disbursement float of Rs 1,00,000. In other words, disbursement float will be the difference between the available balance and the book balance. In this case, the disbursement float will be equal to Rs 1,00,000.

Similarly, cheques received from guests would be considered as collection float. For example, assume that the cheques issued by all your guests amount to Rs 1,00,000, as on 30 January, and therefore, the balance of the book balance and the available balance is Rs 2,00,000. In this case, the collection float would be the difference between your available balance and book balance. Since the guests have paid you, your book balance would increase by Rs 1,00,000 whereas your bank will have to present the cheques for payments before providing you the required credit. In this example, the collection float would amount to Rs 1,00,000.

Net float is the sum of the disbursement float and the collection float. It is simply the difference between the firm's available balance and its book balance. If the net float is positive, it means that the available balance is greater than the book balance, and a negative float means that the available balance is lesser than the book balance.

Since the available balance is material, it is prudent to maximize the net float. This means that one should try to speed up collection and slow down disbursements to a reasonable extent. Hotel and restaurant operations do not really need to worry about collections, as there are few transactions through cheques as compared to cash or credit card. Normally, all the bills are settled within a period of 15 days.

From the above discussion, we may summarize that one of the strategies to manage cash is by playing the float. While all other industries grapple with problems of timely billing, speeding up collections as a part of their cash management strategy, hotels and restaurants can try to maintain liquidity by just slowing down payments to the suppliers within a reasonable limit.

Delaying Payments

While the option of increasing the net float by speeding up collections is unavailable to hotel firms, the other way is to slow down payments. Control of disbursements is essential to the efficient management of cash, which will eventually slow down cash outflows and thereby minimize the time that the cash deposits are idle. A firm with multiple accounts should be able to shift funds to other bank accounts from which the disbursements are made. This will prevent building of cash in one bank. The following points should be considered while maximizing the disbursement float:

- Payments should be made on the due date only, and not before.
- Centralizing disbursements helps in consolidating funds at the corporate office and reduces unproductive cash balances at the units. Many hotel companies have started to use a centralized purchase system where the payment is made by the corporate office.
- Synchronization of cash outflows with inflows helps in better management of cash. It is advisable that the due dates be negotiated with the suppliers in a way that coincides with the cash inflows.

SUMMARY

- Cash is the most liquid of all assets, and management of cash is extremely crucial for the success of any firm.
- Firms hold cash for the purpose of transactions, as precaution for speculation, and as compensating balances.
- The firm should be able to pay cash to the suppliers and other service providers on the specified due date while at the same

time maintain the minimum cash balance required for the smooth operation of the business. Management of cash is aimed at achieving both contradicting objectives.

- Maintaining excessive cash balance does not help the firm, as an opportunity to earn interest is lost. On the other hand, maintaining inadequate cash balance may have fatal consequences.
- Requirement of cash is based on the inflow and outflow of cash. Higher outflow as compared to the relative inflow will compel the firm to hold on to higher cash balance.
- Requirement of cash also depends upon factors such as the cost associated with the shortfall in the cash requirements, cost associated with the excess level of cash maintained, and impact of uncertainties on cash management.
- Cash budget is an important tool for cash management. Cash budget helps a firm to plan and control the use of cash. It presents a clear picture of cash from one period to another.
- Cash budget has three components, viz., cash collections, cash payments, and cash balances (surplus/deficit).
- Cash management strategies are aimed at minimizing operational cash requirements. Increasing net float and slowing down payments augments the process of minimizing cash requirements.

KEY TERMS

Cash budget A management tool that helps in forecasting cash flows over the short and long range.

Cash management The process of matching cash outflows to cash inflows.

Collection float The amount of funds associated with cheques received but not cleared.

Deficit The excess of outflow over inflow.

Disbursement float The amount of funds associated with cheques issued by the firm that are not presented for payment.

Liquidity The ability of the firm to pay bills on due date.

Net float The difference between disbursement float and collection float.

Receipts and payment method The most commonly used method to forecast cash inflows and outflows over a short range.

Surplus cash The excess of inflow over outflow.

REVIEW QUESTIONS

1. State the motives for holding cash.
2. What are the basic objectives of cash management?
3. State the factors that determine the requirements of cash for hotel and restaurant firms.
4. What do you mean by net float?
5. What is cash budget? What are its components?
6. Explain the terms
   - Cash float
   - Short-term cash budget
   - Long-term cash budget

CRITICAL THINKING QUESTIONS

1. Discuss the importance of cash management in the context of hotel and restaurant operations.
2. Compare and contrast long range and short range cash forecasts.
3. Discuss various cash reports used for the purpose of control.
4. Compare and contrast collection and disbursement floats using suitable examples.

REVIEW PROBLEMS

1. From the information provided below for Sharma's Catering, prepare a cash budget for the six months commencing 1 April.

| | Sales | | Purchase | | Others | |
	Food	Beverage	Food	Beverage	Wages	Expenses
February	1,50,000	90,000	2,40,000	4,40,000	1,20,000	1,40,000
March	3,10,000	2,20,000	3,30,000	4,80,000	2,40,000	1,40,000
April	4,34,000	1,80,000	1,63,000	1,45,000	2,60,000	1,80,000
May	3,65,000	2,61,000	1,40,000	1,46,000	1,83,000	1,21,000
June	1,64,000	1,31,800	1,41,600	1,86,000	1,15,000	1,61,000
July	1,50,000	1,61,200	1,66,000	1,28,000	1,84,000	1,41,000
August	1,54,000	1,24,000	1,64,000	1,27,000	1,31,400	1,60,000
September	1,40,800	1,13,000	1,24,000	1,46,000	1,22,000	1,20,000

(a) Assume that all sales are 80% cash and 20% credit. The credit sales are collected in the month after sale.

(b) The annual interest of Rs 22,000 on the restaurant's short-term investments is expected to be received in the month of July.

(c) The time lag in paying suppliers for purchases is two months. For example, February purchases are paid in April.

(d) Wages are paid without any time lag.

(e) Other expenses are paid with one-month delay.

(f) In May, new kitchen equipment will be purchased for Rs 1,00,000. Payment for this will be made in the following month.

(g) The restaurant's bank balance on 1 April is Rs 55,000.

2. Wine and Dine have decided to lease a new restaurant. Rent for the building will be Rs 35,000 a month to be paid on the first day of each month. They initially invested their own money Rs 25,20,000, which was used to finance the business operations.

   Sales are forecast as follows for the first three months after commencing operations in the month of January as follows:

January	Rs 8,40,000
February	Rs 9,00,000
March	Rs 12,00,000

   Sales will be 60% cash and 40% credit with the maximum credit period allowed of 30 days. Food cost is expected to average 35%. All purchases will be cash.

   Wages and salaries will be Rs 1,50,000 a month. All salaries and wages will be paid in the month during which they were earned. Other operating costs are expected to be 10% of sales and will be paid in the same month.

   Prepare a cash budget for the period of January–March using the cash receipts and disbursement method.

3. Use the following information to formulate a simplified cash budget for a large five-star hotel in New Delhi.

		(Rs in millions)		
	December	**January**	**February**	**March**
Sales	4.0	4.0	5.0	7.0
Inventory purchase	1.0	1.5	1.8	3.0
Other cash expenses	1.5	1.5	1.5	2.0
Capital purchases	0.0	0.0	1.0	0.0

Sales: 75% of the sales are cash while the remaining 25% are credit sales. One half of the credit sales are collected in the month of the sale and one half in the next month.

Purchases: 80% of the purchases are paid in the month of the purchase while 25% are paid in the next month.

Inventory: Assume that other cash expenses and the capital purchases are paid for during the month indicated above (for example, other cash expenses of Rs 10,00,000 for December were paid in December).

Assume that the beginning cash balance of 1 January is Rs 10,00,000.

Prepare a cash budget using the cash receipts and disbursements approach for the months of January–March.

4. Ram Sharma, owner of Sharma's Restaurant, needs your assistance to prepare a cash budget for his restaurant. He estimated cash on 1 July will be 1,20,000 and he wants to maintain a minimum of cash at the end of each month equal to one week's disbursements for the next month, not including disbursements related to working capital loans. (Assume that disbursements are made evenly throughout a month.)

Total monthly sales are as follows:

March	Rs 2,50,000
April	Rs 6,00,000
May	Rs 6,00,000
June	Rs 7,50,000
July (estimated)	Rs 7,95,000
August (estimated)	Rs 9,00,000
September (estimated)	Rs 7,10,000
October (estimated)	Rs 4,50,000

The sales are 40% cash and 60% regular credit. Regular credit sales are collected as follows:

Interest income of Rs 5000 is expected in August. In September, the restaurant plans to sell some extra equipment. The chief has told Sharma that the equipment will bring Rs 10,000: the book value of the equipment is Rs 5000. Payments for food are made one month after the sale. The food cost is 35%. Beverages are purchased and paid for in the month of sale and the beverage cost is 35%. Beverage sales are 50% of food sales.

Labour is paid during the month wages are earned and represents 40% of total sales. Fixed expenses, except for insurance, depreciation, and property taxes, are Rs 4000 per month and are paid monthly.

Insurance premium of Rs 15,000 are paid quarterly in January, April, July, and October of each year. The property taxes of Rs 1,00,000 for the year are paid in two instalments of Rs 50,000 each in July and December. Depreciation expense is Rs 15,000 per month. In September the firm plans to acquire fixed assets using cash totalling Rs 10,000.

Prepare a monthly cash budget for Ram Sharma for July–September, using the cash receipts and disbursements approach.

5. Smithson, the owner and the manager of a fine dining restaurant, has provided the following information about his business for July–September 2005. The cash balance on 1 July 2005 is Rs 50,000, and he wants to maintain a minimum balance of Rs 50,000 at the end of each month.

The estimated monthly sales are as follows:

July	5,50,000
August	6,50,000
September	6,00,000

The sales are 30% of cash and 70% of credit. Other expected income is Rs 10,000 from the interest to be received in February. In addition, in February a gas range with a net book value of Rs 15,000 is expected to be sold for cash for a gain of Rs 5,000 on the sale.

Food and beverages are paid for the month following the sale, and they average 40% of sales. Sales in June totalled Rs 6,50,000. Employees are paid on the last day of the month, and the total compensation is 35% of sales.

Other cash expenses approximate Rs 50,000 per month. In the month of September, Rs 2,00,000 is expected to be expended on new equipment. Funding for this expenditure comes in part from a long-term loan of Rs 1,00,000 from a local bank. Prepare the monthly cash budget for the restaurant for July–September 2005 by using the cash receipts and disbursements approach.

6. Prepare a cash budget for the owner of a restaurant for the period July–September 2005, using the following information.

The monthly sales (actual and expected) are as follows:

March	5,00,000
April	7,00,000
May	7,25,000
June	7,15,000
July (estimated)	8,00,000
August (estimated)	7,90,000
September (estimated)	8,25,000
October (estimated)	8,50,000

The sales are 70% cash and 30% regular credit. Regular credit sales are collected as follows:

Month of sale	10%
Month after sale	50%
Second month after sale	30%
Third month after sale	10%
Total	100%

Interest income of Rs 15,000 is expected in August. In September, the restaurant plans to sell some extra equipment. The owner estimates the equipment will bring Rs 25,000; the book value of the equipment is Rs 20,000.

Payments for food are made one month after the sale. The food cost is 45%. Beverages are purchased and paid for one month in advance and the beverage cost is 30%. Beverages sales are 40% of food sales.

Labour is paid during the month wages are earned and represents 40% of total sales. Fixed expenses, except for insurance, depreciation, and property taxes, are Rs 2,80,000 per month and are paid monthly.

Insurance premiums of Rs 45,000 are paid quarterly in January, April, July, and October of each year. The property taxes of Rs 2,00,000 for the year are paid in two instalments of Rs 1,00,000 each in July and December. Depreciation expense is Rs 23,000 per month. He estimates cash on 1 July will be Rs 42, 000.

PROJECT WORK

1. Talk to restaurateurs in your city and find out about cash management practices in the context of their operations.

■ CASE STUDY

CASH MANAGEMENT AT SALUD*

Jimmy Noronha operates a 50-seat Spanish restaurant in a metropolitan city in India. He embarked on the restaurant project after resigning as a *sous chef* at a large five-star hotel in the country. He commenced operations single-handedly and the business has reached its pinnacle in the last two years. The menu served at Salud is exotic and fabulous—authentic Spanish with an amazing eye for detail. Whether it is Gazpacho,** or the Pollo Con Langostinos, or the Bitter Chocolate Mousse, everything is just picture perfect. The variety of rice and pastas served at the restaurant are definitely the talk of the town. Being a chef has helped Jimmy create brand equity in the market and his stint with the five-star hotel has come to his rescue as far as marketing and promotion are concerned. He has invited chefs from Spain, and has perfected the art of making a perfect Cocido.*** Jimmy's hard work in the past seems to have paid off. But there is a problem in this fairy tale. He is acutely aware of his shortcomings as far as managing cash is concerned. Jimmy has consulted his uncle on this issue, who has advised him to go to Mr Jain, a well-known financial consultant and a very good friend. This is what happened at Mr Jain's office this morning.

Jimmy: Good morning, Mr Jain. How are you doing today?

Mr Jain: Very well. Thank you. Good to see you. I talked to your uncle last evening and he mentioned you.

Jimmy: Ahhh! Well! He wanted me to consult you about some of the problems that I'm facing in business.

Mr Jain: I have visited your restaurant You seem to be doing exceedingly well.

Jimmy: Well, Mr Jain, the problem is that I'm unable to manage my cash balance. On certain days, there is excess cash and on some days there is absolutely no cash to pay my suppliers. I had studied at college that there is a way to forecast cash flows. I need your help is establishing a cash forecast for the business.

Mr Jain: That is very easy. Do you have some details as regards to the anticipated future sales, corresponding expenses, and any other receipts and disbursements that you plan in the future? But remember, you will have to provide a definite period for the cash forecasts.

Jimmy: That is not a problem. I have the details with me.

After gaining an understanding of the process of cash budgeting, Jimmy gets up to leave for his restaurant.

---

   * Salud, or as in written Spanish, ¡Salud!, means cheers.

  ** Gazpacho is a cold soup.

*** Cocido is the national dish of Spain.

Jimmy: Thank you, Mr Jain. You have solved a lot of my problems.

Mr Jain: You are always welcome. Good luck.

On his way back, Jimmy reflects on the discussion and there are many questions that emerge in his mind:

1. Is cash budget the only solution to deal with the problems of management of cash? Does this suggest that there would be no deviation in the actual cash flow stream?

2. What is the difference between long range and short range cash forecasting?

3. Can the receipts and disbursement method be used for long range cash forecasting?

4. How to use net cash float to the advantage of the business?

5. What kinds of reports must be maintained in order to resolve some issues as regards cash management?

6. Is it fair to delay payments beyond time? He had been paying the suppliers almost before the due date, as he considered this an ethical issue.

While Jimmy has decided to ask Mr Jain these questions during his next visit, can you help him find answers to the questions in the meantime?

Inventory and Receivables Management

> *Erroneous assumptions can be disastrous.*
>
> **Peter F. Drucker, American management guru**

Learning Objectives

After studying this chapter, you will be able to

➤ Understand the meaning and importance of inventory management
➤ Determine exact quantity and time of ordering inventories
➤ Explore the methods for monitoring and controlling inventories
➤ Discuss the basis for changing credit policy variables
➤ Examine the role of the front office in the credit or receivables management

INTRODUCTION

In Chapter 7, we saw that investment in inventory involves trade-off between profitability and risk. As far as the hospitality business is concerned, the percentage of investments in inventory may be low as compared to non-current assets, but it is important to control and account for inventories from the profitability point of view. Inventory levels largely depend upon sales activity and therefore the crucial aspect is that the inventory must be acquired ahead of sales. Additionally, an incorrect estimation of inventory levels either leads to a loss of sales or adds to the total cost of operations. Therefore, the importance of inventory management cannot be undermined in the context of hospitality operations. Albeit, inventory management is predominantly a production related aspect, we shall try and understand its financial implications in this chapter.

OBJECTIVES OF INVENTORY MANAGEMENT

The goal of inventory management is to ensure that inventories needed to sustain operations are available and that the ordering and carrying costs are kept under complete control. Costs associated with inventory can be classified into three categories— carrying costs, ordering costs, and stockout costs.[*] As an overall part of the hotel's cost control strategy, there is always an emphasis on controlling inventory costs. On one hand, it is necessary to control costs, while on the other, it is necessary to maintain adequate levels of inventories.

Let us begin our discussion with an illustration: Rendezvous, a fine dining restaurant, must order bourbon for its mint julep requirement at the beginning of the month. If Rendezvous stocks incorrectly, then it will either not be able to meet the demand, or will have a lot of unsold inventory towards the end of the period. The effect of inventory changes is demonstrated in Table 9.1.

Table 9.1

Situation 1: Beginning of season			
Capital and liabilities	15,000	Bourbon inventory (base stock)	15,000
Accounts payable	10,000	Bourbon inventory (seasonal)	10,000
	25,000		25,000

Rendezvous anticipates a good sales turnover during the season and expects to sell Rs 10,000 (cost) worth of beverages.

---

[*] The cost incurred if the hotel runs out of inventory.

Rendezvous will sell at a price 30 per cent higher than the cost price. If everything works out as the restaurant has planned, the balance sheet will look as in Table 9.2.

Table 9.2

Situation 2: End of season			
Capital and liabilities	15,000	Bourbon inventory (base stock)	15,000
Reserves and surplus	3,000	Cash	3,000
	18,000		18,000

The restaurant is in a liquid position and is ready to begin a new season. But, if the season was not beneficial and the restaurant had sold only Rs 2000 worth of bourbon, then the balance sheet would look as in Table 9.3.

Table 9.3

Situation 3: End of Season			
Capital and liabilities	15,000	Inventory (base stock)	15,000
Reserves and surplus	600	Inventory	8,000
Accounts payable	8,000	Cash	600
	23,600		23,600

Note that in situation 1, for the sake of simplicity, we have assumed that the inventory of bourbon is procured from suppliers on credit and that the accounts are settled at the end of the season.

Now, suppose that the restaurant is unable to sell the inventory by the end of the season and the suppliers insist on settling the accounts. At this point, the restaurant is in serious trouble as it does not have enough cash to pay the suppliers. The restaurant will have to borrow from some other source to pay the suppliers, which will increase its financial burden. In this example, we have restricted ourselves to only one item, but real time restaurant operations deal with numerous other inventory items. Clearly, poor inventory decisions can be disastrous.

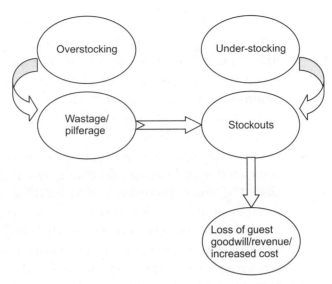

Fig. 9.1 Impact of overstocking and understocking in hotel operations

COSTS ASSOCIATED WITH INVENTORY

We have seen that one of the objectives is to minimize inventory costs. Apart from the cost of merchandise, costs associated with inventories fall into three categories, shown in Table 9.4.

Table 9.4

Ordering costs	Carrying costs	Stockout costs
Ordering, shipping, and receiving costs	Carrying costs	Stockout costs
Storage and handling costs	Cost of placing orders	Loss of sales
Insurance	Shipping and handling costs	Loss of guest good-will
Property taxes	Cost of capital blocked	Disruption in the schedule
Loss arising out of spoilage and wastage		

Ordering Costs

This category of costs arises with the acquisition or ordering of inventory. Hotels place orders with the vendors to replenish inventory of materials. The costs involved in placing orders are called *ordering costs*. Ordering costs include costs incurred on (i) preparing a purchase order or a requisition form and (ii) receiving, inspecting, and recording costs to ensure both quantity and quality. Apart from costs allied to placing orders, costs involved in inter-departmental transfers are also considered as ordering costs.

Ordering costs are generally fixed in nature, that is, costs associated with ordering do change with the increase in order size. The costs, however, would increase with the rise in the number of orders. Thus, ordering costs would be higher as the frequency of the orders increase. Ordering a larger quantity of material with every order would reduce the cost per order. But acquiring larger quantity of materials would increase the carrying costs or costs related to storing and maintaining inventory.

Carrying Costs

The second broad category of costs associated with inventory is the carrying costs. The main component of this category of carrying costs is *storage costs* that include costs of storing and maintaining adequate levels of inventory. Examples of storage costs would be (i) cold storage costs, warehouse charges, utilities, and other costs, (ii) fire or theft insurance charges, and (iii) loss due to fire, wastage, pilferage, etc. Carrying costs also include the cost of funds locked in inventory. This is called *opportunity cost* of funds.

Carrying costs and levels of inventory are positively related. In other words, carrying costs increase or decrease with the rise and fall in inventory levels.

Stockout Costs

When hotels run out of inventory, it is referred as stockout. Stockout costs are basically the cost of running short of inventory. Stockouts result in lost sales, loss of guest goodwill, and disruption in production schedules. Measurement of stockout cost is difficult because effects are short term as well as long term in nature, and are intangible to some extent.

ORDER QUANTITY: EOQ MODEL

In the earlier sections, we have seen the importance and objectives of inventory management. All managers must ideally aim at an optimum level of inventory, based on the costs and benefits associated with different levels of inventory. The two basic questions that must be answered are as follows:

- How much should be the ideal order size?
- What should be the level at which the order must be placed?

Recall that there has to be a balance between the ordering costs and the carrying costs. When a hotel orders large quantities with a view to reduce ordering costs, the average inventory increases and consequently, there is a rise in the carrying costs. Similarly, if the average inventory is reduced, the number of orders would increase, thereby increasing the ordering costs. The EOQ (economic order quantity) model helps managers to ascertain the exact quantity to be ordered that ensures equilibrium between the ordering and carrying costs.

ASSUMPTIONS OF THE EOQ MODEL

The EOQ model assumes that

1. The forecasted usage or demand is known to the managers for the period, which is generally a year.
2. The usage or demand is more or less constant during the year.
3. There is no delay between placing and receiving orders, and the orders can be replenished immediately without any delay.
4. There are only two identifiable costs associated with the inventory—ordering and carrying costs.
5. The cost per order is constant, irrespective of the order size.

Optimum Order Quantity: Formula

The optimal or the economic order quantity to order at one time is that quantity (Q^*). Ordering Q^* units of the inventory will minimize the total inventory cost for the particular period. We can use the following formula to determine the optimal order quantity:

$$Q^* = \sqrt{\frac{2(O)(F)}{C}} \qquad (9.1)$$

where,

Q^* = Optimal or economic order quantity
O = Annual usage
F = Fixed cost per order
C = Carrying cost

To illustrate, assume that a restaurant requires 4000 units of a certain item over a 100-day cycle, ordering costs are Rs 400 per order, and carrying costs are Rs 20 per unit for 100 days. Substituting the values in the formula mentioned above, we have,

$$Q^* = \sqrt{\frac{2(4000)(400)}{20}} = 400 \text{ units}$$

The optimal order quantity that the restaurant must order is 400 units and the restaurant must order 10 times (4000/400), for the period under consideration (100 days). We can conclude from Equation 9.1 that the hotel would order 4000/400 = 10 times during the 100-day cycle. It is evident from the equation that as usage increases the economic order quantity and the average level of inventory increase by a lesser percentage. For example, if the quantity increases to 8000 units, there would a new optimal order quantity and a new average inventory level. In short, it is quite possible to ensure economies of scale. Figure 9.2 shows costs associated with inventory, *total inventory costs*, which is the sum of total ordering and carrying costs. It is clear that there is a direct relationship between the order size and the total carrying costs, while there is an inverse relationship between ordering costs and the order size. Note that the total inventory cost curve declines in the beginning as the fixed costs per order are lower due to fewer orders of large order sizes being placed. But as the number of units per order increase, the carrying costs increase, leading to an overall increase in the total costs. Q^* represents the point where the carrying costs equal the ordering costs. The EOQ model discussed here is indeed an important tool for inventory management.

WHEN TO ORDER: CALCULATING THE ORDER POINT

In addition to order size, the hotel also needs to know when to order. This calls for identification of a signal to place an order for the optimal order quantity. In all the calculations, we have ignored the lead time, that is, the time lag between placing the order and receiving inventory. Suppose this is a resort hotel located away from the mainland and about 5 days elapse between placing and receiving the order. From our earlier illustration we have calculated the EOQ as 400 units, which will be supplied after a lag of 5 days. The order point would be calculated as follows:

Order point (OP) = Lead time x Daily usage

Thus, the order point is

5 days x 20 units per day = 100 units

MAINTAINING PAR LEVEL OF INVENTORY

Hotels must maintain par levels of inventory. They need to maintain an average level of inventory to ensure uninterrupted service to guests. The following are the benefits of maintaining a par inventory:

1. *Continuous services* Chefs and accommodation managers need to maintain an average inventory to provide continuous and uniform level of products and services to the guests.

2. *Safeguard against stockouts* Maintaining par inventory helps in safeguarding against stockout and the resultant consequences. Recall the discussion on the effects of stockout on hotel operations.

3. *Emergency purchase* Maintaining par inventory helps in reducing the frequency of emergency purchases, which ultimately reduces the burden on cash flows and other consequential costs.

4. *Regular guest requests* There are some high profile guests, celebrity guests, or loyal guests who frequently visit the

same restaurant or hotel and may have some typical requests for particular amenities or a certain brand, or other likes or dislikes. It is therefore necessary to maintain par inventory to dazzle and delight such guest segments.

5. *Quality concerns* Standard operating procedures and brand standards would demand use of certain quality products in delivering services. For example, if a restaurant uses butter chiplets, which are easy to serve and are more hygienic than the use of the conventional butter tray, then the chef must ensure a par inventory of these chiplets at all times. Failure to do so will result in deviation from the standards leading to guest complaints.

Factors Influencing Par Inventory Levels

It is also necessary to understand some fundamental factors that affect the par inventory levels required in hotel and restaurant operations. Some of the factors are outlined below:

1. *Location of the hotel* A hotel located in a city, vis-à-vis a resort destination, would require lower level of par stock as the vendors and suppliers are easily accessible and can replenish inventory at short notice, while this may not necessarily be the case with resort hotels.

2. *Average consumption per day* If the hotel or restaurant experiences a high average consumption per day, then the par level of inventory would be high as compared to a restaurant that does not experience a high level of average consumption per day.

3. *Lead time* If the vendors are able to replenish the orders within a short period, then the par level would be lower than when there are bottlenecks or problems with vendors.

4. *Standard operating procedure* Par inventory is also determined by the extent of consistency in the operating procedure. Standard recipes and other operating procedures are extremely important in service delivery and also in determining the level of inventory required for operations.

SAFETY STOCK

In our earlier example, we have assumed constant or fixed usage of units and replenishment of inventory without any time lag or lead time. Under real time hotel operations, the demand or usage of inventory cannot be ascertained with certainty. The inventory requirement depends upon the production schedule and demand, which may be unpredictable. A discrepancy between the assumed (expected) inventory requirement and the actual usage cannot be ruled out. Moreover, the lead time may exceed beyond normal due to some bottlenecks in the transport and logistics system. Thus, a hotel would come across situations where the actual inventory usage is higher than the anticipated level and/or delivery from the vendors is delayed due to some unforeseen circumstances. Owing to these conditions, it is not advisable to allow the level of inventory to fall to zero before an order is replenished. A zero level of inventory would lead to a stockout situation, resulting in alienation of guests. The hotel should keep an additional inventory to safeguard from a state of stockout. Such inventory level is called safety stock. Safety stock can be defined as the minimum additional inventory required for meeting the increase in consumption caused by a surge in demand and/or an increase in time taken by a supplier to replenish inventory requirements.

Owing to the fluctuations and uncertainty in demand for inventory and the changes in lead time, the original formula for calculating order point can be modified as follows:

Order point = (Average lead time × Average daily usage)
+ Safety stock

Determining the amount of safety stock to be maintained depends upon several factors. Just as determining economic order quantity depends on the trade-off between ordering and carrying costs, safety stock is determined by a trade-off between carrying and stockout costs. The more the uncertainty associated with forecasted demand for inventory, the larger would be the safety stock required by the hotel. Put differently, the greater the risk of running out of stock, the larger would be the fluctuations in usage. Similarly, safety stock would also depend on the increase in costs and loss of revenue due to non-availability of inventory. As discussed in the earlier sections, non-availability of inventory would lead to loss of guest satisfaction. In addition to the loss in present sales revenue, future sales would also be endangered as the guests may switch to competition. While it is difficult to exactly measure the opportunity cost involved in such cases, most managers factor this aspect while deciding on the level of safety stock. The final factor to be considered here is the cost of carrying an additional inventory. It is interesting to note that it is the carrying cost that restricts the purchase of additional stock. Given a choice, a housekeeper would keep the stock of bath robes and other amenities to avoid all possibilities of running out of stock. Generally speaking, the carrying cost will increase with the quantity of inventory. Determining the exact amount of safety stock involves calculating the cost of stockout and comparing it to the costs related with carrying enough safety stocks to avoid the possibility of a stockout. In other words, the question here is to reduce the stockout costs by increasing the level of safety stock while not adding to the carrying costs at the same time. Typically, the probability of a stockout reduces at a decreasing rate as additional units of safety stock are added. It is not advisable to add safety stock beyond a point where the incremental carrying costs become greater than the incremental benefits to be derived from avoiding stockouts.

INVENTORY CONTROL

Hotels consume a lot of inventory ranging from small value items like wheat or refined flour to highly expensive items like branded amenities and ingredients like truffles. It is necessary to treat inventory items according to their value. Segregation of inventory items helps in better control of inventory as the hotel can devote more attention to controlling high value items.

ABC Analysis

One of the most common methods followed by hotels to control inventory is the ABC analysis. ABC analysis calls for classifying inventories into three categories—A, B, and C. Category A represents the most important inventory items, generally consisting of 15 to 20 per cent of inventory items and accounts for 60 to 75 per cent of the usage value. The next 25 to 30 per cent of the items come under category B, which represents items of moderate value accounting for 20 to 30 per cent of the value. More than half or 55 per cent of the items account for only 10 per cent of the value. These inventory items are placed under category C. Exhibit 9.1 shows how to list inventory according to usage and consumption.

Exhibit 9.1 *Mise en place*

Item	Description	Quantity (kg)	Price/unit (Rs)
1	Wheat flour	5,000	22
2	Refined flour	3,000	20
3	Dal and lentils	1,000	40
4	Cereal and pulses	600	45
5	Fresh vegetables	3,500	30
6	Fish and shellfish	500	400
7	Imported meat	500	1,000
8	Dry fruits and nuts	100	400
9	Truffles (black mushroom)	3	2,00,000
10	Bordeaux wine	50*	15,000

Modus Operandi

Inventory items are categorized as follows:

- The items of inventory are ranked according to the consumption and are numbered from 1 to n.
- The item-wise consumption values are expressed as a percentage of the total consumption.
- Looking at the total cumulative percentages of consumption value against the cumulative percentages, items are broadly categorized as A, B, or C as discussed earlier. The cut-off levels can be arbitrary and are specific to operations.

Let us continue with the illustration of items in Exhibit 9.2 and their categorization in Exhibit 9.3.

Exhibit 9.2

Category	Item	Description	Quantity	Price/unit (Rs)
A	9	Truffles	3 kg	2,00,000
	10	Bordeaux wine	50 bottles	15,000
	7	Imported meat	250 kg	2,000
B	6	Fish and shellfish	500 kg	500
	8	Dry fruits and nuts	100 kg	400
		New world wines	500 bottles	1,000
		Imported juices, sauces, etc.	300 bottles	400
C	4	Cereal and pulses	600 kg	45
	3	Dal and lentils	1,000 kg	40
	5	Fresh vegetables	3,500 kg	30
	1	Wheat flour	5,000 kg	22
	2	Refined flour	3,000 kg	20

Exhibit 9.3

Class	Number of items	Percentage of items	Percentage of usage value
A	3	30	65.32
B	4	20	22.59
C	5	50	12.07

Some other approaches to inventory control are provided below.

HML Classification

The high, medium, and low (HML) classification is based on the unit value of the inventory item instead of the consumption value. The cut-off point would depend upon the individual items. For example, salt would be considered as a low value item and truffles as high value item. This method focuses on the purchase price of the inventory item.

VED Classification

The vital, essential, and desirable (VED) classification is useful where the consumption pattern is different from regular inventory items. Stocking inventory items according to utility is the focus of this approach. This determines the stocking of inventory in a particular pattern of utility in consumption.

FSN Classification

Classification of inventory items according to fast, slow, and non-moving items forms the basis of FSN classification. FSN analysis helps in identification of obsolete items, thereby guiding the hotel to stock less of slow and non-moving items, thus avoiding wasteful expenditure.

SDE Classification

It is important to remember that inventory levels also depend on the source and this approach will help hotels to stock items that are scarce and extremely important for operations. The SDE (scarce, difficult, easy to obtain) classification here is based on the general availability and the source.

CREDIT MANAGEMENT AND CONTROL

While hotels may always want to sell on cash, there are times when there is pressure from the high-end guests to extend credit. Hotels, normally, would grant credit to facilitate sales. Usually, hotels will have an agreement with corporate guests for a special rate, depending on the volume of business provided. In such cases, the bills are not settled immediately by the guest but are sent for collection as per the terms agreed.

The credit period is usually between 7 days to 15 days. Credit transactions increase the accounts receivable (credit). The amount of accounts receivable would depend upon the extent to which the hotel would sell on credit and the time taken to collect the outstanding payment. For instance, if the credit extended is Rs 3,00,000 per day and the average collection period is 20 days, then the total outstanding would be Rs 60,00,000. Managing credit is an important aspect of working capital in current asset management and hence it is important to manage receivables appropriately.

COST AND BENEFITS ASSOCIATED WITH RECEIVABLES

As seen from the earlier section, credit is an integral part of the modern business system. Credit sales and, in turn, receivables form an aspect of the overall marketing strategy of a hotel. There is an oral promise to pay from the guests and no formal acknowledgment of debt obligation is involved.

While extending credit aims at increased sales and, consequently, higher levels of profit, it also involves some risk and cost. It is necessary to consider the costs and benefits involved before deciding to extend credit to guests. The objective of receivables management is to facilitate sales and profits to a point where the benefit (return on investment) from the increased investment in receivables is lower than the cost of funds raised to finance the receivables. In other words, granting of credit is like lending cash to the borrower. Hence, the cost involved should not exceed the benefits from the transaction. The specific costs and benefits are discussed below:

1. *Collection costs* Collection costs are administrative costs incurred in collecting dues from guests. Additional expenses on creation and maintenance of the credit department, inclusive of manpower and other administrative costs, are included in this category. The cost of obtaining credit information from external sources is also included in this category.

2. *Opportunity cost of funds* Incremental receivable denotes a higher level of investment in current assets. There is a time lag between the sale and receipt of cash, which implies that the hotel has to make arrangements for payment to suppliers and employees in the meantime. Therefore, additional receivables call from incremental funds and the corresponding costs. These additional funds, which could have been invested elsewhere, are the opportunity cost of extending credit to guests.

3. *Cost of delinquent accounts* Delinquent account means that the guest fails to pay dues beyond the credit period. Costs related to delinquent accounts are called delinquency costs. Locking up of funds for an extended period and

costs associated with collection of the overdue amount, legal charges, wherever applicable, and other incidental charges fall under this category of costs.

4. *Default costs/bad-debt loss* The hotel may not recover dues due to reasons that are beyond its control. Such debts are treated as bad and are written-off. There is always a risk of default and consequent costs associated with credit sales and accounts receivable.

We now turn our attention to the benefits associated with credit sales and accounts receivable. The benefits of granting credit are the incremental sales and the profits expected from the higher level of sales revenue. Hotels can grant credit either to increase the clientele base or to provide additional facilities to the existing clientele. The prime motive here is to prevent the existing guests from moving towards competition. The other option is to provide credit to new guest segments with a view to increase sales.

Other things remaining constant, an extension of credit facilities will definitely increase sales revenue. The more liberal a hotel is in granting credit to the guests, the more would be the risk and cost associated with such decisions. The decision to increase the investment in receivables will depend on a cost and benefit analysis of extending credit facility.

CREDIT STANDARDS

The credit policy plays a significant role in generating sales revenue. The marketing effort of a hotel can be negatively influenced by the liberal credit policy of the competition. While credit is an important aspect in generating sales revenue, there are many other factors that influence the demand for hotel products. As a result, sales would be influenced by a number of factors. Theoretically, the hotel should consider lowering its credit standards for accounts as long as profitability of incremental sales is in excess of the cost involved in the transaction.

Let us understand the process of assessing the impact of relaxing credit standards.

We have to assess the incremental sales and profits, the increased average collection period, and the required rate of return to ascertain the profitability of relaxing credit standards. Suppose the annual credit sales is 24 million rupees and is not expected to increase further. The hotel may liberalize credit to increase the number of guests, which will result in an average collection period of one month for the new guest segment while the old guest segment would continue to pay within 15 days. The new credit standards would increase the sales by 25 per cent to Rs 3,00,00,000 per year. Finally, we shall assume that the opportunity cost of funds is 20 per cent before taxes and the variable cost is 40 per cent of the total sales revenue.

The above information will help us to evaluate the cost and the benefit involved in extending credit to the new guest segment. The increased investment is a consequence of new guests who will take a longer period to pay. The cost benefit analysis is presented in a tabular form Table 9.5.

Table 9.5

Profitability of additional sales revenue	(Contribution margin*) × (Additional sales)	0.60 × Rs 6,00,00,000 = Rs 3,60,00,000
Incremental investment in receivables	(Additional sales revenue) ÷ (Receivable turnover for new guest segments)	Rs 6,00,00,000 ÷ 12 = Rs 50,00,000
Investment in additional receivables	(Variable cost percentage) × (Additional receivables)	0.40 × Rs 50,00,000 = Rs 20,00,000
Required pre-tax return on additional investment	(Opportunity cost of funds) × (Investment in additional receivables)	0.20 × Rs 20,00,000 = Rs 4,00,000

As Table 9.5 shows, the hotel can relax credit standards to the extent that the pre-tax return on additional investment does not

---

* Contribution margin = Sales revenue – Variable cost percentage
  = 1 – 0.40 = 0.60

exceed the profitability of additional sales revenue. In this example, an optimal decision would involve relaxing credit standards to a point where it does not reduce the total profit (Rs 3,60,00,000 million) below the required pre-tax return on additional investment (Rs 40,000). However, as the hotel increases investment in receivables, it also gets exposed to additional risk, like variance in the projected cash flow stream, and also bad debt loss, which we discuss in the next sections.

CREDIT TERMS

Credit terms specify the credit period—the time for which credit is available to the guest. Although, the guest would dictate the period of credit, extending the credit is another way to increase the clientele base. Let us assume in our example that the hotel changes its credit period from 15 days to 30 days, thus increasing the average collection period to one month. The new credit period increases the sales by Rs 3,60,00,000 million and the new and old guests would pay by one month. The total receivable consists of two parts. The first part consists of receivables associated with the incremental sales. In the example, Rs 3,60,00,000 is the incremental sales revenue. With the increase in average collection period, the new receivable turnover would be 12 times. Table 9.6 illustrates the problem.

Based on the information provided and the calculations in the table, it is worthwhile to increase the credit period from 15 days to 30 days. Note that the profitability of additional sales is greater than the opportunity cost of additional investment in receivables. The benefit exceeds the costs, and a large portion of this investment in receivables is due to the slowing down of receipts from the existing guest segment.

CASH DISCOUNT

The above discussed prepositions are applicable to the accommodation division, as well as the food and beverage departments. However, by providing a discount the guests can be induced to pay early. We shall factor the element of discount into our discussion while providing credit to the guests. By varying cash discounts it is possible to speed up the collections.

Table 9.6

Profitability of incremental sales	(Contribution margin) × (Additional sales)	0.60 × Rs 36,00,000 = Rs 21,60,000

Part A: Calculation related to additional sales generated due to increase in credit period

Additional receivables related to the new sales	(New sales revenue) ÷ (New receivables turnover)	Rs 36,00,000 ÷ 12 = Rs 3,00,000
Investment in additional receivables associated with new sales	(Variable cost percentage) × (Additional receivables)	0.40 × Rs 3,00,000 = Rs 1,20,000

Part B: Impact of increasing the credit period on the existing receivables

Level of receivables before change in credit period	(Annual credit sales) ÷ (Old receivable turnover)	Rs 2,40,00,000 ÷ 24* = Rs 10,00,000
New level of receivables	(Annual credit sales) ÷ (New receivable turnover)	Annual credit sale Rs 2,40,00,000 ÷ 12** = Rs 20,00,000
Additional investment in receivables	New Investment – Old Investment	Rs 20,00,000 – Rs 10,00,000 = Rs 10,00,000
Total Investment in receivable		Rs 10,00,000 ÷ 1,20,000 = Rs 11,20,000
Required pre-tax return on additional investment	(Opportunity cost) × (Total investment in additional receivables)	0.20 × Rs 11,20,000 = Rs 2,24,000

Let us consider an illustration. A hotel has annual credit sales of Rs 3,00,00,000 and an average collection period of one month. Assume that the maximum credit period granted by the hotel is 45 days without any discount. Consequently, the average

---

* 12 months divided by new average collection period of 30 days or 1 month.
** 12 months divided by old average collection period of 15 days or 0.5 month.

receivables balance is Rs 3,00,00,000/12 = Rs 25,00,000. However, the average collection period can be reduced to 15 days if an additional discount of 2 per cent is offered. Now, the credit terms are altered to 2/10 net 45[*], which will reduce the average collection period to 15 days. Assuming 40 per cent of the guests would avail the discount option and there is a 20 per cent pre-tax rate of return, we shall find the implications of extending a 2 per cent discount to expedite the collection. Table 9.7 provides a step-by-step calculation for the above mentioned situation.

Table 9.7

Level of receivables before charging cash discount	(Annual credit sales) ÷ (Old receivable turnover)	Rs 3,00,00,000 ÷ 12** = Rs 25,00,000
New level of receivables related to cash discount	(Annual credit sales) ÷ (New receivable turnover)	Rs 3,00,00,000 ÷ 24 = Rs 12,50,000
Reduction of investments in accounts receivable	(Old receivable level) – (New receivable level)	Rs 25,00,000 – Rs 12,50,000 = Rs 12,50,000
Pre-tax cost of discount change	(Cash discount) × (Percentage of guests availing the discount facility) × (Annual credit sales)	0.02 × 0.40 × Rs 3,00,00,000 = Rs 2,40,000
Pre-tax opportunity savings on reduction in receivables.	(Opportunity cost) × (Reduction in receivables)	0 .20 × Rs 12,50,000 = Rs 2,50,000

In the above case, the hotel saves about Rs 12,50,000 as per the conditions specified above. The hotel can consider adopting the 2 per cent discount as it results in greater opportunity savings as compared to the cost of cash discount. With an

---

[*] 2/10 net 45 implies that a 2 per cent discount facility can be availed if paid within 10 days of the bill date. The term, net 45, implies that the full payment is due within 45 days from the date of the bill.

[**] Information provided in the problem.

increase in the discount per cent, there is a possibility of the discount cost increasing, leading to an adverse decision.

DEFAULT RISK

In our discussion so far, we have not considered bad debt losses. In this section, we shall deal with decisions pertaining to default. Let us suppose that the hotel has two other liberal credit policies producing the following results. Refer to Table 9.8.

Table 9.8

	Present policy	Policy A	Policy B
Credit sales	Rs 2,40,00,000	Rs 3,00,00,000	Rs 3,30,00,000
Incremental sales		Rs 60,00,000	Rs 30,00,000
Default losses			
Original sales	2%		
Incremental sales		10%	18%
Average collection period	1 month		
Incremental sales		2 months	3 months

We assume that the possibility of default associated with the present policy is 2 per cent, 10 per cent on the incremental sales of Rs 60,00,000 and 18 per cent on the additional sale of Rs 30,00,000 in policy A and B, respectively. In the same way, the average collection period of one month pertains to the present level of sales. The incremental sales of Rs 60,00,000 and Rs 30,00,000 will have an average collection period of 2 months and 3 months, respectively. Also, assuming a contribution margin of 40 per cent, Table 9.9 provides a step-by-step calculation.

From Table 9.9, it can be concluded that the hotel definitely has an advantage of moving from the present policy to Policy P due to the increase in profitability. Policy Q should be ruled out due to decrease in profitability. The hotel can also frame a policy that is in between the current policy and Policy P. To conclude, an optimum policy is the one that provides a maximum incremental profit.

Table 9.9

		Policy P (Rs)	Policy Q (Rs)
1	Profitability of the incremental sales = (Contribution margin) × (Incremental sales)	24,00,000	12,00,000
2	Incremental bad-debt losses = (Incremental sales) × (Bad-debt percentage)	6,00,000	5,40,000
3	Additional receivables = (Additional sales) ÷ (New receivable turnover)	10,00,000*	7,50,000**
4	Additional investment in receivables = (0.60)*** ÷ (Additional receivables)	6,00,000	4,50,000
5	Desired pre-tax return on additional investment = (0.20) × (Additional receivables)	1,20,000	90,000
6	Additional costs involved (row 2 ÷ row 5)	7,20,000	6,30,000
7	Incremental profits (row 1 – row 6)	16,80,000	5,70,000

FRONT OFFICE AND ACCOUNTS RECEIVABLES

Irrespective of continuous monitoring, chances of a guest leaving without settling the bill cannot be ruled out. Some of the instances are inadvertent, where the guest forgets to settle the bill before checking out. Unfortunately, some guests check out of the hotel without an intention of settling their accounts. They are commonly referred to as *skippers*. Whatever the reason, the balances represent accounts receivable.

Late charge is another major concern in the settlement of a guest account. These are the transactions that require posting to a guest account but do not reach the front desk for posting before the guest checks out. Restaurant and telephone bills, etc.

---

  * New receivable turnover for Policy P = 12/average collection period = 12/2 = 6
    Additional receivables = Rs 60,00,000/6 = Rs 10,00,000
 ** New receivable turnover for Policy Q = 12/average collection period = 12/3 = 4
    Additional receivables = Rs 30,00,000/4 = Rs 7,50,000
*** Variable cost: This is calculated as 1 – contribution margin.

are some examples of potential late service charges. The hotel may face a problem in collecting this amount after the guest departs. In certain cases, even if late charges are collected, the cost incurred in the process exceeds the collectible amount. The key to higher levels of profitability is reducing late charges. Most hotels employ computerized systems to reduce or eliminate the problem of late charges. A restaurant point of sale with an interface with the front office can instantly verify room accounts and post all the charges to the guest account before the guest leaves the restaurant. Likewise, a telephone or a call accounting system can help eliminate telephone late charges. Some hotels insist on a key deposit before a guest actually checks into the room with a motive that guests would come to the front desk to retrieve the deposit. This provides for an opportunity for the front office to take a look at the guest account and locate for any late or other incidental charges before the guest actually checks out of the hotel.

COLLECTION POLICY AND PROCEDURE

Guest accounts not settled during check out by cash payment in full are classified as accounts receivable and are transferred from the guest ledger to the city (non-guest) ledger for collection. The hotel determines its overall collection policy by a combination of collection procedures. These procedures could include such things as letters, phone calls, personal visits, and even legal action. One of the important variables is the expense involved in the collection procedure. More often, the higher the collection expense, the lower would be the losses as a result of bad debts. Timing is another variable in determining a collection policy. The sooner the hotel commences its collection process, the higher are the chances of receiving payment on unpaid accounts. Collection schedules can vary from strict to liberal, depending on the hotel's financial requirements, guest profile, collection history, etc. See Exhibit 9.4 for an example of a scheduling chart. In all collection cases, it is important for the hotel staff to be polite but firm in dealing with the guests. Violation of consumer rights during collection activities may prove to be costlier than the original debt.

Irrespective of the collection efforts, there arise problems in collecting accounts receivable. The hotel should have a documented procedure to collect accounts receivable. Hotels can also appoint a credit committee to examine overdue accounts and decide the collection procedure. To be effective, the front office must establish a policy that should determine

1. The number of days between billing
2. The exact due date of outstanding account balances
3. The method to contact departed guests whose accounts are overdue

While monitoring individual accounts is important, it is equally essential to track meeting and tour group accounts. Credit policy for tour groups should be established well in advance. Some hotels insist on deposit to cover some proportion of default risk before the group checks into the hotel. It is also advisable to prepare a preliminary master account folio and review it with the group leader to ensure accuracy of statement and billing details before the group departs from the hotel.

Exhibit 9.4 Scheduling chart

	Timing	Method
1st reminder	Mailed immediately or on a specific date from the transfer of outstanding amount to city ledger	_____ statement with a copy of the bill
2nd reminder	After _____ days	☐ Statement ☐ Phone call ☐ Letter ☐ Personal visit
3rd reminder	After _____ days	☐ Statement ☐ Phone call ☐ Letter ☐ Personal visit
4th reminder	After _____ days	☐ Statement ☐ Phone call ☐ Letter ☐ Personal visit

SUMMARY

- Inventories form a link between the sale and production of a hotel product. Inventories enable a hotel to maintain some flexibility in purchasing, scheduling of production, and fulfilling guest demand.
- While estimating the exact level of investment in inventories, the hotel must balance the benefits of economies of production and purchasing against the cost of carrying additional inventories.
- Ordering costs include the cost of placing an order, receiving material, and inspecting the quality of supplies. Ordering cost does not change with the increase or decrease in the number of units ordered. Carrying cost represents the cost of storing, handling, and other incidental charges.
- The economic (optimal) order quantity for an inventory item depends upon forecasted use, ordering, and carrying cost. The economic order quantity model aids in calculating the optimal order quantity of an inventory item to be ordered.
- Hotels and restaurants should maintain a par stock of certain items for various reasons.
- Hotels also need to maintain a safety stock owing to fluctuations in demand and in lead times.
- Hotels often sell on credit to increase and facilitate sales revenue. The credit period extends from seven days to one month.
- Liberal credit standards attract different categories of guests but increase the incidents of bad debts and higher level of investment in receivables. Stringent credit standards have the opposite effect.
- The front office plays an important role in the management of receivables.

KEY TERMS

Accounts receivable A promise to receive money in future and not immediately after the product or service.

Bad debts Uncollectible amount from the credit extended to guests.

City ledger (non-guest ledger) Ledger used to record details pertaining to transactions of guests who have checked out of the hotel.

Fixed cost Cost that does not change with the change in the level of sales.

Guest ledger Ledger used for recording accounts of guests in the hotel.

Inventory Stock of goods to be used in production.

Late charges Charges billed to the account after the guest's departure.

Overstocking Hoarding more inventory than actually required for operations.

Skippers Guests who check out of the hotel without settling the accounts.

Under stocking Holding lower levels of inventory than required for operations.

Variable cost Cost that changes with the level of sales.

REVIEW QUESTIONS

1. Explain the importance and purpose of inventory management.
2. Explain the costs associated with inventory management.
3. How can a hotel reduce its investment in inventories?
4. Elucidate the costs and benefits associated with receivables or credit management.
5. Explain the principal factors that can be varied in setting a credit policy.
6. Write a note on the ABC analysis.

CRITICAL THINKING QUESTIONS

1. Critically examine the applicability of the EOQ model to the hotel and restaurant operations.
2. Discuss the implications of the inventory ordering and carrying costs on the cost of the food sold.
3. Discuss the procedure for establishing an inventory management policy for hotel and restaurant operations.
4. Discuss in detail the process to allow credit to the guests.
5. Allen has joined a leading hotel chain in India as a sous chef early this year. His earlier assignment was as a junior sous chef wherein no administrative responsibilities were involved. This morning he

was advised by the executive chef to prepare a report on the inventory requirements for the kitchen. The senior chef wants him to think about ways to reduce the inventory costs. He wants more details on the economic order quantity, re-order point, and par levels of stock of each item consumed by the kitchen.

He seeks your advice and help in obtaining information required to complete the report. Can you help him?

PROJECT WORK

Talk to executive chefs on the inventory control policy of the hotel. Talk to general managers and find out the methods they follow to grant credit to specific categories of guests. Write a report on your findings.

Short-term Finance for Hotels and Restaurants

> *Creditors have better memory than debtors, and creditors are a superstitious sect, great observers of set days and times.*
>
> **Benjamin Franklin**

Learning Objectives

After studying this chapter, you will be able to

➢ Understand the meaning of short-term financing
➢ Understand the meaning and importance of trade credit
➢ Examine other sources of short-term finance

INTRODUCTION

There are a number of sources available for hotel and restaurant operations. Most prominent among them are trade credit and short-term borrowings by a firm. The need for financing arises mainly because the investment in working capital tends to fluctuate during the year. While long-term funds may finance the working capital requirements, short-term requirements are predominantly supported by short-term sources, in the context of hotel and restaurant operations. This chapter delves into the main sources of short-term finance.

ACCRUALS

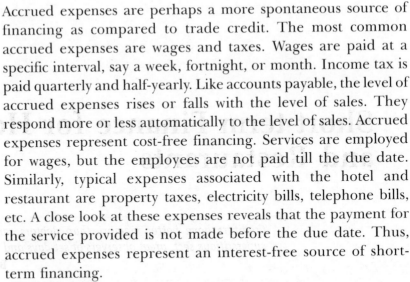

Accrued expenses are perhaps a more spontaneous source of financing as compared to trade credit. The most common accrued expenses are wages and taxes. Wages are paid at a specific interval, say a week, fortnight, or month. Income tax is paid quarterly and half-yearly. Like accounts payable, the level of accrued expenses rises or falls with the level of sales. They respond more or less automatically to the level of sales. Accrued expenses represent cost-free financing. Services are employed for wages, but the employees are not paid till the due date. Similarly, typical expenses associated with the hotel and restaurant are property taxes, electricity bills, telephone bills, etc. A close look at these expenses reveals that the payment for the service provided is not made before the due date. Thus, accrued expenses represent an interest-free source of short-term financing.

Unfortunately, accrued expenses are not at the discretion of any firm. While it may be possible for a financially hard-pressed hotel or restaurant to temporarily postpone dues payable to the government or employees, a regular delay would cause loss of employee morale, penalty by the government, and problems such as disconnection of some services. Therefore, a company must be extremely careful in procrastinating expenses. This is the last resort, but many companies on the edge of a cash-flow crisis have to resort to postponing payment of wages and other expenses.

TRADE CREDIT

Trade credit arises when a hotel or a restaurant purchases supplies from vendors and does not pay cash immediately, thereby creating accounts payable for itself. This deferral represents a source of finance for current assets. Trade credit is also referred to as *spontaneous short-term financing*, because it expands automatically, as hotels and restaurants purchase more inventories. There are also negotiated short-term borrowed funds. However, there is no formal or specific negotiation for trade credit. It is an informal arrangement between the buyer and the seller. There are no legal instruments of debt, as the credit is granted on an open basis. A variant of accounts payable is the bills payable.

Advantages of Trade Credit

- *Easy Access* Trade credit is very easy to access. It is automatically available in the regular course of business. The hotel or restaurant business deals with vendors who supply consumables, or even perishables. A regular supplier would provide credit, ranging from 15 days to 30 days. This is beneficial to the supplier, as there is a guarantee of sales. The bills need not be cleared on a day-to-day basis, and therefore it is beneficial to the hotel and restaurant companies.

- *Flexibility* Trade credit is flexible and depends entirely upon negotiations between the buyers and the sellers. There is no need for extensive documentation or a strict repayment schedule. The amount of credit depends upon the level of sales achieved by the operations. The higher the sales achieved, the higher can be the amount of trade credit. Moreover, there is no time lag between recognizing the need for funds and the actual time of borrowing.

- *Continuity* Trade credit is continuous. It is not necessary to formally arrange finance, as it is already in existence. As old bills are cleared and new purchases made, new bills replace the old bills, and the accounts payable keeps changing accordingly.

- *Freedom from restrictions* In other kinds of short-term financing, it is necessary to negotiate with the lender the terms of loan. The lender may want to impose restrictions and secure his position. Such a situation is unlikely in case of trade credit.

Cost of Trade Credit

From the above discussion, is it possible to conclude that there is no cost involved in obtaining trade credit? Let us assume that you enter into a negotiation with a vendor of kitchen supplies. If the credit terms are 30 days net, then trade credit is free of cost, because the amount payable is same, whenever you decide to pay within 30 days. However, let us further assume that the supplier offers a discount of 2 per cent if paid within 10 days. This situation is represented as 2/10, net 30 days. In this case, there is a cost associated with the trade credit beyond the discount period. In such a case, we may divide the 30-day period into two parts as follows:

- 10 days/Discount period
- 20 days/Non-discount period

There is no cost associated with the trade credit during the discount period, whereas the cost during the non-discount period is computed as follows:

$$\text{Discount\%}/1 - \text{Discount\%} * 360/\text{Credit period} - \text{Discount period} \tag{10.1}$$

In our example, this works out to

$$.02/1 - 0.02 * 360/30 - 10 = 36.7\%$$

Delaying Payables

In the preceding section, we assumed that the payment was made at the end of the credit period. However, you may decide to stretch it beyond the credit period. Stretching accounts payable will generate additional short-term finance by further increasing liabilities. Generally, the cost of additional trade credit is higher, and unless it is absolutely essential, discounts should not be foregone. From the above discussion, it is evident that

- The cost of delaying payment includes the cost of discounts foregone. Therefore, unless the firm is hard-pressed financially, it should not forego discounts offered by suppliers.
- In case, the firm is not able to avail the discount, it must delay the payment till the last day of the net period, and if possible, beyond the net period.
- The cost of delaying payments will also include penalty or interest, as may be the industry practice.
- Delaying payments much beyond the stipulated period may result in deterioration of credit rating and may impede future prospects of obtaining credit.

LOANS FROM COMMERCIAL BANKS FOR WORKING CAPITAL

Working capital assistance from commercial banks is an important source of finance for many hotel companies. The banks provide working capital assistance to hotels and restaurants in the following ways.

Cash Credits/Overdrafts

Under a *cash credit* or an *overdraft* arrangement, the banks generally fix an upper limit for borrowings. There is no limit on borrowings, provided the amount does not exceed the limit specified. The borrower can pay the amount in part or full, as per his convenience. Interest is charged on the amount borrowed and not on the amount specified. This form of assistance is attractive to borrowers, primarily because there is freedom to borrow as per their requirement and the interest is charged on the amount outstanding.

Loans

Loans are fixed amounts advanced to the borrower. The amount is paid in cash or is credited to the account of the borrower. Unlike cash credit, interest is charged on the entire amount. Loans are usually payable in instalments, but in certain cases, loans are also repayable on demand. In case of loans repayable on demand, they are supported by a demand promissory note executed by the borrower. Generally, banks provide an option of renewing the loan in the interest of the borrower.

Issues with Bank Finance

Banks usually seek security for working capital financing in the form of *hypothecation*, which calls for borrowing against security of movable property, usually inventory. Here, the possession remains with the owner. The nature of the agreement decides the rights of the lender and the borrower. In case of default, the lender can file a case against the borrower to recover the dues from the hypothecated item. Restaurants can hypothecate wine stock to get loan. Another arrangement is called a *pledge*, wherein the borrower has to part with the possession of the items. Transfer of the items is a precondition for the pledge. Moreover, banks do not provide 100 per cent assistance. A part of the required amount has to be arranged from some other source. This portion is called the *margin amount*. There is no fixed formula for calculation of margin money, but the requirement may range from 5 per cent to 50 per cent, depending on the purpose of the loan.

SUMMARY

- Accruals are the most important source of short-term finance to hotels and restaurants. Accrued expenses represent a spontaneous source of financing. The major accrued expenses are wages and taxes, and both are expected to be paid on a particular date.
- Trade credit from suppliers can be a significant source of short-term financing for hotels. If a hotel has a strict policy as regards to payment of bills, trade credit becomes a spontaneous source of finance that varies directly with the production cycle.
- When a cash discount is foregone by the buyer, it becomes a cost of trade credit. The longer the period between the end of the discount period and the time of the bill payment, the lesser would be the cost incurred.
- Stretching accounts payable beyond a certain period generates additional benefits. This must be weighed against associate costs. The costs to be considered are (i) the cost of cash discount foregone, (ii) any possible late payment penalties or interest charges, (iii) the possible erosion in credit rating and the firm's ability to obtain future credit.
- Commercial banks also provide some assistance for working capital. Banks provide major assistance in the form of working capital advances, cash credit, overdrafts, and short-term loans.

KEY TERMS

Accrued expenses Expenses due but not paid.

Cash credit Arrangement with the bank for a certain limit of withdrawal.

Overdraft Loan arrangement with the bank to withdraw more than the account balance.

Short-term loans Borrowings on short-term basis.

Trade credit Credit extended by suppliers to hotels and restaurants.

REVIEW QUESTIONS

1. How do accrued expenses become a spontaneous source of finance?
2. What is trade credit?
3. State the methods by which banks provide assistance for working capital.

CRITICAL THINKING QUESTIONS

1. Trade credit from suppliers is a costly source of funds when discounts are lost. Comment.
2. Assess the relative merits and demerits of using trade credit and accrued expenses as methods of short-term financing in the context of hotel and restaurant operations.
3. Discuss the advantages and disadvantages of using working capital assistance from banks.

PROJECT WORK

Visit a commercial bank and collect necessary information on the kind of working capital assistance extended to the hotel and restaurant business.

Basics of Capital Budgeting and Estimating Cash Flows

> Drive thy business or it will drive thee.
>
> **Benjamin Franklin**

Learning Objectives

After studying this chapter, you will be able to
- ➤ Understand and define capital budgeting
- ➤ Categorize capital expenditure decisions
- ➤ Determine the cash flows associated with the capital budgeting process

Burj al-Arab—Epitome of Hotel Business

Dubai, one of the iconic cities of the world, is host to the Burj al-Arab, a hotel that has become synonymous with the name of its country. Built at a cost of US$ 650 millions, it is one of the amazing hotels of the world. Burj al-Arab stands on an artificial island and is the tallest building exclusively used as a hotel.

The construction required over 70,000 cubic metres of concrete and 9000 tons of steel. It took the engineers three years to reclaim the land from the sea and about three years to construct the building. While the exterior of the Burj al-Arab is expressed in terms of ultra-modern sculptural design, the interior guest space is a compilation of lavish and luxurious architectural styles from both the East and the West. The hotel boasts of 8000 square metres of 22-carat gold leaf and 24,000 square metres of 30 different types of marble that epitomizes the Burj al-Arab as the ultimate luxury in hospitality.

INTRODUCTION TO THE CAPITAL BUDGETING PROCESS

Growth is the most exciting feature of any business. Hotels may achieve growth by increasing capacity or by expanding into other markets. Unlike manufacturing companies, hotels have to venture into different locations and geography as part of their expansion strategy. This is a characteristic feature of the hotel business. Experts believe that while managing growth is a difficult task, monitoring and ensuring profitable growth is even more challenging. The first step towards ensuring profitable growth is a detailed planning of capital investment. Whenever a hotel company undertakes capital investment, there is a substantial current cash outlay (outflow) with an expectation to receive future benefits. The benefits actually extend beyond one year in majority of the cases. Examples quintessentially include building a new hotel property, as mentioned at the beginning of the chapter, purchasing a sophisticated range of kitchen equipment from manufacturers such as Hobart, True, or Garland, or creation of state-of-the-art wellness facilities to stay ahead of competition. A number of factors make the process of matching the costs incurred today with the benefits to be received in future, one of the most important functions that financial managers and their staff must execute.

Hotel investments proposals need to be carefully evaluated before implementation, as they involve a great deal of resources and cannot be reversed or diversified. For instance, The Ritz in London, founded by Cisar Ritz, completed a century of operations in 2006. The Taj Mahal Palace and Towers, Mumbai, reached the centenary mark in January 2003. We can, therefore, say that the economic life of a hotel property is far in excess of any other business. Further, the decision to build a hotel, or to create a new facility such as a spa, would also depend upon the sales forecast. Finally, the company's capital budgeting decisions would determine the strategic direction because capital expenditure will precede any move into new products, services, or new markets.

Overestimation or underestimation of parameters may spell a disaster for the company as capital expenditure decisions are seldom reversible. Overinvestment will increase depreciation and other costs, while the company would succumb to competition due to underinvestment in capacity, and regaining lost guests may be easier said than done. Timing is also an essential element of capital budgeting as capital assets must be available when required. For instance, most of the hotel companies in India are acquiring real estate properties in the year 2007 so that they may be ready to meet the surge in demand by 2010 during the Commonwealth Games. Beijing alone will build 110 star-hotels to cope with the demand during the 2008 Olympic Games.

The essential ingredient for attaining precise timing and quality of investment is effective capital budgeting. If a business can foresee its capital requirement, then it can purchase assets before they are actually required. With real estate prices skyrocketing in the major cities of the world, it has become necessary for hotel companies to plan their capital expenditure meticulously. It is noteworthy here that if the sales do not increase, although a business may forecast an increase in demand and then expand to meet the expected demand, then the company would sustain huge losses due to increasing costs. Therefore, a precise sales forecast is absolutely crucial to the success of the process of capital budgeting. It is also necessary for companies to plan for the financing of the capital expenditure programme, well in advance, to ensure timely availability of funds.

GENERATING INVESTMENT PROJECT PROPOSALS

Analysis of capital expenditure proposals may incur different levels of cost. For instance, analysis of a proposal for replacing kitchen equipment may be less expensive than a proposal to construct a new hotel property. Certain proposals may involve complex procedures in terms of collection and analysis of data, whereas others may require a simple procedure. For the purposes of analysis, we may classify the investment proposal into the following categories:

1. *Expansion of existing products or markets* Expenditure involved in enhancing facilities or creation of additional infrastructure to improve guest service is included in this category. Examples typically include increase in the existing capacity of rooms and adding more seats to an existing restaurant to cater to the demands of the existing market. This decision is likely to be made at the higher level of management.

2. *Expanding into new products or markets* These are investments associated with creating a new hotel in an existing market or catering to a new market segment. For instance, Indian Hotels Company Ltd, the brand owner of Taj Hotels Palaces and Resort, has made its presence felt in hotel markets across five continents. The company has a portfolio of over 77 hotels in different countries of the world.

This decision normally requires a huge amount as initial cash outflow and meticulous analysis becomes necessary. The final decision is usually made at the top level by the board of directors as a part of strategy for growth.

3. *Replacement for routine operations* The hotel business may replace worn out housekeeping equipments or kitchen equipments with more modern and efficient equipments. The consideration in these cases may be to replace existing equipments that are damaged and worn out in the regular course of business, or the replacement may be a conscious decision to ensure reduction in material, labour, or other inputs, such as electricity. For example, manufacturers of kitchen equipments have designed an ultra-modern cooking range that includes a variety of facilities from the fat frier to the grill and griddle that ensures reduction in wastage and increases productivity. Replacement decisions in the regular course of business may not involve an elaborate process, whereas the cost reduction proposal may require detailed analysis of the cost involved in the purchase of the equipment versus the savings (benefits) to be acquired in the future. The term 'assets' encompasses more than building or equipment. The material management software Fidelio, used in the reservation process and revenue management software, can also be included as capital expenditure.

4. *Projects associated with safety or environment* Safety and security of guests is one of the foremost factors that determine the sales of any hotel company. The situation in India is viewed very seriously by tourists, particularly in view of the 9/11 crisis. Most of the countries are also very stringent on pollution control norms, and though this may not be directly associated with guests, environment protection is on the priority list for many hotel companies. Installing effluent treatment plants (ETPs) is a part of investment that is typically concerned with projects associated with environment protection.

5. *Other considerations* No five-star hotel is appreciated without a beautifully landscaped frontage. Though landscaping, installing water coolers, locker facilities,

gymnasium, and dining room for employees may not be directly beneficial for the hotel in terms of revenue generation opportunities, such facilities are the basic requirements in any hotel business.

Generally, the capital budgeting process requires simple to compound calculations and a range of supporting documents, depending upon the category of the capital expenditure. Large investment decisions require multifarious analysis and approval from within the company, whereas a smaller quantum of investments may not require intricate calculations and may be decided upon by the general manager of the hotel. Large investment decisions to launch a new property in a completely new market would usually originate in the marketing department, while a proposal to replace an existing or worn-out equipment with an updated model could be the decision of the operations manager. The idea generated must be consistent with the corporate strategy and avoid analysis of projects that are incoherent to the corporate strategy.

Most of the hotel firms screen proposals at different levels of authority before the proposal is finalized. For example, a proposal to renovate the existing kitchen or refurbish rooms would pass through the respective departmental chiefs—the general manager, the chief operating officer, the capital expenditure committee, to the managing director—and then to the board of directors. The magnitude of the expenditure would determine the level at which the expenditure would be finally approved. The level of autonomy would be specific to a company but it is evident that hotel companies are adopting a sophisticated approach to capital budgeting.

CASH FLOW IN CAPITAL BUDEGTING

After the idea for an investment proposal is conceived, the next important task is to estimate future cash flows associated with it. The final results would not be accurate if the cash flow estimates are erroneous (refer to Figs 11.1 and 11.2 for a diagrammatic description). It is important that costs and benefits involved with the capital budgeting process must be measured in terms of cash flow. An organization invests cash in the present with the

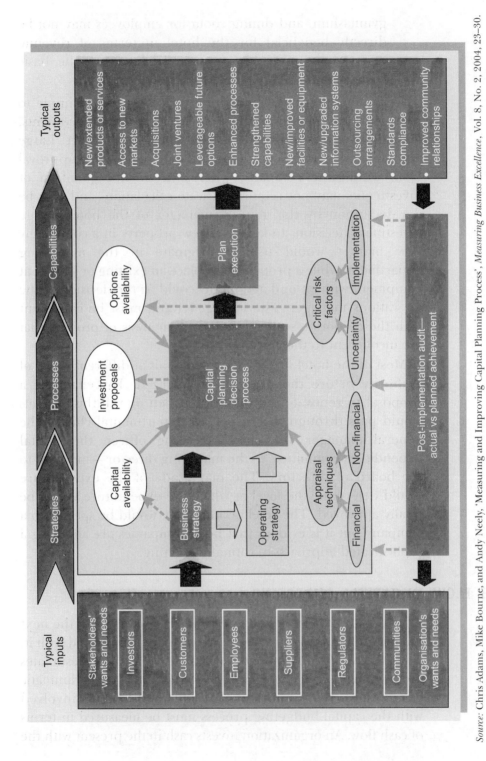

Fig. 11.1 Perspective reflections on the process of capital planning

Source: Chris Adams, Mike Bourne, and Andy Neely, 'Measuring and Improving Capital Planning Process', *Measuring Business Excellence*, Vol. 8, No. 2, 2004, 23–30.

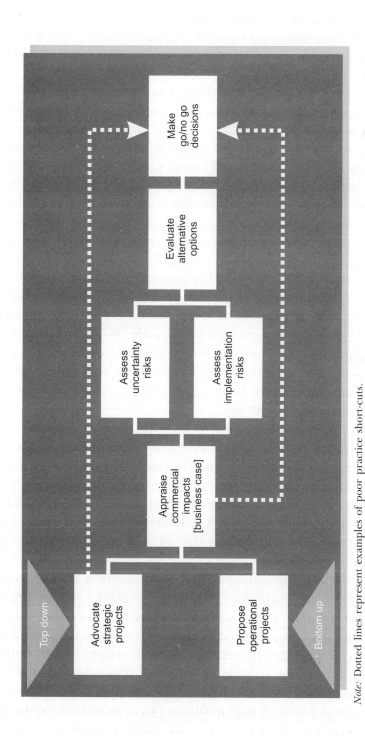

Note: Dotted lines represent examples of poor practice short-cuts.

Source: Chris Adams, Mike Bourne, and Andy Neely, 'Measuring and Improving Capital Planning Process', *Measuring Business Excellence,* Vol. 8. No. 2, 2004, 23–30.

Fig. 11.2 Measuring and improving capital planning process

objective of receiving even more cash in the future. Costs are cash outflows, and benefits are cash inflows. Cash outflows are a reasonable measure of costs and by the same principle, cash inflows are a realistic parameter to gauge benefits.

Cash flows are determined on the post-tax principle. The initial outlay involved and the average cost of capital employed for evaluating cash flow stream is also measured in post-tax terms. Further, the information should be considered on an incremental basis and should take into account all costs incidental to the project. For example, if a hotel adds new rooms to the existing capacity, there is a chance that the newly constructed rooms may adversely affect the demand for old rooms. This is referred to as competitive effect. On the other hand, a complimentary situation may arise in case of new restaurants, enhancing the demand for rooms in certain cases. It is also important to consider the implication on the market share if the investment is not carried out. The key to analysis is to view the situation with and without the investment, and to consider the complimentary and competitive effects of the proposed investment. It is very clear that costs and benefits could be brought to play only when relevant incremental cash flows are considered.

Pragmatically, *sunk costs* must be ignored while dealing with investment decisions. Sunk costs represent costs incurred in the past that are not relevant at the time of evaluating an investment proposal. While it may be essential to ignore sunk costs, it is absolutely logical to consider *opportunity costs*. For example, if there is space allocated in a hotel that can be used for some other purpose, its opportunity cost must be included in the evaluation of the project.

While anticipating capital investments, it is also necessary to anticipate inflation and draft a capital expenditure plan accordingly. There is always a tendency to erroneously assume that price levels would remain constant throughout the life of a project. Since the required rate of return usually reflects the premium on account of inflation, it is essential that the cash flows must also reflect the rate of inflation. The inflows would be affected by a change in future prices as inflows would arise out of the sale of the product. The outflows would also vary with the increase in incidental costs. Finally, the change in the position of current assets and current liabilities, as a fall-out of the investment decisions, is also considered as capital investment, not as a distinct working capital decision. For instance, an investment proposal may lead to increased investment in cash, inventories, or additional receivables, which may be treated as cash outflow, as and when they arise.

Calculating Incremental Cash Outflows

The next important task is to identify specific components that determine the relevant cash flow of the project. It is beneficial to place project cash flows into categories based on timing as follows:

1. *Initial cash outflow* It represents the total cash outflow associated with investment in various project components.
2. *Operational cash flow* The cash flow expected during the operational phase of the project.
3. *Terminal cash flow* The cash flow expected at the termination of the project. This is given special attention due to the set of cash flows that occur towards the end of the project.

Illustrations: New project

The following cases illustrate the calculation of cash flows in a hotel business environment, while dealing with a new project and a replacement project.

Case I The Phoenix Hotel Corporation is considering an overseas expansion project. The following information is available as regards to the investment proposal.

1. The total outlay on the project will be 100 million rupees. This consists of 80 million rupees on building and equipment and 20 million rupees on gross working capital.
2. The project will be financed with 40 million rupees of equity capital, 30 million rupees of long-term debt (in the form of debentures), 10 million rupees of short-term bank borrowings, and 20 million rupees of trade credit. This means that 80 million rupees of investor funds (equity +

debt) will be applied towards plant and equipment (600 million rupees) and working capital margin (200 million rupees). Working capital margin is defined as gross working capital minus current liabilities. The interest rate on debentures will be 13.5 per cent and the interest rate on short-term borrowings will be 20 per cent.

3. The project will increase the revenues by 80 million rupees per year. The increase in expenses on account of the project will be 400 million rupees per year (this includes all items of expenses other than depreciation, interest on debentures, and taxes). The effective tax rate will be 50 per cent.

4. Equipments will be depreciated @ $33\frac{1}{3}$ per cent per year as per the written-down value method. So, the depreciation charges will be

	(Rs in millions)
First year	20.00
Second year	13.33
Third year	8.89
Fourth year	5.93
Fifth year	3.95

Given the above details, the post-tax incremental cash flows relating to investor claims are shown in the following table. Some clarifications about this table may be given. The initial outflow, occurring at the end of the year 0, is 80 crore rupees. This represents the commitment of investor funds to the project. (Note that the total outlay on the project is 100 crore rupees. However, our focus is only on cash flows relating to investors.) The operating cash inflow, relating to investor funds, at the end of year 1 is 30 crore rupees. This is calculated as

Profit after tax + Depreciation
$$= Rs\ 10,00,00,000 + Rs\ 20,00,00,000$$
$$= Rs\ 30,00,00,000$$

Note that in determining the operating cash inflow relating to investor claims, we have excluded interest on debt and computed the taxes as if the project were all equity financed. The operating cash inflows for the subsequent years have been calculated similarly.

Table 11.1   Cash flows for the new project

	Year	0	1	2	3	4	5
			(Rs in million)				
Building and equipment		(85.00)					
I Revenue and Operating Expenses							
Revenues			24.00	26.00	28.00	30.00	32.00
Costs (other than depreciation and interest)			14.00	14.70	15.44	16.21	17.02
Depreciation			17.00	13.60	10.88	8.66	6.91
II Operating Profit							
Profit before tax			(7.00)	(2.3)	1.68	5.13	8.07
Tax					(0.672)	(2.05)	(3.23)
Profit after tax			(7.00)	(2.3)	1.01	3.08	4.84
Net salvage value of plant equipment							20.00
III Cash Flow generated by the project							
Initial flow (Row 1)		(85.00)					
Operating flow (Row 7 + 4)			10.00	11.3	11.89	11.74	12.91
Working capital requirement at 20% of the sales revenue			4.80	5.20	5.60	6.00	6.40	0.00
Change in working capital requirement from the previous year			4.80	0.40	0.40	0.40	0.40	(6.40)
Terminal flow (Row 8)							20.00*
Net cash flow (Row 9 + 10 • 12 + 13)		(89.8)	14.8	16.5	11.49	11.34	32.91

*It has been assumed that 20 million rupees would be realized from the sale of equipment after five years.

Terminal cash flow relating to long-term funds = Net salvage value of plant and equipment + Net recovery of working capital margin

Note that when the project is terminated, the

Liquidation value = Net salvage value of plant and equipment + net recovery of working capital

The first component belongs to the investors. The second component, first applied to repay the current liabilities, is called the net recovery of working capital margin, which belongs to the investors.

Case II   A large five-star hotel is interested in assessing the cash flows associated with the replacement of an old machine by a new machine. The old machine bought a few years ago has a book value of Rs 90,000 and it can be sold for Rs 90,000. It has a remaining life span of 5 years after which its net salvage value is expected to be Rs 20,000. It is being depreciated annually @ 20 per cent (written down value method).

The new machine costs Rs 4,00,000. It is expected to fetch a net salvage value of Rs 2,00,000 after 5 years, when it will no longer be required. It will be depreciated annually @ $33\frac{1}{3}$ per cent (written down value method). The new machine is expected to bring a saving of Rs 1,00,000 in manufacturing costs. Investment in working capital would remain unaffected. The tax rate applicable to the firm is 50 per cent.

Given the above information, the incremental post-tax cash flows associated with replacement project are worked out in Table 11.2.

Table 11.2   Cash flows for the replacement project

							(Rs in million)
Year	0	1	2	3	4	5	
Net investment in equipments	(2.9)						
I Revenue and Cost							
Savings in costs		3.00	3.00	3.00	3.00	3.00	
Depreciation on old equipment		1.52	1.22	0.97	0.78	0.62	
Depreciation on new equipment		3.20	2.56	2.05	1.64	1.31	
Incremental depreciation on new equipment (Row 3 • 4)		1.68	1.34	1.08	0.86	0.69	
II Profit							
Incremental taxable profit (Row 2 • 5)		1.32	1.66	1.92	2.14	2.31	
Incremental tax (40%)		0.53	0.66	0.77	0.86	0.92	
Incremental profit after tax		0.79	1.00	1.15	1.28	1.39	
III Cash Flow generated by the project							
Net incremental salvage value						0.69	
Initial flow (Row 1)	(2.9)						
Operating flow (Row 8 + 5)		2.47	2.34	2.23	2.14	2.08	
Terminal flow (Row 9)						0.69	
Net cash flow	(2.9)	2.47	2.34	2.23	2.14	2.77	

Elements that would make a difference to the process of capital planning:

1. Capital planning decisions must be guided by corporate or business unit strategy execution.

2. The risk involved in the capital planning process must be adequately defined before final investment decisions are made.

3. There needs to be consistency as regards cost of capital and value of money over time, when carrying out analysis of capital project proposals.

4. Other projects, such as the infrastructure projects, should realistically reflect the negative cash flows and the repercussion of non-implementation of the project.

5. Capital planning should address a range of stakeholder issues and not consider the short-term demands of investors alone, and therefore, project proposals should be supported by relevant non-financial information as well.

6. Alternative options must also be evaluated when larger investments are concerned.

7. All capital plans need to have measurable outcomes. This is necessary to track the project before and after implementation.

8. Capital planning and implementation must be documented and, if appropriate, must be shared with the staff. This reduces the chances of errors and leads to a better planning and implementation of capital project proposals.

SUMMARY

- Capital budgeting in hotels is the process of identifying, analyzing, and planning expenditures on assets whose returns (cash flows) extend beyond a period of one year.

- Accuracy in determining capital expenditures helps in managing profitable growth, particularly in the age of globalization, when hotels are entering transnational and cross-border markets.

- The process involves generating investment project proposals that are in line with the firm's strategy and vision, which is followed by estimating and evaluating post-tax incremental operating cash flows for the project in question, selecting projects based on their intrinsic ability to maximize value to the company.
- An important aspect of capital expenditure decisions is the incremental cash flow. The post-tax effects of the tax flows are considered.
- It is necessary that only the incremental effect is considered. Sunk costs are ignored whereas opportunity costs are considered.
- It is pertinent to categorize cash flows on the basis of timing into initial outflows, interim incremental net cash flows, and terminal-point incremental net cash flows.

KEY TERMS

Cash flow Refers to the amounts of cash being received and spent by a business during a defined period of time, sometimes tied to a specific project.

Investment A term with several closely-related meanings in business management, finance, and economics, related to saving or deferring consumption.

Working capital Represents the amount of day-to-day operating liquidity available to a business.

REVIEW QUESTIONS

1. Discuss the guidelines to be followed while estimating incremental cash flows associated with a new hospitality project.
2. Explain the important phases of the capital budgeting process in the hospitality business.
3. Explain the key elements to be considered while planning capital expenditure decisions.

REVIEW PROBLEMS

1. A hotel company is presently using a crane for a major project. This crane was bought 2 years ago for Rs 10,00,000 and has been depreciated at the rate of 20 per cent per annum, as per the written down value method. The company requires such a crane for 3 more years. An improved version of this crane is available now for Rs 20,00,000. Determine the cash flows associated with the replacement of the existing crane by the improved crane, given the following information:

   (i) The salvage value of the existing crane is equal to its book value.

   (ii) The improved crane can be sold after 3 years for Rs 12,00,000. The existing crane, if used for 3 years, will have nil salvage value.

   (iii) The annual savings in operating expenses with the improved crane will be Rs 3,00,000.

   (iv) The depreciation rate for the improved crane is $33\frac{1}{3}$ per cent p.a., as per the written down value method.

   (v) The effective tax rate for the company is 50 per cent.

2. The Marriott Company is considering the proposal to replace one of its equipments. The following information is available:

   (i) The existing equipment was bought 5 years ago for Rs 10,00,000. It has been depreciated at the rate of 10 per cent p.a., as per the written down value method. It can presently be sold for Rs 8,00,000. It has a remaining life of 5 years after which it would, on disposal, fetch Rs 2,00,000.

   (ii) The new equipment costs Rs 16,00,000. It will be subjected to a depreciation rate of $33\frac{1}{3}$ per cent. After 5 years, it is expected to fetch Rs 10,00,000 on disposal. The replacement of the old equipment would increase revenues by Rs 1,00,000 per year and reduce operating costs (excluding depreciation) by Rs 1,20,000 per year.

   Compute the cash flows associated with the replacement proposal, assuming a tax rate of 50 per cent.

3. Taj Ventures is considering investment in a new product. The following information is available:

Annual sales	Rs	30,00,000
Manufacturing costs (excludes depreciation but includes Rs 1 lakh of allocated fixed costs)	Rs	12,00,000
Selling and distribution expenses (includes Rs 80,000 of allocated costs)	Rs	6,00,000
Loss of contribution of other products	Rs	1,00,000

The capital cost for plant and equipment needed to manufacture the new product will be Rs 20,00,000 and the working capital margin will be Rs 8,00,000. Short-term bank borrowing of Rs 20,00,000 will be needed. This will carry 18 per cent interest. Define the cash flow associated with the new product. Make suitable assumptions.

Capital Budgeting Techniques

> *The general who wins the battle makes many calculations in his temple before the battle is fought. The general who loses makes but few calculations beforehand.*
>
> **Sun Tzu**

Learning Objectives

After studying this chapter, you will be able to

➢ Understand the importance of capital budgeting in the context of hospitality operations

➢ Critically assess accounting rate of return (ARR) and payback period (PBP) as investment criteria

➢ Evaluate net present value (NPV), internal rate of return (IRR), and methods of project appraisal

➢ Differentiate between traditional and discounted cash flow techniques in evaluating various capital expenditure decisions

2007—The Year of the Hotelier

The year 2000 was about the Internet burn-out, while 2004 was about the telecom boom. 2007 seems to have turned into a year for hotel build-out. Corporations, real estate developers, and investment funds are ready to pay any amount of money to build a hotel. Hotel Leela Ventures is shelling out the highest price ever paid for a hotel property in Delhi—Rs 611 crore. Emaar-MGF paid Rs 388 crore for two plots in Jasola at a recent DDA auction.

Reliance Industries is developing a hotel. Bombay Dyeing is entering the supply-deficient hospitality sector, and is in talks with Peninsula, Walt Disney, Ritz Carlton, and Four Seasons for managing some of its hotels. Not to be

outdone, private equity players have put money into the sector. Recently, Warburg Pincus picked up 27% stake in Delhi-based Lemon Tree Hotels for Rs 280 crore, ICICI Venture Funds picked up a stake in Hyderabad's Viceroy Hotels for Rs 100 crore, WestBridge Capital Partners acquired 10% stake for Rs 250 million in Royal Orchid Hotels, Sarovar Hotels inked a Rs 100 crore agreement with US-based Bessemer Venture Partners and New Vernon. All these investors are betting on the scarcity of hotel rooms and consequently, healthy rates of return.

There is an immediate requirement for approximately 1,00,000 new hotel rooms across cities in India, and only 75% of this demand is being met by the projects that are currently underway. On account of the supply lag, average room rates (ARRs) and occupancy rates have been on the rise, and are expected to increase by 20–25% over the next two years, and stabilize thereafter. In 2006, occupancy rates across 10 major cities in the country touched 74.5% and ARR was about Rs 7800.

While it may be too early to comment on the success or failure of these projects, it is clear that the capital investments made today will have far-reaching consequences on a company's performance. Each of the investments mentioned above requires careful analysis, based to a large extent on the tools and techniques discussed in this chapter. As you read through this chapter, think about the ways some of the successful hotel companies use capital budgeting analysis to make better investment decisions.

Source: Based on an article by Lijee Philip, *The Economic Times*, 3 May 2007.

CAPITAL BUDGETING IN ACTION

After estimating relevant cash flows associated with new project proposals, it is necessary to evaluate the potential viability of the proposals. The entire process would culminate into a decision to either accept or reject the capital expenditure proposal. This chapter seeks to examine alternative methods of project evaluation and address some of the potential difficulties in implementing these methods.

CAPITAL BUDGETING MODELS

Managers in the hospitality industry use a variety of capital budgeting models, ranging from the simple to the complex. The models discussed in this chapter are

1. Accounting rate of return (ARR)
2. Payback period (PP)
3. Net present value (NPV)
4. Internal rate of return (IRR)

The above models can be classified as the discounted cash flow (DCF) and the non-discounted cash flow techniques. While the ARR and the PP are typically non-discounted cash flow techniques, the NPV and the IRR are referred to as DCF techniques.

Accounting Rate of Return

Accounting rate of return, also referred to as average rate of return, is determined as

$$\text{Post-tax profits} \div \text{Book value of the investment} \qquad (12.1)$$

Consider the illustration associated with the investment proposal of a large five-star hotel in New Delhi, shown in Table 12.1. The accounting rate of return is

$$\frac{\frac{1}{5}(20 + 22 + 24 + 26 + 28)}{\frac{1}{5}(90 + 80 + 70 + 60 + 50)} = 34 \text{ per cent}$$

Accept/reject criteria

The higher the accounting rate of return, the better would be the project. While ranking or comparing two investment

Table 12.1

Year	Book value of fixed investment (Rs in millions)	Post-tax profit (Rs in millions)
1	90	20
2	80	22
3	70	24
4	60	26
5	50	28

proposals, the project with a higher accounting rate of return is preferred over the project with a lower accounting rate of return.

Evaluation

The relative merits and demerits have to be considered before selecting the accounting rate of return as a criterion to accept/reject investments in the projects. The most favourable aspect of the ARR method is the simplicity in calculation, and it does not demand intricate details. It just requires the accounting post-tax profits that are easily obtainable from the books of accounts. Furthermore, it is simple to understand and use when compared with other techniques of evaluation. Finally, the post-tax profits associated with the projects can be considered for the lifetime of the project.

Though simple to calculate and easy to understand, the method suffers from serious drawbacks. *First*, the ARR method considers the post-tax accounting profits and not the cash flows. From Chapter 1, we know that cash flow is an important aspect from the financial management perspective, when compared with accounting profits or earnings. The *second* area of deficiency is that it does not consider the time value of money.[*] The timing of cash inflows and outflows plays an important role in the process of financial decision making. The *third* drawback is that the ARR method does not differentiate between the size of investment required for each project. It would be difficult for the firm to choose from projects with the same ARR but different initial investments. Consider the situation in Table 12.2.

[*] Refer to Chapter 3 for a detailed discussion on the concept of time value of money.

Table 12.2

Equipments	Average annual earnings	Average investment	ARR (%)
A	Rs 60,000	Rs 3,00,000	20
B	Rs 20,000	Rs 1,00,000	20
C	Rs 40,000	Rs 2,00,000	20

Finally, this method does not take into consideration the benefits that would accrue from the sale, or by abandoning the equipment to be replaced by the new investment. From a financially correct perspective, the new investment should be measured in terms of incremental cash flows, i.e., new investment minus sales proceeds of the existing equipment, with due tax consideration. But the ARR disregards any adjustments while determining the level of average investment. The acquisition cost of the assets is considered for all practical purposes. Due to these reasons, there arises a need for some sophisticated tools for evaluation of investment projects.

Payback Period

The time required to recover the initial cash outlay on the project is called the payback period. Consider the following example. A proposed investment in a spa requires an initial outflow of Rs 6,00,00,000 and generates cash inflows of Rs 1,00,00,000, Rs 1,50,00,000, Rs 1,50,00,000, and Rs 2,00,00,000, in the first, second, third, and fourth year, respectively. Then, in this case, the payback period is 4 years because this is the time required to recover the initial investment of Rs 6,00,00,000. When the annual inflow is a constant sum, the payback period will be the initial investment divided by the annual cash inflow. For example, if the initial investment is Rs 1,00,00,000 and constant annual cash flows are of Rs 30,00,000 million, the payback period will be 31/3 years.

Accept/reject criteria

Projects with shorter payback period are preferred over projects with longer payback period. The firms using payback period as a tool to evaluate capital projects may also specify the maximum acceptable payback period. In the case of restaurants, the maximum period could range between three to five years.

This method is also used

(a) To evaluate the investment project on a preliminary basis. The project would be subject to a detailed scan process if it successfully clears this requirement.

(b) In proposed projects where the element of risk is high due to the speculative nature, or due to the short life-span of the project.

(c) When the firm is short of cash and meeting immediate cash requirements is important, as compared to long-term profitability.

Evaluation

The payback period method is easy to calculate and comprehend. The payback period, in a way, is superior to the ARR method because it considers the cash flows in the calculations. It is also useful in differentiating between two projects involving the same initial investment. This point is illustrated in Table 12.3.

The above comparative shows that project X should be chosen over project Y due to the short time-span involved in the recovery of the initial investment.

The limitations or caveats of this method should be considered before using the payback method for investment appraisal. The drawbacks of the method can be summarized as follows:

1. This method does not consider cash flows after the payback period. Consider the illustration in Table 12.4. Though both the projects show the same payback period, there is a difference in the amount of cash flows generated by the individual projects. The cash flows for project X stop at year 3, whereas the cash flows for project Y continue beyond year 3. Rationally, project Y would be preferred to project X, but the payback period would rank both the projects as equal. Hence, it cannot be regarded as a measure of profitability. The major failure lies in the fact that the method fails to consider the total benefits accruing from the project.

2. Another drawback of the payback period is that it does not measure correctly the cash flows occurring during the

Table 12.3

Particulars	Project X (Rs in millions)	Project Y (Rs in millions)
Initial investment	40	40
Post-tax cash inflows		
1	14	10
2	16	10
3	10	10
4	04	10
5	02	12
6	01	16
7	Nil	17
Payback period (years)	3	4

Table 12.4

Particulars	Project X (Rs in millions)	Project Y (Rs in millions)
Initial investment	150	150
Post-tax cash inflows		
1	50	40
2	60	50
3	40	60
4	0	60
5		30
6		30
Payback period (years)	3	3

payback period. It considers only the recovery period as a whole. This method does not consider the time value of money. To illustrate this point, consider the cash flows in Table 12.5. Although the payback period of both projects is the same, project A would be chosen because of its ability to generate larger cash flows during the initial phase of the project. The payback method of project evaluation fails to highlight this situation.

Table 12.5

Particulars	Project A (Rs in millions)	Project B (Rs in millions)
Total cost of the project	150	150
Post-tax cash flows:		
Year 1	10	01
Year 2	04	04
Year 3	01	10

Discounted Cash Flow (DCF)/Time-adjusted Techniques

The distinguishing feature about the sophisticated capital budgeting techniques is that they take into account the time-value of money while evaluating the costs and benefits associated with the investment proposals. These methods also take into consideration the cash flows associated with the project throughout the life of the project. The ensuing discussion considers discounted cash flow techniques such as the net present value (NPV), internal rate of return (IRR), profitability index (PI), and benefit cost ratio (BCR).

Present value (PV)

The present value or the discounted cash flow procedure recognizes the fact that cash flow streams at different time periods differ in value and can be compared only if they are expressed in terms of a common denominator, the present value. In other words, it is impossible to compare a certain amount of money received today with the amount of money received one year hence, unless the present value of the amount is ascertained. In the discounted cash flow method, all cash flows are expressed in terms of their present value, which makes comparison easy and logical.

Net Present Value Method

As the flaws in the traditional methods surfaced, there was a requirement to search for ways to improve the effectiveness of project evaluations. One such method is the net present value (NPV) method. The net present value is described as the summation of the present values of all cashflows in each year. Net present value calculations involve the following three steps.

Step 1: Find the present value of each of the cash inflows and outflows at a predetermined discount rate.

Step 2: Sum these discounted cash flows. This sum is called the projects NPV.

Step 3: If the NPV is positive, the project would be accepted. The project would be rejected if the NPV is negative.

The equation for the NPV is as follows:

$$\text{NPV} = CF_0 + \frac{CF_1}{(1+i)^1} + \frac{CF_2}{(1+i)^1} + \frac{CF_n}{(1+i)^n} \qquad (12.2)$$

Let us consider cash inflows and outflows associated with an expansion project of a large five-star hotel company, shown in Table 12.6.

Table 12.6

Year	Cash flows (Rs in millions)
0	(100)
1	35
2	39
3	40
4	32

Applying Equation 12.2, the NPV for the project at 12% discount rate would be

$$\text{NPV} = \frac{CF_1}{(1+i)^1} + \frac{CF_2}{(1+i)^2} + \frac{CF_n}{(1+i)^n}$$

$$\text{NPV} = \frac{35}{(1+12)^1} + \frac{39}{(1+12)^2} + \frac{40}{(1+12)^3} + \frac{32}{(1+12)^4} - 100$$

Alternatively,

$$\text{NPV} = 35\,(\text{PVIF}_{12,\,1}) + 39\,(\text{PVIF}_{12,\,2}) + 40\,(\text{PVIF}_{12,\,3})$$
$$+ \; 32\,(\text{PVIF}_{12,\,4}) - 100$$
$$= 35\,(0.893) + 39\,(0.797) + 39\,(0.712) + 32\,(0.636) - 100$$
$$= 31.255 + 31.083 + 27.768 + 20.352 - 100 = \text{Rs } 10.458$$

Accept/reject criterion

If an investment project's net present value is zero or more, the project is accepted. The project is rejected if the net present value is less than zero. In other words, the project is accepted if the present value of the cash inflows exceeds the present value of the cash outflows. NPV of zero signifies that the project's cash flows are exactly sufficient to repay the invested capital and to provide the requisite rate of return. If the NPV is positive, the project is able to generate more cash than required to return to the shareholders, and this excess cash would belong to the shareholders solely. Hence, there will be an increase in shareholder wealth if the company takes on projects with a positive NPV.

Evaluation

The net present value criterion has considerable merits:

- It takes into account the time value of money.
- It considers the cash flow stream in its entirety.
- It squares neatly with the financial objective of maximization of wealth of the shareholders. The net present value of various projects measured at today's value of rupee can be added. For example, the net present value of a package consisting of two projects, A and B, will simply be the sum of the net present value of these projects individually:

$$\text{NPV (A+B)} = \text{NPV (A)} + \text{NPV (B)}$$

Due to this property of the net present value, a poor project (one which has a negative net present value) will not be accepted just because it is combined with a good project (which has a positive net present value).

The advantages discussed here make the net present value a formidable investment appraisal criterion. Indeed, conceptually the net present value is virtually unassailable. However, from a practical point of view, the net value suffers from a limitation. As it is expressed as an absolute number, it is not very appealing to decision-makers who may think in relative terms (like, rate of return or profitability index).

Internal Rate of Return

The internal rate of return of a project is the discount rate, which makes its net present value equal to zero. It is the discount rate in the equation:

$$\text{Intial investment} = \sum_{t=1}^{N} \frac{C_t}{(1 + IRR)^t} \qquad (12.3)$$

Or

In the net present value calculation, we assume that the discount rate is known and determine the net present value of the project. In the internal rate of return calculation, we set the net present value equal to zero and determine the discount rate (internal rate of return) that satisfies this condition.

To illustrate the calculation of internal rate of return, consider the cash flows of a project, shown in Table 12.7.

Table 12.7

Year	0	1	2	3	4
(Rs in millions)	(1,00,000)	30,000	30,000	40,000	45,000

The internal rate of return is the value of r, which satisfies the following equation:

$$\frac{30,000}{(1+r)^1} + \frac{30,000}{(1+r)^2} + \frac{40,000}{(1+r)^3} + \frac{45,000}{(1+r)^4} = \text{Rs } 1,00,000$$

The calculation of r involves a process of trial and error. We try different values of r till we find that the left side of the above equation (which represents the present value of benefits) is equal to 1,00,000 (the initial investment). Let us, to begin with, try $r = 15$ per cent. This makes the left side equal to

$$\frac{30,000}{(1+1.5)^1} + \frac{30,000}{(1+1.5)^2} + \frac{40,000}{(1+1.5)^3} + \frac{45,000}{(1+1.5)^4} = \text{Rs } 1,00,802$$

This value is slightly higher than our target value 1,00,000. So, we increase the value of r from 15 per cent to 16 per cent. (In general, a higher r lowers and a smaller r increases the left side value). The left side becomes

$$\frac{30,000}{(1+1.6)^1} + \frac{30,000}{(1+1.6)^2} + \frac{40,000}{(1+1.6)^3} + \frac{45,000}{(1+1.6)^4} = \text{Rs } 98,641$$

Since this value is now less than 1,00,000, we conclude that the value of r lies between 15 per cent and 16 per cent. To get a more precise estimate, we can resort to linear interpolation in this range, using the following formula:

$$L + \frac{(PVB)\,L - I}{(PVB) - (PVB)\,U} * (U - L)$$

where, $\quad\quad L$ = Lower discount rate

$(PVB)\,L,\,(PVB)\,U$ = Present value of benefits at the lower and upper discount rates

I = Initial investment

U = Upper discount rate

Applying the above formula to our example, the value of r is

$$\frac{1,00,802 - 1,00,000}{15\% + 1,00,802 - 98,641}\,(16\% - 15\%)$$

$$= 15\% + 0.37\% = 15.37\%$$

Accept/reject criterion

The internal rate of return is generally compared to a predetermined rate of return, known as the cut off or the *hurdle rate*. For the purpose of understanding, we assume that the required rate of return is known to us. The project is accepted if the internal rate of return exceeds the required rate of return, else the project is rejected. In the illustration provided above, if the required rate of return is equal to 12 per cent, and the internal rate of return method is employed, the project would be accepted. The return expected by the investors can be termed as the required rate of return.

Evaluation

The internal rate of return criterion, a popular discounted cash flow method, has several points worth consideration:

- It takes into account the time value of money.
- It considers the cash flow stream in its entirety.
- It makes sense to businessmen who think in terms of rate of return and find an absolute quantity like net present value somewhat difficult to work with.

The internal rate of return criterion, however, has its own limitations:

- The internal rate of return may not be uniquely defined. If the cash flow stream of a project has more than one change in sign, there is a possibility that there are multiple rates of return.
- The internal rate of return figure cannot distinguish between lending and borrowing. Hence, a high internal rate of return need not necessarily be a desirable feature.

Consider projects A and B (shown in Table 12.8).

Table 12.8   Cash flows

Year	0	1
Project A (Rs in million)	(400)	600
Project B (Rs in million)	400	(700)

The internal rate of return for A is 50 per cent, whereas the internal rate of return for B is 75 per cent. Does this mean that B is more attractive than A? Certainly not. A is a very attractive project, whereas B is a highly undesirable project. Why? A involves investing 400 at a rate of return of 50 per cent, whereas B involves borrowing 400 at a rate of return of 75 per cent. Yet, if we go by the internal rate of return figures, B seems more attractive than A.

Conflicting Rankings with NPV versus IRR

Both NPV and IRR methods will always give the same accept or reject decision for any single proposal. However, if a number of proposals that are mutually exclusive projects are evaluated and ranked, then there might be a difference in the rankings of the NPV method and the IRR method. This may be an outcome for any of the following reasons:

1. The scale of investment or the cost of the projects is different. The NPV and IRR would produce conflicting results when two projects with unequal initial investments are considered; for example, when we compare constructing a restaurant to building a hotel.

2. The cash flow pattern may vary. Consider an example of two projects wherein the cash flows of one project increase with time, whereas there is a decrease in the cash flows of the other project.

3. The projects have an unequal life period. For example, we are dealing with a project that provides returns for a period of ten years, whereas the other ceases to exist by the fifth year.

Theoretically, the NPV method is considered to be a better method because it uses the same discount rate for alternative proposals, and that rate would normally represent the minimum rate acceptable for investments to be made by the company. On the other hand, the use of IRR is advocated due to the ease in interpretation, does not require a predetermined discount rate, and allows more meaningful comparison of alternatives.

Potential Problems

The techniques discussed in this chapter provide a cost benefit analysis of the capital expenditure to be incurred and the difficulties encountered while carrying out a cost benefit analysis of the capital expenditure decision. The following are some caveats in the context of budgeting for capital expenditure.

Project review

It is only possible to approximate the investment rate to be achieved. This is one of the major difficulties associated with the process of capital investment decision making. Investment proposals are based on estimated cash flows and the decisions based on the cash flows can only be judged for success or failure after the actual cash flows are known. Therefore, it is necessary that a review of all capital proposals is carried out at the end of every project. This will ensure refinement in the process of forecasting future cash flows and will benefit investment decisions in the future.

In all our calculations so far, we have either not considered the risk factor, or assumed that the discount or the investment rate adequately considers the risk element. *Risk* is also defined as the deviation of estimated cash flows from the actual cash flows.

Risk factor in investments

Our illustrations consider short periods. Determining cash flows over a longer time period is difficult as compared to forecasting cash flows over a short period. Therefore, risk plays a dominant role when the period is five years or less. In reality, investments in restaurant or hotel building investments involve a longer time span.

Therefore, while ascertaining the cash flows, it is also necessary to ascertain the level of risk associated with the project. This will help in obtaining a better perspective of the costs and benefits associated with the project.

Intangible benefits

The results obtained from the techniques mentioned here may not be the only criteria for making investment decisions. Some information may be vital in the process of decision making, but may not easily be quantifiable. There are implications of factors such as prestige, reputation, employee acceptability, and social or environment responsibility on the capital investment decision. For example, redecorating the hotel lobby, fulfilling the statutory norm of installing an effluent treatment plant (ETP), expenditure on landscaping, and installing equipments and devices for employee satisfaction may not yield quantifiable benefits, but are extremely necessary in the regular course of business. Personal judgment must come into play in such cases.

CONCLUSION

It is evident that capital budgeting techniques provide important information to decision makers. While impetus has to be given to the NPV, it is also worthwhile considering the information provided by the other methods.

SUMMARY

- Accounting rate of return or average rate of return (ARR) and the payback period are considered traditional methods of capital budgeting. Net present value (NPV) and internal rate of return (IRR) are discounted cash flow techniques.

- Accounting rate of return compares the average annual net income (after taxes) resulting from the investment to the average investment.

- The payback period (PBP) of an investment tells us the time period (number of years) required to recover our initial cash investment. This is a good tool to measure the liquidity of a project, but is a poor judge of profitability. The deficiency particularly arises because the method ignores cash flows accruing post payback period, ignores time-value of money, and makes use of an arbitrary cut-off point.

- The net present value (NPV) of an investment proposal is the present value of the future cash flows associated with the investment proposal less the initial cash outflow. The project should be accepted only if the NPV is positive or equal to zero.

- The internal rate of return (IRR) for an investment proposal is the discount rate that equates the present value of the expected cash flows with the initial cash outflows. The project should be accepted if the IRR is equal to or higher than the required rate of return.

KEY TERMS

Accounting rate of return Also known as the average rate of return, it is obtained by dividing the profit after tax by the book value of investments.

Internal rate of return (IRR) The rate at which the NPV is zero. The project is accepted if the IRR is greater than some predetermined rate.

Net present value (NPV) method The technique of capital budgeting that discounts all cash flows and then sums them up. The project with a positive NPV is accepted.

Payback period The number of years required to recoup the cost (initial investment) associated with a project.

REVIEW QUESTIONS

1. Define the following:
   - (a) Accounting rate of return
   - (b) Payback period
   - (c) Net present value
   - (d) Internal rate of return
   - (e) Discounted cash flow technique

2. State the reasons for the NPV and the IRR methods to provide different rankings.

3. State the accept/reject criteria for the different methods of investment appraisal examined in this chapter, viz., accounting rate of return, payback period, net present value, and internal rate of return.

4. State the potential problems associated with capital budgeting techniques.

CRITICAL THINKING QUESTIONS

1. Discuss the importance of capital budgeting decisions in the context of hospitality operations.

2. Evaluate average rate of return as a method of project appraisal.

3. Critique the use of payback period in evaluating hospitality investment projects.

4. Examine the importance of discounted cash flow techniques in the process of capital investment decisions.

5. Assess the relative merits and demerits of the net present value (NPV) method of investment appraisal.

6. Appraise the internal rate of return (IRR) as a method to evaluate investment proposals in the context of hospitality operations.

7. Compare and contrast the net present value (NPV) method of project evaluation and the internal rate of return method (IRR) for selection.

REVIEW PROBLEMS

1. The International Hotel Company Ltd has two investment proposals, which have the following characteristics:

	Project A (Rs in millions)			Project B (Rs in millions)		
Period	Cost	Profit after taxes	Net cash flow	Cost	Profit after taxes	Net cash flow
0	900	-	-	1200	-	-
1		100	5000		1000	5000
2		100	4000		1000	5000
3		100	3000		4000	8000

For each project, compute the payback period and the net present value using a discount rate of 15%.

2. The following exercises are on internal rate of return:

   (a) An investment of Rs 1000 today will return Rs 2000 at the end of 10 years. What is the internal rate of return?

   (b) An investment of Rs 1000 will return Rs 500 at the end of each of the next 3 years. What is the internal rate of return?

   (c) An investment of Rs 1000 today will return Rs 900 at the end of 1 year, Rs 500 at the end of 2 years, and Rs 100 at the end of 3 years. What is the internal rate of return?

   (d) An investment of Rs 1000 will return Rs 130 per year, forever. What is the internal rate of return?

3. Two mutually exclusive projects have projected cash flows as follows:

End of year

	0	1	2	3	4
			(Rs in millions)		
Project A	(2000)	1000	1000	1000	1000
Project B	(2000)	0	0	0	6000

   (a) Determine the internal rate of return for each project.

   (b) Determine the net present value for each project at discount rates of 0%, 5%, 10%, 20%, 30%, and 35%.

   (c) Plot a graph of the net present value of each project at the different discount rates.

   (d) Which project would you select? Why? What assumptions are inherent in your decision?

4. Naveen Hotels is considering two mutually exclusive projects with the following cash flow streams:

Year	Project A (Rs)	Project B (Rs)
0	(300)	(300)
1	60	130
2	100	100
3	120	80
4	150	60

(a) If the cost of capital to the firm is 12 per cent, rank the two projects in terms of (a) payback period and (b) net present value. Which criterion will you use for selecting a project? Why?

(b) If the cost of capital is 16 per cent and you have to choose a project, which project will you choose? Is your choice different from the one chosen in (a)? If so, why?

PROJECT WORK

Many hotel companies provide information about investments in projects of environmental concern. Search the Internet and/or your library for information about global hotel companies including the contribution made towards cleaning-up of the environment. Prepare a report encompassing the benefits associated with such investments, though they may not be viable according to the capital budgeting techniques discussed in this chapter.

CASE STUDY

DILEMMA AT THE MANGO TREE HOTEL COMPANY

The top management at the Mango Tree Hotel Company enthusiastically rolled out the expansion plans in the current financial year. The company has embarked on an ambitious plan to acquire and build two hotels overseas. In a co-ordination meeting, it was decided that a team of four senior executives, along with the CEO, would monitor the activities. All team members were advised to use the code Mission Overseas in all formal communication as regards to the project. The chief executive officer asked a member of the evaluating team, Alok Varma, to carry out a careful analysis to ascertain the viability of the projects.

The task of collecting relevant data was far more complex than Alok had imagined. Nonetheless, he was very happy with the estimates he had gathered. The second task was to rank the projects, for which he decided to seek the help of his sub-ordinate Naveen Deshpande. 'Here we go. I hope you exceed my expectations, as always ', thought Alok, as he clicked the send button on the computer screen. The excerpt of the e-mail communication to Naveen is as follows:

From: Alok Varma <alok.varma @ themangotree.com>
To: Naveen Deshpande <naveen.deshpande@ themangotree.com>
Subject: Mission Overseas
Dear Naveen,

... the relevant figures with respect to the projects are attached herewith. Evaluate the projects based on the payback and accounting rate of return as required by the existing capital budgeting system of the company. However, you may also consider the results obtained from discounted cash flow techniques. Ensure that you use a 7 per cent discount rate as this is the interest paid by our bankers on time deposited ...

Let me know if you have any questions regarding the same.
Alok Varma.

The mail triggered off numerous questions in Naveen's mind. 'The company uses payback method and the accounting rate of return to rank investments in capital projects. Something's definitely amiss with the company's capital budgeting system', he said to himself, as he perused carefully through the details of the e-mail. Being very organized, Naveen made a list of questions immediately. The questions on his notepad were

(a) What criteria is to be used to evaluate investments in capital projects?
(b) Is it rational to compare two projects with different lives?
(c) What discount rate is to be used in this case?
(d) Is the discount per cent specified by Alok justified because investing in a project is riskier than depositing money in a bank?

Valuation of Hotel Real Estate

> *Price is what you pay. Value is what you get.*
> **Warren Buffett, American investment entrepreneur**

INTRODUCTION

The value of a property is very important for both the buyer and seller. Buying and selling is an ongoing process in the hotel industry today. Owners may want to sell some property to invest in properties elsewhere. Buyers would want to buy to gain benefits in the future. Sometimes it is beneficial to acquire a property rather than investing in a totally new project. Heritage and palace hotels are an example of acquisition for the historical or antique value of the property. Determining value is a subjective process that varies with the purpose. In this chapter we shall take a closer look at the valuation process.

DEFINITION OF VALUE

While there are many dimensions of value, we shall focus on the market value for the purpose this chapter. Market value is what the knowledgeable buyers would pay and the informed sellers will accept after negotiations under conditions of fair sale and without any pressure.

METHODS OR APPROACHES TO VALUATION

This chapter provides a thorough overview of lodging valuation models. Hotel valuation, like all real estate valuation, must be seen in the context of establishing a point estimate that represents the value of a unique, illiquid asset in an environment with noisy and conflicting information. This gives rise to the use of multiple approaches that must be reconciled. Appraisers are charged with estimating market value using the classic troika of the cost approach, the sales comparison approach, and the income approach. Appraisers use 'market' indicators of return requirements and other valuation parameters to produce their estimates. Investors, on the other hand, wish to estimate investment value, which includes the effects of income taxes, the investor's unique cost of capital, and other investor-specific conditions. Investors typically rely on a modified income approach tailored to their circumstances, augmented with recent transaction information, to estimate value and form their bidding strategy.

THREE APPROACHES TO HOTEL VALUATION

There is a choice of three methods available to value hotels, namely the income capitalization, sales comparison, and cost approach. Although all three valuation approaches are generally given consideration, the inherent strengths of each approach and the nature of the hotel in question must be evaluated to determine which approach will provide supportable value estimates. This chapter seeks to explain all the three methods briefly.

Income Capitalization Approach

The income capitalization approach is based on the principle that the value of a property is indicated by its net return, or what is known as the 'present worth of future benefits'. We have seen in Chapter 12 that the future benefits in the case of hotels is the income stream estimated by a forecast of income and expense, along with the anticipated proceeds from a future sale. These benefits are converted into an indicative market value through a capitalization process and discounted cash flow analysis.

The forecast of income and expense is expressed in nominal or inflation-adjusted currency for each of the three years. The stabilized year is intended to reflect the anticipated operating results of the hotel over its remaining economic life, given any or all applicable stages of in the life cycle of a hotel. The income capitalization approach involves three steps.

The foremost step is to project the income stream over the life of the property or over a specified period. The second step involves determining an appropriate capitalization rate. The third and final step calls for application of the capitalization to the income stream.

Projecting the income stream This involves the projection of revenues and expenses, except depreciation and interest expense. Refer to the discussion on cash flows in Chapter 11. Projection of the future income (cash) stream is a challenging task. The projections consider relevant factors that would affect the business in the future. For example, the projection would consider competition, and the income stream would be adjusted accordingly. Further, the income stream considers expected costs instead of assuming that the costs would remain at the current level. This method also assumes that the income stream will not increase indefinitely. It is most likely that any hotel business will increase for a certain period of time and then decline.

Determining the capitalization rates The next step of the income capitalization approach is deriving the overall capitalization rate. One way to derive the market capitalization rate is to divide the average annual income stream by the market value. For instance, if a hotel property with average annual income stream of Rs 20,00,000 was sold for Rs 2,50,00,000, the overall capitalization rate would be 0.08 or 8 per cent. The overall capitalization rate can be determined by using sales prices and the income streams of comparable properties that have been sold in the time period relevant to the property under consideration.

This means that due consideration has to be given to terms of finances, income stream calculations, and the market conditions.

This approach ignores the time value of money and assumes that the income stream is infinite in terms of the time frame. Therefore, these are considered as drawbacks of this approach to arrive at the capitalization rate.

The other approach is to look at the debt and equity components to arrive at the capitalization rate. This approach considers the relative components and the required returns and hence appears to be a reasonable way to determine the appropriate rate for capitalization. The formula for arriving at the capitalization rate can be expressed as follows:

$$(D\% \times M) + (1 - DF\%) \times K_e$$

where, $D\%$ = the percentage of debt financing to total financing

M = the mortgage constant used to finance the hotel property

$1 - D\%$ = the equity component used to finance the hotel property

K_e = the annual required returns on the owners (equity) investment

Consider a loan for 75 per cent (D%) for a period of 20 years at an annual interest rate of 14 per cent and a mortgage constant[*] of 0.11 and the equity investors require a return of 15 per cent. Substituting the above values in the equation, we have

Capitalization rate = $(0.75 \times 0.11) + (1 - 0.75) \times 0.15$

= 0.12 or 12%

Therefore, the appropriate capitalization rate to value the above hotel would be 12 per cent.

Discounting the income stream   The last step is to discount the income stream. We shall discuss ways to discount the value of the property.

A straight way to discount the income stream is to *capitalise the stabilised year's income*. The stabilised year's income refers to the

---

[*] The mortgage constant is equal to the amount paid annually divided by the principal (initial loan amount). Refer to the section on amortization of loan in Chapter 3 to arrive at the amount paid annually.

assumed average annual income. Once the average annual income is determined, the capitalised value can be ascertained by dividing the average annual income by the overall capitalization rate. While this method is simplistic and easy to apply, the major problem with this approach is the selection of one average annual income. While it may be arithmetically possible to average the income streams over the life of the hotel property, we know that the income streams from the remote years have to discounted more since the income streams are distant and are therefore risky.[*] In addition, projections over a longer period tend to loose accuracy. Using this approach we can determine the capitalised value as follows:

Let as assume the average annual income to be Rs 1,00,00,000 and the capitalization rate to be 12 per cent as calculated from the earlier section.

Capitalization rate = Average annual income ÷ Overall capitalization rate

= Rs 1,00,00,000 ÷ .12 = Rs 8,33,30,000

Since the limitations are substantial, we must think about some other methods.

The other approach is the use of capitalization rate to *discount the property's income stream over its life*. The calculations are same as those used for calculating the net present value (NPV) discussed in Chapter 12. The same can be illustrated as follows:

Year	Income stream (Rs in million)	PVIF @ 12%	Discounted income stream
(1)	(2)	(3)	(4) (2 × 3)
1	10	0.8929	8.9290
2	12	0.7972	9.5665
3	12	0.7118	8.5416
4	11	0.6335	6.9685
5	10	0.5674	5.674
		Total	Rs 36.67 million

This approach is more realistic, but one drawback herein is the projecting of income stream for long time periods. Risk associated with the income stream increases and the probability

---

[*] Refer to the section on discounting in Chapter 3.

of realising the income stream decreases with the increase in time period. Moreover, this approach is useful to investors who would be interested in the hotel property for the lifetime. This approach assumes that the land alone will have value towards the end of the life of the hotel property or facility.

The problem of unduly long periods can be resolved by the third method, *discounting the property's income over the investment period*. This approach considers the investment period and not the economic life of the hotel property. While this approach does not consider long time periods, it does take into account the expected sales value at the end of the investment period. The sales price can be considered by assuming the present value of the remaining years at the time of sale. For example, if the economic life of a hotel property is estimated as 20 years and the property is expected to be sold at the end of year 7, then the sale value would be the present value of the future income streams from year 8 to year 20. Again the overall capitalization rate is used to discount the income streams generated in the future.

To conclude, we can say that the income capitalization approach generally provides the most conclusive and supportable conclusions when valuing a hotel facility. Experts suggest that using a 10-year forecast and an equity yield rate to discount the income stream most accurately reflects the actions of typical hotel buyers, who purchase properties based on their leveraged discounted cash flow.

Sales Comparison Approach

The sales comparison approach is based on the comparison of the sales value of the property under consideration with the value (sales) of similar properties that have been sold in the recent past. This approach would be helpful only when certain adjustments are considered, such as the difference in the sales prices due to factors such as location, physical state during the time of sale, terms and conditions of the sale, etc. The following steps summarise this approach to value hotels.

The first step is to collect information with respect to several comparable properties that have been sold in the recent past including details such as the sales price, terms of financing, etc. The second step calls for collection of other details such as the date of sale, size and number of rooms, guest amenities, age of facility, etc. The third step is to adjust the sales price to account for differences between the property or the facilities that ought to be compared. Finally, the appraisal value is calculated by establishing an average price per room and multiplying it with the number of rooms. Hotel investors are interested in the information contained in the sales comparison approach. However, this method is not necessarily employed to arrive at any conclusion. Factors such as the lack of recent sales data, the numerous insupportable adjustments that are necessary, and the general inability to determine the true financial terms and human motivations of comparable transactions often make the results of this technique unreliable and questionable. Nonetheless, the sales comparison approach is most useful in providing a range of values indicated by prior sales and in establishing an indicator of movement and direction of prices. Over reliance on this method beyond the establishment of broad parameters is not justified. The market-derived capitalization rates sometimes used by appraisers are susceptible to the same shortcomings inherent in the sales comparison approach.

Cost Approach

This approach considers the cost incurred to rebuild a property in the present condition. However, the cost of land is ascertained distinctly. The key issue in valuation using this method is the cost of reproducing the existing hotel facility. The amount of depreciation is deducted from the cost of reproduction to arrive at the net reproduction cost. The cost of land is ascertained based on the sales comparison approach. The value of the furniture, fixtures, and equipments is determined and depreciated by 90 per cent. In other words, the value of furniture, fixtures, and equipment is only 10 per cent. The cost of the reproducing the hotel can be ascertained by considering the original cost and multiplying it with appropriate value of inflation. The next and the most crucial step is to calculate the amount of depreciation. Ascertaining depreciation is important from an appraisal point of view to reflect economic conditions during the time of sale. The accrued depreciation is then deducted from the reproduction cost to arrive at the appraised value. The cost approach provides a reliable estimate of value in the case of new properties, but as buildings and other improvements grow older and begin to deteriorate, it becomes increasingly difficult to quantify the loss in value. Most hotel buyers would prefer to base their purchase decisions on economic factors such as projected net income and return on investment. The cost approach does not reflect these income-related considerations and requires a number of highly subjective estimates and hence this approach is given minimal weight in the hotel valuation process. However, it is useful in establishing a benchmark for buy versus build decisions and for relative pricing over time.

SUMMARY

- The definition of value varies with the context of valuation. There are many connotations of value but this chapter focuses on the 'market value'.
- Three major approaches to hotel valuation are the cost, the sales comparison, and the income capitalization approach.
- There are many methods of applying the capitalization rate to the income stream. On one hand, the stabilized year's income is divided by the band of investment, while on the other hand, 20 to 30 years of future income is discounted to determine the market value.

KEY TERMS

Appraiser A person who deals with the determining the value of a hotel property.

Cost approach An approach to value hotels based on the cost incurred.

Income capitalization approach A method used for valuing hotel property. It focuses on the future income generating capabilities of the hotel.

Market value The price that buyers and sellers mutually agree upon during negotiations without any pressure.

Sales comparison approach A method used to value hotel property, which provides a range of sales figures.

Valuation process The process of ascertaining the exact market value of a property.

REVIEW QUESTIONS

1. State different approaches to hotel valuation.
2. Write a note on income capitalization approach.
3. Explain the cost approach to value hotel properties.

CRITICAL THINKING QUESTIONS

1. In your opinion, which is the best approach to value hotel real estate?
2. Discuss why the income capitalization approach is preferred for appraising hospitality real estate.

PROJECT WORK

Talk to hotel consultants and find out the most widely used approach to value hotel real estate in India.

Risk in the Hospitality Industry

> *If we don't succeed we run the risk of failure.*
>
> **Dan Quayle**

Learning Objectives

After studying this chapter, you will be able to

➢ Understand the meaning of the term return
➢ Understand the meaning of the term risk
➢ Appreciate alternatives to measure risk
➢ Examine the trade-off between risk and return

INTRODUCTION

The value of any investment is affected by two factors: *risk* and *return*. We begin our discussion with the premise that individuals prefer higher return and lower risk. Therefore, all other things being constant, people demand higher return for higher risk. It is necessary that we understand the interlocking between the concept of risk and return. We shall explore the following dimensions in this chapter.

Risk analysis can be simple if the following aspects are kept in mind before exploring the risk associated with an asset or portfolio:

• The first and foremost characteristic is that the risk associated with an asset is measured with its ability to generate cash flows, since all assets are expected to produce cash flows.

- Stand-alone risk refers to the risk associated with one asset only, whereas portfolio risk refers to the risk associated with a combination of assets (portfolio).
- An asset with a higher degree of risk must provide a relatively higher level of expected return to be attractive to the investors. Investors are risk averse and will not invest in assets that are risky unless and until the assets provide enough to compensate for the risk.
- The concepts discussed in this chapter are applicable to financial assets such as shares, debentures, etc. and also to physical assets. The return and risk associated with a single asset is examined first.

RETURN

Every individual or business spends money with the sole objective of earning money in the future. The concept of return is a measure to express financial performance of an asset or an investment. One approach is to take a look at the absolute return that is provided by an investment. For instance, you may buy shares worth Rs 10,000 and at the end of year, sell the same for Rs 11,000. The gain in this transaction is Rs 1000. In other words, it is the amount received *minus* the amount invested. If you decide to sell the stock at Rs 9000, your return, in terms of currency value, would have been Rs 1000. This is a crude method of determining return because, for a meaningful assessment, it is necessary to ascertain the scale of investment. For instance, Rs 1000 in return for Rs 1000 is very good indeed, but Rs 10 for Rs 1000 would be considered a poor return. It is also necessary to know the duration of the investment. In the preceding example, Rs 1000 on Rs 1000 at the end of one year is very lucrative, but the same return in 10 years may not be good at all.

How do we resolve the problem of expressing both aspects of quantum and time? The solution lies simply in expressing return as a percentage of the total investment for a year. Therefore, when you receive Rs 100 for an investment of Rs 1000, the rate of return would be calculated as follows:

Amount received – Amount invested/Amount invested

In the above example, 100/1000 signifies a return of 10 per cent.

By using percentage, it is possible to standardize the return. This also helps in comparing the investment with different initial investments. By expressing return annually, we are also able to take into consideration the period of the investment. Although we have used simple examples, the illustrations can be extended to multiple cash inflows and outflows.

RISK

While it is very easy to define and quantify return, it is extremely difficult to quantify and measure risk. Risk is normally defined as a hazard or peril, exposure to loss or injury. Going by the above definition, we know that risk refers to the probability of an unfavourable occurrence. Scuba diving is risky because you risk losing your life. Gambling is risky because you are risking your money. Therefore, risk can be understood as the exposure to a potential hazard involved in any activity (in our case, investment).

The risk involved in investment (asset) can be viewed from two angles:

- *Stand-alone basis* In this case, the asset is considered in isolation. In other words, it is the risk the investor would face as regards to this particular asset only.
- *Portfolio* This considers the risk of many assets held in one basket.

Let us understand the risk in the context of assets. Suppose an investor deposits Rs 1,00,000 in a bank at 9 per cent per annum. We can consider this investment to be to be risk-free, as there is very little risk involved in bank deposits. Suppose he decides to invest in shares of a company, another avenue that gives him 20 per cent interest, there is, however, a possibility of him losing the money.

Investments will be attractive only if the expected rate of return is high enough to compensate the investor for the perceived risk of investment. Assets that are risky seldom produce results. Risky assets are characterized by disproportionate returns as compared to expected returns. If the returns are as expected, then they shall no longer be called risky assets.

MEASUREMENT OF RISK

The risk associated with a single asset is measured using a behavioural and statistical tool. The behavioural point of view can be ascertained using sensitivity analysis and probability distribution, whereas standard deviation and coefficient of variation are some of the statistical techniques used for analysing risk.

Sensitivity Analysis

Sensitivity analysis takes into account a number of possible outcomes/return estimates while evaluating an asset, or while assessing the risk involved in investment in an asset. In order to have variability among return estimates, a possible approach is used to estimate the worst (pessimistic), the most likely (expected), and the best outcomes. Let us look at the example in Table 14.1.

Table 14.1   Sensitivity analysis

Particulars	Asset X	Asset Y
Initial outlay (TO)	50	50
Annual return per cent		
Pessimistic	14	8
Expected (most likely)	16	16
Optimistic	18	24
Range (optimistic *minus* pessimistic)	4	16

On the basis of the above return characteristics, it is evident that asset Y is more risky. Though the sensitivity analysis provides a range, it still remains a crude method of calculating risk.

Probability Distribution

The risk associated with an asset can be assessed with precision using a probability distribution. The *probability* of an event represents the likelihood or chance of its occurrence. For example, if the expectation is that a given outcome will happen at all times, the probability of its occurrence is 100 per cent. On the other hand, an outcome that will never happen is said to have a probability of zero.

Depending on the probabilities assigned, it is possible to ascertain the expected value of the return to be computed. The *expected rate of return* is the weighted average of all the possible returns multiplied by their respective probabilities. Thus, the probabilities of various outcomes are used as weights.

Ki = return for the *ith* possible outcome

Pri = probability associated with its return

n = number of outcomes

Table 14.2 illustrates the expected rates of return.

Table 14.2   Actual and expected rate of return

Possible outcomes	Probabilities	Returns (%)	Expected returns
Asset X			
Worst (pessimistic)	0.20	14	2.8
Moderate (normal)	0.60	16	9.6
Optimistic (best)	0.20	18	3.6
Asset Y			
Worst (pessimistic)	0.20	8	1.6
Moderate (normal)	0.60	16	9.6
Optimistic (best)	0.20	24	4.8

In this case, both the assets produce the same expected rate of return.

Standard Deviation of Return

Standard deviation is the most commonly and widely used measure of risk for an asset. It is calculated as shown in Table 14.3.

Table 14.3   Calculating standard deviation

I	E	Mean	E-mean	$(K - K)^2$	Pri	$(K - K) \times Pr$
1	14	16	(−2)	4	0.20	0.80
2	16	16	0	0	0.60	0
3	18	16	2	2	0.20	0.20
						1.6

The greater the standard deviation of return, the greater would be the variability/dispersion of return, and the greater the risk of asset/investment. Standard deviation is an absolute measure of deviation and does not consider variability of return in relation to the expected value.

Risk and Return Trade-off

In the earlier sections, we have discussed some of the important characteristics of risk and return. Risk can be reduced by using a proper spread and through proper diversification. Risk has two dimensions: (i) systematic risk, and (ii) unsystematic risk. *Systematic risk* is the fallout of risk factors that affect the overall market. No investor can claim to be free from systematic risk. *Unsystematic risk* is unique to a particular industry. Investors can reduce or eliminate unsystematic risk.

CONCLUSION

Risk is an important aspect in the area of finance. It is defined as the probability of occurrence of an unfavourable event. We can ascertain risk associated with an individual asset and a portfolio (combination of assets). Rational investors believe that by holding a portfolio of assets, they would be able to reduce the overall risk.

SUMMARY

- Return can be measured in two terms: absolute and relative.
- Risk refers to the variability of expected returns associated with a given security or an asset.
- Risk has two dimensions—stand-alone risk and risk associated with a portfolio.
- Sensitivity analysis and probability distribution explain the behavioural point of risk, whereas standard deviation and co-efficient of correlation present a statistical analysis of risk.

KEY TERMS

Co-efficient of variation A relative measure of dispersion pertaining to standard deviation.

Probability The chance of an event happening. Probability is always expressed between 0 and 1. The chance of an event always happening is 1, whereas the chance of something not happening is zero.

Return The financial consideration for investing in an asset. Return is measured in terms of per cent per annum.

Risk Peril or hazard associated with any investment.

Standard deviation A measure used to determine variance from the mean. It is a reliable measure of dispersion.

REVIEW QUESTIONS

1. Explain the concept of risk and return.
2. What is the relationship between risk and return?
3. What are the different methods available to assess risk?
4. State the terms systematic and unsystematic risk.

CRITICAL REVIEW QUESTIONS

1. Holding a portfolio of assets reduces the overall risk. Comment.
2. Discuss the methods available to the investors for assessing the risk involved in an asset in hotel operations.
3. Elucidate the relationship between standard deviation and project risk.

PROJECT WORK

Refer to reports (such as the HVS International) and list the risks associated with the hotel business in India.

The Financial System

> *Any informed borrower is simply less vulnerable of fraud and abuse.*
> **Alan Greenspan**

Learning Objectives

After studying this chapter, you will be able to

➢ Understand the meaning and importance of the financial system in an economy
➢ Understand the functions of financial markets
➢ Understand the importance and functions of securities market

INTRODUCTION

Modern economies are based on sound financial systems that help in economic growth by mobilizing funds to the productive sectors like the manufacturing, service, and trade from the household and other segments. The financial system encompasses both credit and cash transactions. A financial system, therefore, is a set of institutions that helps in mobilizing funds from segments that generate surplus of funds and transfers them to other segments that are in need of the funds. The financial system consists of a gamut of financial institutions such as banks, stock exchanges, intermediaries, and other range of financial instruments. Various factors influence the growth and development of the financial market. The prime factors are level of savings in the economy, the taxation policy, the industrial development, the development in the economy, etc. The GDP (gross domestic product) determines the strength and growth of the economy. Recall from Chapter 5 that the forms of financing include using the internal resources and also borrowings (debt financing). The growth in financial performance of companies has led to the high amount of popularity for equity investments.

In order to gain a better understanding of the financial markets, we must understand the functions of the financial markets. A good financial system carries out

- Banking functions
- Agency functions and is the custodian of cash reserves
- Management of international currency reserves
- Control of credit within the economy
- Administration of national, fiscal, and monetary policies
- Maintenance of liquidity
- Supply and deployment of funds for productive usage

FINANCIAL SYSTEM: ORGANIZATION AND STRUCTURE

The financial system is organized into various components such as financial markets and market participants and instruments.

Financial Markets

Financial markets ensure that the resources are transferred from the areas having surplus funds to areas that have pressing requirements for funds. In other words, financial markets channel savings to investments. Financial markets thereby provide a choice of assets to people who want to save. On the other hand, people who want funds for productive purposes are also provided with a lot a options by the financial markets. The growth of the economy depends to a large extent on the financial markets.

The money market and the capital markets are the two major components of the financial markets.

Money market

Money markets refer to transactions between lenders and borrowers of short-term funds. The instruments used for such borrowings have low default risk, maturity under one year, and high marketability.

Capital market

Markets that facilitate flow of financial investments that are direct or indirect claims to capital are referred to as capital markets and encapsulate all forms of lending and borrowings. The capital markets help in transferring securities that already exist with individuals.

The capital markets are an indicator of the performance of the economy. The policy of the government is also directed towards creation of wealth through products and services and the excess of funds is reinvested in the economy through the operations of capital markets.

Securities market

The securities market refers to a market condition where the financial instruments are generally transferable by sale. The securities market has two interdependent segments known as the primary (new or first time issue of securities) and the secondary (stock) market.

Primary market The primary market provides an opportunity to sell new securities, whereas the secondary market deals with securities already existing with the investors. In other words, the market wherein resources are channelized by companies through the issue of new securities is called the primary market. These resources are required for new projects, expansion, modernization, diversification, or to fulfil any other financial obligation.

Companies use the following methods to mobilise funds from the investors:

1. Initial public offer (securities issued for the first time to the public by the companies)
2. Further issue of capital
3. Rights issue to the existing shareholders (if the existing shareholders decline, then the shares are sold to others)
4. Allotment of securities to foreign partners, mutual funds, banks, overseas investors, employees, etc.
5. Bonus issue

The primary market is of great importance to the economy of any country because it ensures the flow of funds to entrepreneurs from investors. The strength of the economy is also gauged through the performance of the stock exchanges. The primary market is the basis for operations of the secondary market.

Secondary market   The secondary market facilitates the resale of securities. This helps in providing liquidity to the individuals who have invested in the primary markets. The price of securities in the secondary markets is an indicator of the risk and return profile of the issuer and it benefits the primary market in allocation of the funds. The secondary market comprises of the stock exchanges that provide for the sale and purchase of securities. It is important to note that trading is confined to the stock exchanges only.

The stock exchange ensures free marketability and liquidity to all the investors. The stock exchange is therefore referred to as the nerve centre of the capital markets. The secondary market can further be divided into two components—*spot market* and *futures market*. The spot market is where securities are traded for immediate delivery and payment, and the future market refers to trading in securities settlement (delivery of securities and payment) in future.

MARKET PARTICIPANT AND INSTRUMENTS

Securities as defined by the Securities Contracts (Regulation) Act connote shares, scrips, stocks, bonds, debenture, debenture stock, or other marketable securities, government securities, derivatives of securities, units of collective investment schemes, security receipts, interest and rights in securities, and any other instrument so declared by the central government. From the above definition, it is clear that the securities are a complex range of financial products and a key to savings and investment within an economy. There are some segments of the economy that demand securities against payment of funds, and other segments that require funds against securities.

It is virtually impossible to make a precise match of the requirements of the people who demand securities to the conditions of the people who require funds. For example, the amount of funds available with the supplier of the funds may not be equal to the amount of funds required by the supplier of securities. Similarly, other characteristics such as the risk, liquidity, and maturity characteristics may not match the preference of the supplier of funds. A search for the exact buyers and sellers would entail phenomenal cost. This problem is resolved by intermediaries who establish a contact between the buyers (suppliers of funds against securities) and sellers (who require funds against securities). The intermediaries act as agents who aid in matching the requirements of both the parties. Smooth functioning of security markets depends upon the services provided by the intermediaries, such as merchant bankers and brokers, in bringing together the buyers and sellers for a variety of transactions. While the intermediaries carry out the important task of bringing the parties together, the onus of risk falls on the transacting parties and not on the intermediaries.

The securities market has three categories of participants—the issuers of securities, the investors in securities, and the intermediaries. The issuers of securities and the individuals who invest in the securities need a reassurance regarding the safety of their respective interests. This reassurance is provided by a legislation often enforced by a regulatory authority. It is the duty of the regulator to develop fair market practices, regulate the proceedings in the market, and thereby ensure transparency in the transactions.

ROLE OF THE SECURITIES MARKET

Individuals are able to drive their rupee an extra mile due to the presence of securities market. It also helps entrepreneurs convert their dreams to reality. In formal terms, savings are mobilized through securities into preferred enterprise.

The securities market also enables the repurchase and resale of securities, thereby ensuring the transferability of securities of joint stock companies. The securities market conforms to the need of the entrepreneurs for capital and the investors' require-ment of liquidity. The securities markets encourage savings by providing a range of investment options with lucrative returns and thereby help in sharing wealth. The securities markets also help in diversify risk among many business ventures and thereby ensure longer tenure and overall success of business activities.

Economic Growth

Numerous studies have shown a robust relationship between development of securities market and economic development. Moreover, the securities markets support the quantities of savings and capital formation at all levels, increase capital inflow across borders, raise the productivity of investment by improving resource allocation, and optimize cost of capital. Therefore, it is logical to expect savings and formation of capital to be in tandem to each other.

Internationalization

The securities markets connect an economy to the rest of the world and facilitate internationalization to a large extent. There is flow of investments across borders in the form of portfolio investments. Furthermore, a strong domestic stock market forms the basis for well-performing domestic business enterprises to mobilize funds from foreign capital markets. This means that the domestic economy has to face challenges from international competitive pressures. This will ensure competitive returns to the domestic investors.

Range of Investment Opportunities and Associated Costs

An organized securities market is the basic requirement for a competitive financial sector that promotes incremental and more innovative measures of financing. This increases opportunities for specialization and reduces costs of financial activities. The securities markets along with other components ensure optimum cost of capital.

Optimum Allocation

Economic development is achievable only when the investment opportunities are well segregated. Many experts argue that distribution is the key to economic development. Huge difference in returns hampers the process of capital formation and does not contribute to development. A developed capital market monitors the efficiency of the deployment of capital stock.

THE INDIAN FINANCIAL SYSTEM

In this section, we take a closer look at the Indian financial markets. We shall discuss the components of the banking sector, the money markets, and the capital markets to get a perspective of the overall financial sector.

Beginning from the nationalization of banks in 1969, the Indian financial system has undergone a complete metamorphosis. The last few decades have experienced a significant expansion in the activities of development financial institutions (DFIs). The role of the DFIs is certainly commendable in providing medium and long-term financial assistance to the industrial sector. The DFIs also have a major share in financing corporate business houses. The DFIs have their nominees on the boards of the companies, and they also provide guidance and assistance in management and deployment of financial resources. Overall, the growth in the Indian banking sector has been noteworthy in the past few decades.

The Indian money market consists of the Reserve Bank of India (RBI), various commercial banks, and co-operative banks, etc. that form a part of the formal money market. On the other hand, chit funds, *nidhis*, commercial bills, and certificates of deposits form a part of the informal money market. Indian money markets have also seen an upward trend with the current monetary and trade policies across the globe. Post liberalization, the demand for capital mobilization has increased tremendously, which has given rise to many innovation and reforms.

The Indian capital market consists of individual investors, mutual funds, banks, companies, financial institutions, etc. This section requires the services of various intermediaries such as merchant bankers, brokers, stock exchanges, etc. Like any economy, the investors in India also require information about the various investment avenues and institutions before actually making an investment. The investors are also expected to be aware of the basic regulatory provisions applicable to the investments and institutions. The investors generally choose investments based on various factors such as safety, liquidity, and return on the investment.

Securities Market

The past decade has seen exponential growth in securities market with respect to the amount of money raised from the market, the number of listed companies on the stock exchanges, volume of trade, and investor population. The market also has experienced changes in transaction costs, efficiency, transparency, and safety of investment avenues.

SUMMARY

- The financial system, comprising of a variety of institutions, markets, and instruments related in a systematic manner, provides the principal means for transformation of savings into investments.
- Financial assets represent claims against future income and wealth of others. A financial liability—the counterpart of financial assets—represents promises to pay some portion of wealth to others.
- A financial market is a market for creation and exchange of financial assets. Financial markets facilitate price discovery, provide liquidity, and reduce cost of transactions.
- Securities market aid in buying and selling of securities.

KEY TERMS

Financial markets A mechanism that aids trading of financial instruments.

GDP (gross domestic product) A sum total of all goods and services produced in an economy, and indicator for the growth of the economy.

REVIEW QUESTIONS

1. What are the functions of the financial system?
2. State the divisions of the financial markets.
3. Explain the functions of financial markets.
4. Write a note on primary and secondary markets.
5. Write a note on the evolution, growth, and functions of financial system in India.

CRITICAL THINKING QUESTIONS

1. Discuss the growth and trends in the Indian financial system.
2. Discuss the impact of the financial sector reforms on the financial system in India.

PROJECT WORK

Scan through financial dailies (*The Economic Times, Business Standard,* etc.) and list down the important developments in the financial system.

Sources of Long-term Finance

> *Gentlemen prefer bonds.*
>
> **Andrew Mellon**

Learning Objectives

After studying this chapter, you will be able to

➢ Understand the meaning of the term 'Capital'

➢ Understand the meaning of 'Debt' and 'Equity'

➢ Examine different classes of 'Shares' and 'Debentures'

INTRODUCTION

Can you identify the similarity between the Leela Palace at Bangalore and the Taj Mahal Palace and Towers at Mumbai. Both are luxury hotels. Suppose you decide to form a hotel company immediately after graduation and want to build a hotel of a similar magnitude. You will definitely require a large investment before the dream project turns into reality. In Chapter 15, we have seen the importance the importance of capital markets in aiding hotels to raise capital. In this Chapter, we shall see broad sources of raising long-term finance to augment hotel operations.

Let us commence with the fundamental sources. Debt and equity are two major sources of capital for your company. Debt (loans) consists of term loans, debentures, and short-term borrowings, whereas equity refers to the shareholders funds. The fundamental difference between debt and equity are as follows:

1. Equity investors have a claim on the cash flows after paying all claims and liabilities, whereas the company is bound by a contractual agreement to pay the investors. Debt investors are entitled to a set of cash flows (principal and interest).

2. Interest paid to debt investors is a tax deductible expense, whereas the dividends are paid after settlement of all claims of the stakeholders.

This chapter discusses the following:

- Equity capital
- Preference capital
- Debentures

MEANING OF CAPITAL

The term 'capital' has variety of meanings in different contexts. In the hotel industry, it means the money to meet the requirements such as property and inventory. The phrase 'loan or borrowed capital' is sometimes used to mean money borrowed by the company and secured by issuing debentures. This, however, is not the proper use of the word capital.

In relation to a company limited by shares, capital means the share capital, that is, the capital in terms of rupees divided into specified number of shares of a fixed amount each. We also use it in the same sense as 'share capital' or the money raised by issue of shares by a company limited by shares.

Share capital is not an essential clause for the formation of a company under the Companies Act, but where the memorandum provides for share capital, it is synonymous with the term capital and the memorandum must state the amount of capital and its division into various types, denominations, and value of shares. Companies limited by guarantee or unlimited companies or companies under Section 25 need not have share capital.

Capital—A Different Connotation

As mentioned earlier, there are many aspects of the term capital. In this section we take a closer look at the term capital.

Nominal, authorized, or registered capital   This is the total amount stated in the memorandum of association of a company limited by shares as the capital of the company. This is the amount committed during the initial stages of formation (incorporation) of the company. This is the maximum amount that the company is authorized to raise by issuing shares. It is also known as the registered capital, as it is registered with this amount. The company has to pay an additional fees with the increase in the share capital. This share capital is divided into shares of uniform denominations. The amount of nominal capital is ascertained according to the projections of fund requirements of the company for its business activities.

Issued capital   This is a segment of the authorized or nominal capital that the company issues for the time being for the public to subscribe. This is computed at the face or nominal value.

Subscribed capital   It is the portion of the issued capital at face value that has been subscribed for or taken up by the subscribers of shares in the company. It must be noted that the entire issued capital may or may not be subscribed.

Called-up capital   It is that portion of the subscribed capital which has been called up or demanded on the shares by the company. For example, where Rs 8 has been called up on each of 4,00,000 shares of a nominal value of Rs 10, the called-up capital is Rs 32,00,000.

Uncalled capital   It is the total amount not called up or demanded by the company on the shares subscribed as on a particular date. However, the shareholders are liable to pay as and when called. Note in the above example that the uncalled capital would be Rs 8,00,000.

Paid-up capital   It is the part of the total called-up amount that is actually paid by the shareholder.

Unpaid capital   It is the total of the called-up capital remaining unpaid. In other words, it is the difference between called-up and paid-up capital.

Reserve capital It is that part of the uncalled capital of a company which the limited company has decided by a special resolution, in accordance with Companies Act 1956, not to call except in the event and for the purpose of the company being wound up. Note that reserve capital should not be confused with capital reserve, which is created out of profits.

Capital reserve Capital reserve is created of profits or earnings that are not ordinarily distributable among shareholders of the company as opposed to revenue reserve which is free for distribution to members. Non-statutory capital reserve may arise in many ways; for example, where a fund is set aside out of the profits to replace assets that are wearing out, such as equipment and other assets for hotel companies, or where the reserve is created out of profits made on sale or revaluation of assets. Reserve created after revaluation of assets is also known as capital reserve.

Capital assets These assets constitute fixed capital and circulating or working capital. Fixed capital assets comprises of assets acquired for retention and use, for example, land and buildings, food and beverage equipment, etc.

Preference and equity share capital The share capital of a public company including hotel companies, consists of only two kinds of shares—preference shares and equity shares. According to the Companies (Issue of Share Capital with Differential Voting Rights) Rules, 2001, which has come into force on 9 March 2001, equity share capital may be with similar rights or with different rights as to dividend, voting, or otherwise. A preference share, on the other hand, has a preference in regard to payment of dividend and preferential right of the repayment of capital in the event of winding up of company. The payment of dividend on preference shares may be cumulative or non-cumulative. Equity shareholders have the last claim on divisible profits after the commitment to the preference shareholders.

Debenture capital It is the money raised by a company by the issue of debentures. This is a borrowing and not capital as far as the meaning of the term capital is concerned. It is the money borrowed and so is a debt due to the creditors.

KINDS OF SHARES

Companies Act 1956 permits a company limited by shares to issue two classes of shares, namely

- Equity share capital
- Preference share capital

Equity Shares

We have seen in the earlier section that companies are permitted to issue a variety of equity shares with differential rights and so on to meet the requirements of investors. Due to certain amendments in the regulatory process in the recent past, companies are also permitted to issue shares with differential rights. Here the law makes a distinction between differential rights and disproportionate rights. While companies are permitted to issue equity shares with differential rights with respect to dividend, voting, or otherwise in accordance with the legislation, they are not permitted to issue shares with disproportionate rights.

According to the Companies Act, 'equity share capital refers to all share capital which is not preference share capital'. Thus, a share or share capital that does not qualify as preference share capital is equity (ordinary) share capital. Equity shareholders receive dividends out of profits as recommended by the company and as declared by the shareholders in an annual general meeting, after due consideration to depreciation and after dividend on preference shares has been paid.

The principal advantages obtaining finance through this source is that there is no compulsion on payment of dividends. If the company does have sufficient cash flow, then it can skip the payment of dividends without any legal complications. Equity shares are not bound by any maturity period and the company does not have any obligation to redeem (payback) amount raised through equity shares. The amount of equity share capital enhances the creditworthiness of the company.

The disadvantage associated with this source is that the sale of equity shares to outsiders dilutes control of the existing owners. Moreover, the cost of equity capital is usually the highest. The investors also assume a greater amount of risk and therefore demand a larger amount of return. Finally, the expenses such as underwriting commission and brokerage costs associated with issuing equity shares is generally higher than the cost of issuing other types of securities.

Sweat Equity Shares

Sweat equity shares are equity shares given to the company's employees in recognition of their work. As per the legislation, companies are permitted to issue sweat equity shares pertaining to a class of shares already issued. A company may proceed with the issue of sweat equity shares if the issue is authorized by a special resolution passed by the company in the general meeting. The resolution specifies the number of shares, current market price, consideration, if any, and the class or classes of directors or employees to whom such equity shares are to be issued.

The conditions for sweat equity issue are

- As on the date of the issue, not less than one year has elapsed since the company was entitled to commerce business.
- The sweat equity shares of a company whose equity shares are listed on a recognized stock exchange are issued in accordance with the regulations made by the Securities and Exchange Board of India in this behalf.
- Provided that in case of a company whose equity shares are not listed on any recognized stock exchange, the sweat equity shares are issued in accordance with the prescribed guidelines by the legislation.

Preference Shares or Preference Share Capital

The Companies Act provides that a preference share or preference share capital is that part of share capital which should fulfil the following requirements:

- It must carry a preferential right to a fixed amount or an amount calculated at a fixed rate, which may be either free of or subject to income tax as regards to payment of dividends.

- On a company being wound up or during the re-payment of capital, it has a preferential right to be repaid the initial amount of the capital.

Types of preference shares

Preference shares may be of the following types:

Participating or non-participating Participating preference shares are those shares that are entitled to a fixed preferential dividend. They carry a right to participate in the surplus profits, along with equity shareholders, after payments of dividends to equity shareholders. For example, after 25 per cent dividend has been paid to equity shareholders, the preference shareholders may share the surplus profit equally with equity shareholders out of the remaining amount. In the event of winding up, if after paying back both the preference and equity shareholders, any surplus is distributed to the preference shareholders. Preference shareholders get only the fixed preferential dividend and nothing more unless explicitly provided. The right to participate may be given either in the memorandum or the articles of association or by virtue of their terms of issue.

Cumulative and non-cumulative shares Preference shares may be cumulative or non-cumulative as far as the payment of dividends is concerned. A cumulative preference shareholder is entitled to claim fixed dividend of the past and the current year(s) and out of future profits. The preference shareholder keeps accumulating dividend till such time it is fully paid. The company is obliged to pay the non-cumulative preference shareholder a fixed amount or a fixed percentage of dividend out of the profits of each year. If no profits are available in any year, then the shareholders are not entitled to get dividends nor can they claim any unpaid dividend in any subsequent year.

Preference shares are cumulative unless explicitly stated to be non-cumulative. Dividends on preference shares, like equity shares, can be paid only out of profits.

Redeemable and irredeemable preference shares Subject to an authority in the articles of association, a public limited company may issue redeemable preference shares to be redeemed either at a fixed date or after a certain period of time during the lifetime of the company, provided the company complies to certain conditions such as provision in the articles of association, profits available for dividends, etc.

PREFERENCE SHARES COMPARED WITH EQUITY SHARES

Preference shares are more like debentures as compared to equity shares. Preference shareholders are entitled to a fixed rate of dividend like the interest payable at a fixed rate on debentures issued by companies.

The rate of dividend on equity shares depends upon the amount of profit available and the funds requirements of the company for future expansion, etc. Dividend on the preference shares is paid in preference to the equity shares. In other words, the dividend on equity shares is paid only after the preference dividend has been paid.

The preference shares have preference to equity shares with regard to the payment of capital on winding up. If the preference shares are cumulative, the dividend not paid in any year are accumulated and until such arrears of dividend are paid, the other equity shareholders are not paid any dividend.

Redeemable preference shares may be redeemed by the company but equity shares cannot be redeemed except under a scheme involving reduction of capital or buyback of its own shares.

The voting rights of preference shareholders are restricted. An equity shareholder can vote on all matters affecting the company, but a preference shareholder can vote only when his special rights as a preference shareholder are being varied or their dividend is in arrears. A company may issue rights shares or bonus shares to the company's existing equity shareholders, but this is not so in case of preference shareholders.

DEBENTURES

A debenture is a document given by a company under its seal as an evidence of a debt to the holder, usually arising out of a loan and most commonly secured by a charge. A debenture is a document that either creates a debt or acknowledges debt. It does not carry any voting rights at any general meeting of the company. The term 'debenture' has been defined in Section 2(12) of the Companies Act to include debenture stock, bonds, and any other securities of a company, whether constituting a charge on the assets of the company or not. The conditions regarding transfer and mode of repayment of the principal amount are mentioned in the debentures. Section 82 of the Act provides that debentures, alongwith shares, in a company shall be a movable property transferable in the manner provided by the articles of the company.

The following kinds of documents have been held to be debentures: a legal mortgage of freehold and leasehold land,a series of income-bonds by which a loan to the company was repayable only out of its profits, a note by which a company undertook to pay a loan but gave no security, and a receipt or a certificate for a deposit made with a company (other than a bank) when the deposit was repayable after a fixed period after it was made. The point to be noted as regards the definition of debenture is that it is so wide as to include any security of a company, whether constituting a charge on the company's assets or not. The Department of Company Affairs has clarified that a fixed deposit receipt may be regarded as a security but not as a debenture.

Characteristics of Debentures

The usual features of a debenture are as follows:

- A debenture is usually in the form of a certificate (like a share certificate), issued under the common seal of the company. The company acknowledges the indebtness to the holder through a debenture certificate.
- A debenture usually provides for the payment of a specified principal sum at a specified date. But that is not essential. A company may issue perpetual or irredeemable debentures with no undertaking to pay. A debenture usually provides for payment of interest until the principal sum is paid back.

- A debenture generally contains a charge on a undertaking of the company, or on some class of its assets or on some part of its profits. However, this is not an essential element and a debenture that creates no such charge is perfectly valid.
- The debentures carry no voting rights at any meeting of the company.

Kinds of Debentures

Debentures may be of different kinds.

Redeemable debentures   Debentures are generally redeemable. In other words, they are issued on the terms that the company is bound to repay the amount of the debenture either on a fixed date on demand, after notice, or under a system of periodical drawings. However, redeemable debentures can be re-issued. This power is expressly given by the statute. The law provides that unless any contrary provision is contained in the articles or in the conditions of issue or unless there is a resolution showing an intention to cancel the redeemed debentures, the company has the power to re-issue the same debentures or issue other debentures instead.

Perpetual or irredeemable debentures   Irredeemable debenture is a debenture in which no time is fixed for the company to pay back the money, although the company may pay back at any time it chooses.

Registered and bearer debentures   Registered debentures are marked to a particular person. The name of such a person appears on the debenture certificate, who is registered by the company as holder of debentures on the register of debenture holders. Such debentures are transferable in the same manner as shares—by means of a proper instrument of transfer duly stamped and executed and satisfying the other requirements specified in Section 108 of the Act. Bearer debentures, on the other hand, are made out to the bearer, and are negotiable instruments, and so transferable by mere delivery like share warrants. The person to whom a bearer debenture is transferred becomes a 'holder in due course', unless the contrary is shown, and is entitled to receive and recover the principal and the interest accrued thereon.

Secured and unsecured or naked debentures   Where debentures are secured by a mortgage or a charge on the property of the company, they are called secured debentures. Where they are not secured by any mortgage or charge on any property of the company, they are said to be naked or unsecured debentures.

Convertible debentures   Where the debentures are convertible, partly or wholly, into the shares of a company after a specified time, either as a result of exercise of option or in terms of the issue, they are called convertible debentures.

In this chapter, we have seen some of the important forms of raising long-term capital for hotel operations. The major sources discussed are equity shares, preference shares, and debentures. Equity share capital refers to ordinary share capital. Debentures are borrowings. Preference shareholders are given preferential treatment when the company makes a payment of dividends and at the time of winding up of the company.

SUMMARY

- Equity share capital represents ownership capital and its owners.
- The ordinary shares are entitled to some special features in terms of the rights and claims of their holders, such as the last claim on income and assets and the right to control limited liability.
- Share capital may be divided into equity shares with voting rights or with differential voting rights to dividends and preference capital.
- Companies may also issue sweat equity for a category of shares already issued.
- Preference shares are divided into participating and non-participating shares.
- Preference share capital involves high cost, does not dilute owners control of the company, has negligible risk, and does not impede managerial functions.

- Debentures represent indebtedness of the company towards the debenture holders. As compared to equity shares, debentures have some contrasting features as compared to equity shares.

KEY TERMS

Equity shares ordinary shares used as a mode to raise money.
Preference shares Preferential capital distributed as shares.
Debentures An instrument that allows companies to borrow money from the general public.
The Indian companies act The law governing companies in India.

REVIEW QUESTIONS

1. Explain the meaning of capital and the kinds of capital.
2. Explain the meaning of equity shares and preference shares.
3. State the differences between equity and preference shares.
4. State the meaning of the term 'debentures'.
5. State differences between equity and preference shares.

CRITICAL THINKING QUESTIONS

1. Equity shareholders provide risk capital. Comment
2. In your opinion, what is the best way for hotel companies to raise money for their business operations?

Franchising

Learning Objectives

After studying this chapter, you will be able to

- ➢ Understand the term franchising
- ➢ Review the importance of franchising as an important aspect of expansion
- ➢ Appreciate the franchise agreement and franchise fees.

INTRODUCTION

Hotel companies expand their scope of operations by building additional properties. Recall from Chapter 16 that the principal source of financing such expansion programmes is either issue of equity shares or additional borrowings. Since 1950s one more method came into existence known as franchising. This method is so popular that most of the well-known hotel and restaurant chains have made extensive and successful use of the franchising model of expansion. The world of franchising is growing exponentially every day. Most of us may not even realize that the businesses we support every day are part of a system of franchises. For example, in the morning you might pick up your daily coffee at a local Starbucks. For lunch you may choose to enjoy a sandwich or salad from McDonalds. On the way home from work, you drop off at a multiplex for a recent blockbuster, and for dinner you pick up a piping hot pizza from Pizza Hut. All of these businesses are a part of the franchisee system. We shall try and understand the basics of the franchising arrangement in this chapter.

While it is difficult to pinpoint the exact origin of the business of franchising, it is clear that this business model can into existence post-World War II.

Franchising is a business model that incorporates all the aspects of business—finance, management, and marketing. In this model the franchisee arranges for the cost of the franchised property that will be put to use in distributing the franchisors products. The management or the expertise is provided by the franchisor. The franchisor also provides the right to market products and/or services for a definite period of time as per mutually agreed terms. It is clear that there are two parties—the franchisor (one who owns the concept, e.g., McDonalds) and the franchisee (one who purchases the right to sell the concept). This business model has the advantage of higher levels of profitability combined with lower risk and therefore has been very popular for the reason that it enables individuals to have more profitable business.

TYPES OF FRANCHISES

Franchises may be classified according to the control exercised by the franchisor and also on the basis of the franchisee's right to expand business operations. Let us take a look at the different types of franchises.

- *Product franchises* These are the most prevalent with respect to sales units and numbers. The main purpose is to deliver a product to the ultimate consumer in various locations. Most of the soft drink companies provide franchises for bottling beverages as per geographic locations.
- *Format franchises* This is a common format followed by the commercial food service and lodging operations. The franchisor provides all the business requirements such as the brand, methods, and standards along with organiza-

tional and technical skills required to maintain efficient business operations. The franchisor exerts tremendous control over the franchisee to ensure uniformity in all the outlets.

- *Other types* The other classification of franchise on the basis of ability to expand operation is *single franchise* where the franchisee is with a single location. Many hotels and restaurant companies have the history of extending single franchise. On the other hand, *multi-unit franchise* is an outcome of the franchisor granting a territory for development. *Master franchise* is another arrangement where the franchisor provides a legal right to offer subfranchise. In other words, the franchisee can further appoint franchisees.

BENEFITS TO THE FRANCHISEE

The franchisor receives royalty and in return he provides the right to market products and services under a prescribed business format for a predetermined period to the franchisee. The other benefits of franchising can be enumerated as follows:

1. *Potentially viable business proposition* In most cases the business model is perfected by the franchisor in terms of the profitability and other operational parameters. The risk of failure in such cases in such a business is far lower as compared to new business venture.
2. *Operational assistance* The franchisee gets a complete set of operational systems including recipes, production systems, etc. Since the operational process and procedures are well defined, the franchisee receives the benefit of all the business.
3. *Financing assistance* Certain franchisors directly provide financial assistance to the franchisees. In all other cases, the name of the franchisor acts as a guarantee and influences banks and other financial institutions to lend financial assistance to the franchisee.
4. *Training and development* The franchisee is also trained by the franchisor before the commencement of business operations. Franchisors provide intensive pre-franchise

training to ensure that the franchisee understands the systems provided by the franchisor to deliver the required standards of product or service. Some franchisors also provide follow-up and continuous training and development to the franchisees to ensure the highest level of guest satisfaction.

5. *Market research* Most franchisors carry out extensive market research with respect to various aspects of the business. The franchisees can benefit from this research and do not need to carry out the exercise of market research.

6. *Demarcated territory* The franchisee often gets an area or territory to operate his business. The size of the area depends on the concept and the market. This also ensures that there is no undue competition.

ADVANTAGES AND DISADVANTAGES TO FRANCHISORS

The first advantage to the franchisor is the franchisee fees received from the franchisees. The second is that the business can grow more quickly, as the franchisor does not have to invest his resources directly in the expansion of the project. There are no mundane operational issues and the franchisor can concentrate on higher goals.

The disadvantage to franchisors is loss of control. As the business operations expands, it become exceedingly difficult to the franchisors to monitor the quality, of the products and services sold by their franchisees. Given this drawback, we do find that some hotel operations have grown at record pace while others have refrained from the franchising approach to expansion. The other disadvantage to the franchisor is the loss in terms of operating income. The franchisee pays only the franchisee fees, while the business has the potential to earn much more. Finally, there is always a chance of discord between the franchisor and the franchisee that could upset business relationship and future earning potential for both the parties.

FRANCHISE FEES AND AGREEMENT

In the earlier section, we have seen that the franchisee has to pay a particular amount to the franchisor. In addition, there could also be other fees, such as the initial fee during the set up of the business, royalty, and other fees as applicable.

The initial fee is generally paid to obtain the franchise rights and is paid at the commencement of the business. The royalty is paid continuously throughout the franchising period and covers all the services provided by the franchisors. Additionally, the franchisees also need to pay some other fees such as the advertising or marketing fees, as applicable.

The franchise document plays an important role in deciding the contractual relationship between the franchisor and the franchisee. It contains provisions as regards to the rights, duties, and responsibilities of both the contracting parties. It further contains details as regards to the term of the franchise. This clause specifies the tenure of the franchise relationship and expiry and renewal of the contract. The agreement also specifies the working hours and days in accordance with the local legislative provisions. The contracting parties mutually agree on other clauses such as training and development. Many franchise agreements prohibit the franchisees from operating similar kind of business in the same area for a particular time period.

We see that franchising has gained a lot of popularity and has proved to be a successful business model for some of the leading hotel and restaurant companies all around the globe. Franchising provides numerous advantages to both the franchising parties. The franchisees get a tested and proven business model that is high on return and comparatively low on risks. The franchisors, on the other hand, get a fixed amount as royalty and other fees. The franchisee agreement forms the basis for the contractual relationship between the franchisor and franchisee.

KEY TERMS

Franchising Franchising is a method where the product or business name is lent to the borrower.

Expansion Growth in the business plans.

Strategy Actions carried out with some specific reason or purpose.

CHAPTER REVIEW QUESTIONS

1. What is the importance of franchising in the hotel industry?
2. State the reasons for hotels and restaurants to franchise.
3. Write a note on franchising as a strategy.

CRITICAL THINKING QUESTIONS

1. Comment on the McDonald's model of franchising.
2. Would you opt to become a franchisee for a well-known brand or set up your own brand? State the reasons for your choice.

PROJECT WORK

Visit a McDonalds outlet and find out the benefits and disadvantages of opting to be a franchisee.

Leasing

> *Why pay a dollar for a bookmark? Why not use a dollar for book mark?*
> **Steven Spielberg**

INTRODUCTION

A lease is an arrangement where the lessor grants the lessee the right to use an asset in return for periodical rents. While leasing of land and buildings has been known from times immemorial, the leasing of hotel equipments is a recent phenomenon.

A hire-purchase involves the purchase of an asset on the understanding that the hirer (called the hirer) will pay in equal periodic installments, spread over a period of time. In essence, a hire-purchase represents debt financing in a different scenario.

Leasing and hire-purchase are additional sources of intermediate long-term finance. They are provided mainly by non-banking financial companies, financial institutions, and other organizations.

With the advent of mixed-use formats, hotels can now benefit by leasing additional space to retail agencies and can earn some additional revenue.

This chapter discusses various aspects of leasing, hire-purchase, and project finance.

The following aspects are covered in this chapter:

- Types of lease arrangements
- Mechanics of leasing
- Other considerations in leasing
- Hire-purchase arrangement

TYPES OF LEASE ARRANGEMENTS

The following are the different types of lease arrangements:

- Operating leases
- Financial leases
- Sale and leaseback
- Leveraged lease

Operating Leases

An operating lease or service lease has following features:

1. The lease period in a short-term lease is less than the useful life of the asset.
2. The lease rentals payable during the lease period are not adequate to cover fully the cost of the asset along with an acceptable return thereon.
3. The lease can usually be terminated at a short notice.
4. The lessor bears the cost for maintenance, insurance, and other incidental expenses.

Businesses interested in leasing their own products enter into a operating leases. Tea and coffee vending machines are examples of very commonly leased assets under operating lease arrangements. Though popular overseas, operating leases are not common in India.

Financial Leases

A financial lease or capital lease is essentially a form of borrowing. The salient characteristics of a financial lease are

1. It is an intermediate-term to a long-term arrangement that cannot be terminated. During the initial period,

referred to as the primary lease period, which is usually 3 years or 5 years or 8 years, the lease cannot be terminated.

2. The lessee is responsible for maintenance, insurance, and the incidental costs.
3. During this period, the lessor recovers, through the lease rentals, his investment in the equipment along with an acceptable rate of return.
4. The lessee has the option of renewing the lease rentals.

Sale and Leaseback

This is a special financial arrangement by which a firm sells an asset to another firm and, simultaneously, the two firms enter into a financial lease by which firm B leases the asset to firm A. As a result, the seller receives the purchase consideration for the asset and also retains the use of the asset in return for periodic lease payments. This avoids heavy outflow of each initially.

Leveraged Lease

Under a leveraged lease arrangement, the lessor borrows a portion of the purchase price of the asset from a lender (a commercial bank or a financial institution). The loan is secured against the asset and the lease payment. The lender is paid back from the lease payments, often directly by the lessee, while the surplus, after setting the claims of the lender, goes to the lessor. As an owner of the asset, the lessor is entitled to tax shelters associated with the ownership.

Leases in India are typically financial leases. Hence, subsequent discussion will focus on the aspects of financial leases.

MECHANICS OF LEASING

As a hotel manager evaluating the possibility of leasing, you should be familiar with the following:

- Legal aspects of leasing
- Typical contents of a lease agreement
- Income tax provisions related to leasing
- Sales tax provisions related to leasing

- Procedural aspects of leasing
- Accounting treatment of leases.

Legal Aspects of Leasing

There is no separate statute for equipment leasing in India, and the provisions relating to bailments in the Indian Contract Act cover equipment leasing agreements as well. Section 148 of the Indian Contract act defines bailment as 'The delivery of goods by one person to another, for some purpose, upon a contract that they shall, when the purpose is accomplished, be returned or otherwise disposed of according to the directions of the person delivering them.' The person delivering the goods is called the bailor, and the person to whom they are delivered is called the bailee.

Since an equipment lease transaction is regarded as a contract of bailment, the obligations of the lessor and the lessee are similar to those of the bailor and the bailee, as defined by the provisions of the Indian Contract Act. Essentially, these provisions have the following implications for the lessor and the lessee:

1. The lessee has the duty to pay the lease rentals, as specified in the lease agreement, to protect the lessor's title, to take reasonable care of the asset, and to return the leased asset on the expiry of the lease period.
2. The lessor is obliged to deliver the asset to the lessee, to legally empower the lessee to use the asset, and to leave the asset in possession of the lessee during the currency of the agreement without any disturbance.

Contents of a Lease Agreement

The lease agreement specifies the legal rights and obligations of the lessor and the lessee. It typically contains terms relating to the following:

1. Description of the lessor, the lessee, and the asset
2. Amount, time, and place of lease rental payments

3. Time and place of equipment delivery
4. Lessee's responsibility for maintenance, repairs, registration, etc., and the lessor's right in case of default by the lessee
5. Lessee's right to enjoy the benefits of the warranties provided by the equipment manufacturer/supplier
6. Insurance to be taken by the lessee on behalf of the lessor
7. Option of lease renewal for the lessee
8. Return of equipment on expiry of the lease period
9. Arbitration procedure in the event of dispute

Income Tax and Income Tax Leasing

The main income tax provisions relating to leasing are as follows:

1. The lessor can benefit from depreciation on the investment made in leased assets.
2. The lessee can claim lease rentals as tax-deducting expenses. In other words, lease rentals are deducted before calculating income tax.
3. The lease rentals received by the lessor are taxable under the head 'profits and gains of business profession' under the Income Tax Act 1961.

Sales Tax Provisions Related to Leasing

The major sales tax provisions for leasing are as follows:

1. The lessor does not get the benefit of concessional rate of central sales tax, since the asset is not meant for re-sale nor for use in manufacturing.
2. The 46th Amendment Act has brought lease transactions under the purview of sale and has empowered the central and state governments to levy sales tax on these transactions.

While the Central Sales Tax Act is yet to be amended in this respect, several state governments have amended their Sales Tax Act on lease transactions.

Lease Accounting

The accounting treatment of lease transactions in India is as follows:

1. Finance leases must be shown as assets in the books of the lessee. This means that (a) at the time of inception, the leased equipment is shown as an asset on the balance sheet of the lessee, its value is equated to the present value of the committed lease rentals, and the leased asset is associated with a corresponding liability called 'lease payable', (b) lease payments are split into two parts—finance charges and principal amount—and the finance charge is treated as an expense on the income statement and the principal amount is deducted from the liability 'lease payable', and (c) the leased asset is depreciated in the books of the lessee as per the depreciation policy followed.

2. Operating leases are a part of capital in the books of the lessor. While lease payments are treated as income of the lessor and expense of the lessee, the depreciation of leased assets should be on a basis consistent with the normal depreciation policy of the lessor for similar assets.

CONCLUSION

Leasing is a popular way to use assets without incurring a huge investment in the initial stages. Restaurants and food service operators lease rental spaces for business. With the real estate prices skyrocketing, leasing is the best way to use assets without incurring huge cash flows.

SUMMARY

- A lease represents a contractual agreement between the lessor, who grants the lessee the right to use an asset, and the lessee.
- Lease arrangements can be divided as operating lease and financial lease.
- A leasing decision is commonly a finance decision.

KEY TERMS

Financial lease A long-term lease that is completely amortized.

Lease agreement An agreement that specifies the legal obligations of the lessor and the lessee.

Lessee An individual or a firm who hires an asset.

Lessor An individual or a firm who leases an asset.

Operating lease A short-term lease that is not completely amortized.

REVIEW QUESTIONS

1. What do you understand by the term lease?
2. What do you mean by a lease agreement?
3. State different types of leases.

CRITICAL THINKING QUESTIONS

1. Compare and contrast operating lease with financial lease.
2. Discuss the legal aspects of leasing.
3. Discuss the principal income tax and sales tax provisions related to leasing in India.

PROJECT WORK

Make a list of items that you can lease, instead of buying, for hotel or restaurant operations.

Future Value of a Lump Sum

Future value interest factor of Re 1 per period at *i*% for *n* periods, *FVIF(i,n)*

Period	1%	2%	3%	4%	5%	6%	7%	8%	9%	10%
1	1.010	1.020	1.030	1.040	1.050	1.060	1.070	1.080	1.090	1.100
2	1.020	1.040	1.061	1.082	1.103	1.124	1.145	1.166	1.188	1.210
3	1.030	1.061	1.093	1.125	1.158	1.191	1.225	1.260	1.295	1.331
4	1.041	1.082	1.126	1.170	1.216	1.262	1.311	1.360	1.412	1.464
5	1.051	1.104	1.159	1.217	1.276	1.338	1.403	1.469	1.539	1.611
6	1.062	1.126	1.194	1.265	1.340	1.419	1.501	1.587	1.677	1.772
7	1.072	1.149	1.230	1.316	1.407	1.504	1.606	1.714	1.828	1.949
8	1.083	1.172	1.267	1.369	1.477	1.594	1.718	1.851	1.993	2.144
9	1.094	1.195	1.305	1.423	1.551	1.689	1.838	1.999	2.172	2.358
10	1.105	1.219	1.344	1.480	1.629	1.791	1.967	2.159	2.367	2.594
11	1.116	1.243	1.384	1.539	1.710	1.898	2.105	2.332	2.580	2.853
12	1.127	1.268	1.426	1.601	1.796	2.012	2.252	2.518	2.813	3.138
13	1.138	1.294	1.469	1.665	1.886	2.133	2.410	2.720	3.066	3.452
14	1.149	1.319	1.513	1.732	1.980	2.261	2.579	2.937	3.342	3.797
15	1.161	1.346	1.558	1.801	2.079	2.397	2.759	3.172	3.642	4.177
16	1.173	1.373	1.605	1.873	2.183	2.540	2.952	3.426	3.970	4.595
17	1.184	1.400	1.653	1.948	2.292	2.693	3.159	3.700	4.328	5.054
18	1.196	1.428	1.702	2.026	2.407	2.854	3.380	3.996	4.717	5.560
19	1.208	1.457	1.754	2.107	2.527	3.026	3.617	4.316	5.142	6.116
20	1.220	1.486	1.806	2.191	2.653	3.207	3.870	4.661	5.604	6.727
25	1.282	1.641	2.094	2.666	3.386	4.292	5.427	6.848	8.623	10.835
30	1.348	1.811	2.427	3.243	4.322	5.743	7.612	10.063	13.268	17.449
35	1.417	2.000	2.814	3.946	5.516	7.686	10.677	14.785	20.414	28.102
40	1.489	2.208	3.262	4.801	7.040	10.286	14.974	21.725	31.409	45.259
50	1.645	2.692	4.384	7.107	11.467	18.420	29.457	46.902	74.358	117.391

Future value interest factor of Re 1 per period at *i*% for *n* periods, *FVIF(i,n)*

Period	11%	12%	13%	14%	15%	16%	17%	18%	19%	20%
1	1.110	1.120	1.130	1.140	1.150	1.160	1.170	1.180	1.190	1.200
2	1.232	1.254	1.277	1.300	1.323	1.346	1.369	1.392	1.416	1.440
3	1.368	1.405	1.443	1.482	1.521	1.561	1.602	1.643	1.685	1.728
4	1.518	1.574	1.630	1.689	1.749	1.811	1.874	1.939	2.005	2.074
5	1.685	1.762	1.842	1.925	2.011	2.100	2.192	2.288	2.386	2.488
6	1.870	1.974	2.082	2.195	2.313	2.436	2.565	2.700	2.840	2.986
7	2.076	2.211	2.353	2.502	2.660	2.826	3.001	3.185	3.379	3.583
8	2.305	2.476	2.658	2.853	3.059	3.278	3.511	3.759	4.021	4.300
9	2.558	2.773	3.004	3.252	3.518	3.803	4.108	4.435	4.785	5.160
10	2.839	3.106	3.395	3.707	4.046	4.411	4.807	5.234	5.695	6.192
11	3.152	3.479	3.836	4.226	4.652	5.117	5.624	6.176	6.777	7.430
12	3.498	3.896	4.335	4.818	5.350	5.936	6.580	7.288	8.064	8.916
13	3.883	4.363	4.898	5.492	6.153	6.886	7.699	8.599	9.596	10.699
14	4.310	4.887	5.535	6.261	7.076	7.988	9.007	10.147	11.420	12.839
15	4.785	5.474	6.254	7.138	8.137	9.266	10.539	11.974	13.590	15.407
16	5.311	6.130	7.067	8.137	9.358	10.748	12.330	14.129	16.172	18.488
17	5.895	6.866	7.986	9.276	10.761	12.468	14.426	16.672	19.244	22.186
18	6.544	7.690	9.024	10.575	12.375	14.463	16.879	19.673	22.901	26.623
19	7.263	8.613	10.197	12.056	14.232	16.777	19.748	23.214	27.252	31.948
20	8.062	9.646	11.523	13.743	16.367	19.461	23.106	27.393	32.429	38.338
25	13.585	17.000	21.231	26.462	32.919	40.874	50.658	62.669	77.388	95.396
30	22.892	29.960	39.116	50.950	66.212	85.850	111.065	143.371	184.675	237.376
35	38.575	52.800	72.069	98.100	133.176	180.314	243.503	327.997	440.701	590.668
40	65.001	93.051	132.782	188.884	267.864	378.721	533.869	750.378	1051.668	1469.772
50	184.565	289.002	450.736	700.233	1083.657	1670.704	2566.215	3927.357	5988.914	9100.438

Present Value of Lump Sum

Present value interest factor of Re 1 per period at *i*% for *n* periods, *PVIF(i,n)*

Period	1%	2%	3%	4%	5%	6%	7%	8%	9%	10%
1	0.990	0.980	0.971	0.962	0.952	0.943	0.935	0.926	0.917	0.909
2	0.980	0.961	0.943	0.925	0.907	0.890	0.873	0.857	0.842	0.826
3	0.971	0.942	0.915	0.889	0.864	0.840	0.816	0.794	0.772	0.751
4	0.961	0.924	0.888	0.855	0.823	0.792	0.763	0.735	0.708	0.683
5	0.951	0.906	0.863	0.822	0.784	0.747	0.713	0.681	0.650	0.621
6	0.942	0.888	0.837	0.790	0.746	0.705	0.666	0.630	0.596	0.564
7	0.933	0.871	0.813	0.760	0.711	0.665	0.623	0.583	0.547	0.513
8	0.923	0.853	0.789	0.731	0.677	0.627	0.582	0.540	0.502	0.467
9	0.914	0.837	0.766	0.703	0.645	0.592	0.544	0.500	0.460	0.424
10	0.905	0.820	0.744	0.676	0.614	0.558	0.508	0.463	0.422	0.386
11	0.896	0.804	0.722	0.650	0.585	0.527	0.475	0.429	0.388	0.350
12	0.887	0.788	0.701	0.625	0.557	0.497	0.444	0.397	0.356	0.319
13	0.879	0.773	0.681	0.601	0.530	0.469	0.415	0.368	0.326	0.290
14	0.870	0.758	0.661	0.577	0.505	0.442	0.388	0.340	0.299	0.263
15	0.861	0.743	0.642	0.555	0.481	0.417	0.362	0.315	0.275	0.239
16	0.853	0.728	0.623	0.534	0.458	0.394	0.339	0.292	0.252	0.218
17	0.844	0.714	0.605	0.513	0.436	0.371	0.317	0.270	0.231	0.198
18	0.836	0.700	0.587	0.494	0.416	0.350	0.296	0.250	0.212	0.180
19	0.828	0.686	0.570	0.475	0.396	0.331	0.277	0.232	0.194	0.164
20	0.820	0.673	0.554	0.456	0.377	0.312	0.258	0.215	0.178	0.149
25	0.780	0.610	0.478	0.375	0.295	0.233	0.184	0.146	0.116	0.092
30	0.742	0.552	0.412	0.308	0.231	0.174	0.131	0.099	0.075	0.057
35	0.706	0.500	0.355	0.253	0.181	0.130	0.094	0.068	0.049	0.036
40	0.672	0.453	0.307	0.208	0.142	0.097	0.067	0.046	0.032	0.022
50	0.608	0.372	0.228	0.141	0.087	0.054	0.034	0.021	0.013	0.009

Present value interest factor of Re 1 per period at *i*% for *n* periods, *PVIF(i,n)*

Period	11%	12%	13%	14%	15%	16%	17%	18%	19%	20%
1	0.901	0.893	0.885	0.877	0.870	0.862	0.855	0.847	0.840	0.833
2	0.812	0.797	0.783	0.769	0.756	0.743	0.731	0.718	0.706	0.694
3	0.731	0.712	0.693	0.675	0.658	0.641	0.624	0.609	0.593	0.579
4	0.659	0.636	0.613	0.592	0.572	0.552	0.534	0.516	0.499	0.482
5	0.593	0.567	0.543	0.519	0.497	0.476	0.456	0.437	0.419	0.402
6	0.535	0.507	0.480	0.456	0.432	0.410	0.390	0.370	0.352	0.335
7	0.482	0.452	0.425	0.400	0.376	0.354	0.333	0.314	0.296	0.279
8	0.434	0.404	0.376	0.351	0.327	0.305	0.285	0.266	0.249	0.233
9	0.391	0.361	0.333	0.308	0.284	0.263	0.243	0.225	0.209	0.194
10	0.352	0.322	0.295	0.270	0.247	0.227	0.208	0.191	0.176	0.162
11	0.317	0.287	0.261	0.237	0.215	0.195	0.178	0.162	0.148	0.135
12	0.286	0.257	0.231	0.208	0.187	0.168	0.152	0.137	0.124	0.112
13	0.258	0.229	0.204	0.182	0.163	0.145	0.130	0.116	0.104	0.093
14	0.232	0.205	0.181	0.160	0.141	0.125	0.111	0.099	0.088	0.078
15	0.209	0.183	0.160	0.140	0.123	0.108	0.095	0.084	0.074	0.065
16	0.188	0.163	0.141	0.123	0.107	0.093	0.081	0.071	0.062	0.054
17	0.170	0.146	0.125	0.108	0.093	0.080	0.069	0.060	0.052	0.045
18	0.153	0.130	0.111	0.095	0.081	0.069	0.059	0.051	0.044	0.038
19	0.138	0.116	0.098	0.083	0.070	0.060	0.051	0.043	0.037	0.031
20	0.124	0.104	0.087	0.073	0.061	0.051	0.043	0.037	0.031	0.026
25	0.074	0.059	0.047	0.038	0.030	0.024	0.020	0.016	0.013	0.010
30	0.044	0.033	0.026	0.020	0.015	0.012	0.009	0.007	0.005	0.004
35	0.026	0.019	0.014	0.010	0.008	0.006	0.004	0.003	0.002	0.002
40	0.015	0.011	0.008	0.005	0.004	0.003	0.002	0.001	0.001	0.001
50	0.005	0.003	0.002	0.001	0.001	0.001	0.000	0.000	0.000	0.000

Future Value of an Annuity

Future value interest factor of an ordinary annuity of Re 1 per period at *i*%
for *n* periods, *FVIFA(i,n)*

Period	1%	2%	3%	4%	5%	6%	7%	8%	9%	10%
1	1.000	1.000	1.000	1.000	1.000	1.000	1.000	1.000	1.000	1.000
2	2.010	2.020	2.030	2.040	2.050	2.060	2.070	2.080	2.090	2.100
3	3.030	3.060	3.091	3.122	3.153	3.184	3.215	3.246	3.278	3.310
4	4.060	4.122	4.184	4.246	4.310	4.375	4.440	4.506	4.573	4.641
5	5.101	5.204	5.309	5.416	5.526	5.637	5.751	5.867	5.985	6.105
6	6.152	6.308	6.468	6.633	6.802	6.975	7.153	7.336	7.523	7.716
7	7.214	7.434	7.662	7.898	8.142	8.394	8.654	8.923	9.200	9.487
8	8.286	8.583	8.892	9.214	9.549	9.897	10.260	10.637	11.028	11.436
9	9.369	9.755	10.159	10.583	11.027	11.491	11.978	12.488	13.021	13.579
10	10.462	10.950	11.464	12.006	12.578	13.181	13.816	14.487	15.193	15.937
11	11.567	12.169	12.808	13.486	14.207	14.972	15.784	16.645	17.560	18.531
12	12.683	13.412	14.192	15.026	15.917	16.870	17.888	18.977	20.141	21.384
13	13.809	14.680	15.618	16.627	17.713	18.882	20.141	21.495	22.953	24.523
14	14.947	15.974	17.086	18.292	19.599	21.015	22.550	24.215	26.019	27.975
15	16.097	17.293	18.599	20.024	21.579	23.276	25.129	27.152	29.361	31.772
16	17.258	18.639	20.157	21.825	23.657	25.673	27.888	30.324	33.003	35.950
17	18.430	20.012	21.762	23.698	25.840	28.213	30.840	33.750	36.974	40.545
18	19.615	21.412	23.414	25.645	28.132	30.906	33.999	37.450	41.301	45.599
19	20.811	22.841	25.117	27.671	30.539	33.760	37.379	41.446	46.018	51.159
20	22.019	24.297	26.870	29.778	33.066	36.786	40.995	45.762	51.160	57.275
25	28.243	32.030	36.459	41.646	47.727	54.865	63.249	73.106	84.701	98.347
30	34.785	40.568	47.575	56.085	66.439	79.058	94.461	113.28	136.31	164.49
35	41.660	49.994	60.462	73.652	90.320	111.43	138.24	172.32	215.71	271.02
40	48.886	60.402	75.401	95.026	120.80	154.76	199.64	259.06	337.88	442.59
50	64.463	84.579	112.80	152.67	209.35	290.34	406.53	573.77	815.08	1163.9

**Future value interest factor of an ordinary annuity of Re 1 per period at *i*%
for *n* periods, *FVIFA (i,n)***

Period	11%	12%	13%	14%	15%	16%	17%	18%	19%	20%
1	1.000	1.000	1.000	1.000	1.000	1.000	1.000	1.000	1.000	1.000
2	2.110	2.120	2.130	2.140	2.150	2.160	2.170	2.180	2.190	2.200
3	3.342	3.374	3.407	3.440	3.473	3.506	3.539	3.572	3.606	3.640
4	4.710	4.779	4.850	4.921	4.993	5.066	5.141	5.215	5.291	5.368
5	6.228	6.353	6.480	6.610	6.742	6.877	7.014	7.154	7.297	7.442
6	7.913	8.115	8.323	8.536	8.754	8.977	9.207	9.442	9.683	9.930
7	9.783	10.089	10.405	10.730	11.067	11.414	11.772	12.142	12.523	12.916
8	11.859	12.300	12.757	13.233	13.727	14.240	14.773	15.327	15.902	16.499
9	14.164	14.776	15.416	16.085	16.786	17.519	18.285	19.086	19.923	20.799
10	16.722	17.549	18.420	19.337	20.304	21.321	22.393	23.521	24.709	25.959
11	19.561	20.655	21.814	23.045	24.349	25.733	27.200	28.755	30.404	32.150
12	22.713	24.133	25.650	27.271	29.002	30.850	32.824	34.931	37.180	39.581
13	26.212	28.029	29.985	32.089	34.352	36.786	39.404	42.219	45.244	48.497
14	30.095	32.393	34.883	37.581	40.505	43.672	47.103	50.818	54.841	59.196
15	34.405	37.280	40.417	43.842	47.580	51.660	56.110	60.965	66.261	72.035
16	39.190	42.753	46.672	50.980	55.717	60.925	66.649	72.939	79.850	87.442
17	44.501	48.884	53.739	59.118	65.075	71.673	78.979	87.068	96.022	105.93
18	50.396	55.750	61.725	68.394	75.836	84.141	93.406	103.74	115.27	128.12
19	56.939	63.440	70.749	78.969	88.212	98.603	110.28	123.41	138.17	154.74
20	64.203	72.052	80.947	91.025	102.44	115.38	130.03	146.63	165.42	186.69
25	114.41	133.33	155.62	181.87	212.79	249.21	292.10	342.60	402.04	471.98
30	199.02	241.33	293.20	356.79	434.75	530.31	647.44	790.95	966.71	1181.9
35	341.59	431.66	546.68	693.57	881.17	1,120.7	1,426.5	1,816.7	2,314.2	2,948.3
40	581.83	767.09	1,013.7	1,342.0	1,779.1	2,360.8	3,134.5	4,163.2	5,529.8	7,343.9
50	1,668.8	2,400.0	3,459.5	4,994.5	7,217.7	10,436	15,090	21,813	31,515	45,497

Present Value of an Annuity

Present value interest factor of an (ordinary) annuity of Re 1 per period at *i*% for *n* periods, *PVIFA (i,n)*

Period	1%	2%	3%	4%	5%	6%	7%	8%	9%	10%
1	0.990	0.980	0.971	0.962	0.952	0.943	0.935	0.926	0.917	0.909
2	1.970	1.942	1.913	1.886	1.859	1.833	1.808	1.783	1.759	1.736
3	2.941	2.884	2.829	2.775	2.723	2.673	2.624	2.577	2.531	2.487
4	3.902	3.808	3.717	3.630	3.546	3.465	3.387	3.312	3.240	3.170
5	4.853	4.713	4.580	4.452	4.329	4.212	4.100	3.993	3.890	3.791
6	5.795	5.601	5.417	5.242	5.076	4.917	4.767	4.623	4.486	4.355
7	6.728	6.472	6.230	6.002	5.786	5.582	5.389	5.206	5.033	4.868
8	7.652	7.325	7.020	6.733	6.463	6.210	5.971	5.747	5.535	5.335
9	8.566	8.162	7.786	7.435	7.108	6.802	6.515	6.247	5.995	5.759
10	9.471	8.983	8.530	8.111	7.722	7.360	7.024	6.710	6.418	6.145
11	10.368	9.787	9.253	8.760	8.306	7.887	7.499	7.139	6.805	6.495
12	11.255	10.575	9.954	9.385	8.863	8.384	7.943	7.536	7.161	6.814
13	12.134	11.348	10.635	9.986	9.394	8.853	8.358	7.904	7.487	7.103
14	13.004	12.106	11.296	10.563	9.899	9.295	8.745	8.244	7.786	7.367
15	13.865	12.849	11.938	11.118	10.380	9.712	9.108	8.559	8.061	7.606
16	14.718	13.578	12.561	11.652	10.838	10.106	9.447	8.851	8.313	7.824
17	15.562	14.292	13.166	12.166	11.274	10.477	9.763	9.122	8.544	8.022
18	16.398	14.992	13.754	12.659	11.690	10.828	10.059	9.372	8.756	8.201
19	17.226	15.678	14.324	13.134	12.085	11.158	10.336	9.604	8.950	8.365
20	18.046	16.351	14.877	13.590	12.462	11.470	10.594	9.818	9.129	8.514
25	22.023	19.523	17.413	15.622	14.094	12.783	11.654	10.675	9.823	9.077
30	25.808	22.396	19.600	17.292	15.372	13.765	12.409	11.258	10.274	9.427
35	29.409	24.999	21.487	18.665	16.374	14.498	12.948	11.655	10.567	9.644
40	32.835	27.355	23.115	19.793	17.159	15.046	13.332	11.925	10.757	9.779
50	39.196	31.424	25.730	21.482	18.256	15.762	13.801	12.233	10.962	9.915

Present value interest factor of an (ordinary) annuity of Re 1 per period at *i*% for *n* periods, *PVIFA (i,n)*

Period	11%	12%	13%	14%	15%	16%	17%	18%	19%	20%
1	0.901	0.893	0.885	0.877	0.870	0.862	0.855	0.847	0.840	0.833
2	1.713	1.690	1.668	1.647	1.626	1.605	1.585	1.566	1.547	1.528
3	2.444	2.402	2.361	2.322	2.283	2.246	2.210	2.174	2.140	2.106
4	3.102	3.037	2.974	2.914	2.855	2.798	2.743	2.690	2.639	2.589
5	3.696	3.605	3.517	3.433	3.352	3.274	3.199	3.127	3.058	2.991
6	4.231	4.111	3.998	3.889	3.784	3.685	3.589	3.498	3.410	3.326
7	4.712	4.564	4.423	4.288	4.160	4.039	3.922	3.812	3.706	3.605
8	5.146	4.968	4.799	4.639	4.487	4.344	4.207	4.078	3.954	3.837
9	5.537	5.328	5.132	4.946	4.772	4.607	4.451	4.303	4.163	4.031
10	5.889	5.650	5.426	5.216	5.019	4.833	4.659	4.494	4.339	4.192
11	6.207	5.938	5.687	5.453	5.234	5.029	4.836	4.656	4.486	4.327
12	6.492	6.194	5.918	5.660	5.421	5.197	4.988	4.793	4.611	4.439
13	6.750	6.424	6.122	5.842	5.583	5.342	5.118	4.910	4.715	4.533
14	6.982	6.628	6.302	6.002	5.724	5.468	5.229	5.008	4.802	4.611
15	7.191	6.811	6.462	6.142	5.847	5.575	5.324	5.092	4.876	4.675
16	7.379	6.974	6.604	6.265	5.954	5.668	5.405	5.162	4.938	4.730
17	7.549	7.120	6.729	6.373	6.047	5.749	5.475	5.222	4.990	4.775
18	7.702	7.250	6.840	6.467	6.128	5.818	5.534	5.273	5.033	4.812
19	7.839	7.366	6.938	6.550	6.198	5.877	5.584	5.316	5.070	4.843
20	7.963	7.469	7.025	6.623	6.259	5.929	5.628	5.353	5.101	4.870
25	8.422	7.843	7.330	6.873	6.464	6.097	5.766	5.467	5.195	4.948
30	8.694	8.055	7.496	7.003	6.566	6.177	5.829	5.517	5.235	4.979
35	8.855	8.176	7.586	7.070	6.617	6.215	5.858	5.539	5.251	4.992
40	8.951	8.244	7.634	7.105	6.642	6.233	5.871	5.548	5.258	4.997
50	9.042	8.304	7.675	7.133	6.661	6.246	5.880	5.554	5.262	4.999

Foreign Exchange

Foreign exchange (Forex) currency trading allows an investor to participate in profitable fluctuations of world currencies. Forex trading works by selecting pairs of currencies and then measuring the profit or loss by comparing the fluctuations of the market activity of one currency against that of the other. For example, fluctuations in the value of the rupee is measured against other world currencies such as the US dollar, British pound, euro, Japanese yen, etc. Being able to discern price trends in market activity is the essence of all profitable trading and this is what makes foreign currencies so exciting—currencies are the world's 'best trending' market. This gives Forex investors a profit-making edge that is unavailable in most other markets.

Forex trading is being called 'today's exciting new investment opportunity for the savvy investor'. The reason is that the forex trading market only began to emerge in 1978, when worldwide currencies were allowed to 'float' according to supply and demand, seven years after the Gold Standard was abandoned. Up until 1995, forex trading was only available to banks and large multinational corporations, but today, thanks to the proliferation of the computer and the new era of Internet-based communication technologies, this highly profitable market is open to everyone. The forex trading market's growth has been unprecedented, explosive, and unequaled by any other trading market.

Unlike traditional trading, which brings buyers and sellers together in a central location (trading floors), in forex trading there is no need for a centralized location. Forex is a market where traders worldwide conduct business, using high-speed Internet connections, with the Interbank Foreign Currency Exchange via forex clearinghouses (also called forex brokerage firms). Forex has not only become the fastest growing trading market, but also the most profitable trading marketplace in the world.

Simply stated, forex is the most profitable trading because it is the world's largest marketplace. The foreign currency market as a whole accounts for over 1.2 trillion dollars of trading per day (as determined by the Fourth Central Bank Survey of Foreign Exchange and Derivatives Market Activity, 1998, and this figure is understood to be significantly higher today). To put this into perspective, on any given day the foreign currency exchange market activity is vastly greater than the stock market. It is 75 times greater than the New York Stock Exchange, where the average total daily value (using 1998 figures) of both foreign and domestic stocks is $16 billion, and much greater than the daily activity on the London Stock Exchange, with $11 billion.

Furthermore, in addition to being the world's largest and most profitable market, the foreign currency exchange market is the world's most powerful and persistent trading market regardless of negative economic indicators. This is because currencies 'trend' better than every other market due to their macro-economic nature. Unlike many commodities whose supply and demand fundamentals can literally change overnight (as we found in the sudden dotcom 'market adjustment' and even more abruptly on 11 September 2001), currency fundamentals are much less random and far more predictable. This is well illustrated in the way interest rates are changed gradually and only in small increments.

Other examples of fundamental predictability are illustrated by the following statistics. Of the $1.2 trillion day trading in foreign currency exchange, 83 per cent of spot foreign exchange activity and 95 per cent of swap activity involves US dollars. The euro is the second most active currency at 37 per cent. The Japanese yen at 24 per cent and the British pound sterling at 10 per cent are ranked third and fourth. The Swiss franc is 7 per cent, and the Canadian and Australian dollars account for 3 per cent.

Spot forex is the type of forex trade in which self-traders concentrate most of their investment activity for reasons that are self-explanatory. By definition, a spot forex transaction is a currency trade transaction that has a settlement (liquidation) within a maximum of two working days following the closing of the trade. Therefore, spot forex allows the self-trader high liquidity. Another popular feature for well-advised spot forex self-traders is the strong profit potential from continual market fluctuations by buying a specific currency when it is weaker and selling it when it is stronger, and the continual pairing of strong currencies against weak ones. This potential for profit or loss is amplified by the effect of leverage. Leverage is a term that describes what can be achieved when a smaller amount of money controls a much larger amount of money. For example, in forex trading, a leverage factor of 100 can allow the trader to hold a 1,00,000-US dollar position with a modest 1000-US dollar margin deposit. Online forex day trading focuses its investment activity largely on spot forex because of the 'risk manageability' of in-and-out trading and the potential to generate excellent and highly liquid profits.

Few financial industries generate as much excitement and profit as currency exchange. Traders around the world enter trades for weeks, days, or split seconds, generating explosive moves or steady flows, and money changes hands quickly at a staggering daily average of a trillion US dollars. Forex profitability is legendary. A fund manager realized a profit in excess of 1 billion dollars for a couple of days work in September 1992. Another netted $28 million for 1993. Despite its high trading volume and its fundamental role in the world, the forex market is rarely in the media limelight because its method of trading transaction is less visible than the trading on the floor of a stock exchange. However, trading on the foreign currency exchange market is today surging into the public awareness, and flocks of Internet traders are attracted by the market's inherent profitability and risk manageability. Add to this the absence of geographic or temporal boundaries and a vibrantly active forex market is open to all players.

Further Reading

BOOKS

1. Ahmad, N. (1998). *Management Accounting*. New Delhi: Anmol Publications Pvt. Ltd.
2. Andrew, W. and R. Schmidgall (1993). *Financial Management for Hospitality Industry*. East Lansing, MI: Educational Institute of the American Hotel and Motel Association.
3. Arnold, J. (1996). *Accounting for Management Decisions*. Hertfordshire, UK: Prentice Hall.
4. Baker, R., V. Lembke, and T. King (1989). *Advanced Financial Accounting*. New York: McGraw-Hill Inc.
5. Bhalla, V. (2005). *Working Capital*. New Delhi: Anmol Publications Pvt. Ltd.
6. Brigham, E. and J. Houston (2004). *Fundamentals of Financial Management*, 10th edn. New Delhi: Thomson Business Information India Pvt. Ltd.
7. Brockington, R. (1993). *Financial Management*. London: DP Publications Ltd.
8. Chakraborty, H. and H. Chakraborty (1997). *Management Accountancy*. New Delhi: Oxford University Press.
9. Chakraborty, K. (1993). *The Essence of Finance*. IBH Publishers: Bombay.
10. Chandra, P. (1989). *Financial Management—Theory and Practice*. New Delhi: Tata McGraw-Hill.
11. Chandra, P. (2000). *Financial Management and Policy*. New Delhi: Tata McGraw-Hill.

12. Chandra, P. (2003). *Finance Sense*. New Delhi: Tata McGraw-Hill.

13. Coltman, M. (1994). *Hospitality Management Accounting*. New York: Van Nostrand Reinhold.

14. Cote, R. (1999). *Understanding Hospitality Accounting*. East Lansing, MI: Educational Institute of the American Hotel and Motel Association.

15. Cypert, S.A. (1991). *Following the Money*. New York: Amalom.

16. Damodaran, A. (2001). *Corporate Finance*. New York: John Wiley & Sons.

17. Davis, E. (1994). *Finance and the Firm—An Introduction to Corporate Finance*. New York: Oxford University Press.

18. Dickey, T. (1992). *The Basic of Budgeting*. Menlo Park, CA: Crisp Publications.

19. Drury, C. (1985). *Management and Cost Accounting*. London: Chapman & Hall Ltd.

20. Gill, J.O. (1990). *Financial Statements*. Menlo Park, CA: Crisp Publications.

21. Harris, P. and P. Hazard (1996). *Accounting and Finance for the International Hospitality Industry*. London: British Library Publishing.

22. Hawawini, G. and C. Viallet (2001). *Finance for Executives—Managing for Value Creation*. New York: South-Western Publishers.

23. Hawken, P. (1993). *The Ecology of Commerce*. London: The Orion Publishing Group.

24. Horngren, C.T. (1978). *Introduction to Management Accounting*. New Jersey: Prentice Hall.

25. Khan, M. and P. Jain (1992). *Management Accounting*. New Delhi: Tata McGraw-Hill.

26. Khan, M. and P. Jain (2003). *Financial Management—Text and Problems*. New Delhi: Tata McGraw-Hill.

27. Kotas, R. (1981). *Accounting in the Hotel and Catering Industry*. London: International Textbook Co.

28. Kotas, R. (1995). *Management Accounting for Hotels and Restaurants*. London: International Textbook Co.

29. Littlejohn, D. (2003). 'Hotels' in B. Brotherton, ed., *The International Hospitality Industry*. London: Elsevier Butterworth-Hienemann.

30. Martin, J., W. Petty, A. Keown, and D. Scott (1999). *Basic Financial Management*. New Jersey: Prentice-Hall.

31. Messenger, S. and H. Shaw (1993). *Financial Management for Hospitality, Tourism and Leisure*. London: McMillan.

32. Negi, J. (2000). *Hotel 7 Tourism Laws*. New Delhi: Frank Bros & Co.

33. Ohmae, K. (1990). *The Borderless World*. New York: Harper Business.

34. Owen, G. (1994). *Accounting for Hospitality, Tourism and Leisure*. London: Pittman Publishers.

35. Pandey, I.M. (2003). *Financial Management*. New Delhi: Tata McGraw-Hill.

36. Pandey, I. and R. Bhat (2000). *Cases in Financial Management*. New Delhi: Tata McGraw-Hill.

37. Pinches, G.E. (1984). *Fundamentals of Financial Management*. New York: Harper Collins.

38. Roy Choudary, A.B. (1991). *Financial Ratios and Working Capital*. Calcutta: Management Technologists.

39. Roy Choudary, A.B. (1991). *Sources and Application of Funds*. Calcutta: Management Technologists.

40. Roy Choudary, A.B. (1991). *Working Capital Management*. Calcutta: Management Technologists.

41. Roy Choudary, A.B. (1992). *A Professional Management Guide—Cash Flow Management*. Calcutta: Management Technologists.

42. Roy Choudary, A.B. (1992). *Controlling Financial Performance*. Calcutta: Management Technologists.

43. Schmidgall, R. (1990). *Hospitality Industry Managerial Accounting*. East Lansing, MI: Educational Institute of the American Hotel and Motel Association.

44. Schmidgall, R. and J. Damitio (1994). *Hospitality Industry Financial Accounting*. East Lansing, MI: Educational Institute of the American Hotel and Motel Association.

45. Singh, A. (2004). *Company Law*, 14th edn. Lucknow: Eastern Book Company.

46. Turmer, D., P. Turner, and D. Voysey (1996). *Financial Service Today*. London: McMillan Press.
47. Vale, P. (1988). *Financial Management Handbook*. New Delhi: Jaico Publishing House.
48. Van Horne, J. and J. Wachowicz (2001). *Fundamentals of Financial Management*. New Delhi: Pearson Education (Singapore) Pte. Ltd.
49. Van Horne, J. (2003). *Financial Management and Policy*. New Delhi: Prentice Hall of India.

WEBSITES

1. www.teachmefinance.com (for calculations involved in the study of finance).
2. www.winninginvesting.com (for details in the investment scenario).
3. www.finance.yahoo.com (for general update from the world of finance).
4. www.fool.com (for latest news from the Wall Street).
5. www.duke.edu/~charvey/Classes/wpg/glossary.htm (for meaning of terms in finance, money, and investment).
6. www.ft.com/ (for online issue of the *Financial Times*).
7. www.bloomberg.com/ (for latest and current news on politics, economy, and investment).
8. www.studyfinance.com/ (for excel spreadsheet and templates on future and present value of money, net present value, and internal rate of return).
9. www.moneychimp.com (for additional information on reading and understanding annual reports).
10. www.investorwords.com/ (for comprehensive glossary on finance).
11. www.nasdaq.com/ (for news, views, and expert comments from the Nasdaq).
12. www.sebi.gov.in (for current information on securities and financial markets in India).
13. www.riskglossary.com (for comprehensive resource in trading, financial engineering, and financial risk).

Index